ANTIQUES
INVESTIGATOR

ANTIQUES
INVESTIGATOR

JUDITH MILLER

DK

LONDON, NEW YORK, MELBOURNE,
MUNICH, and DELHI

A joint production from **DK** and
THE PRICE GUIDE COMPANY

DORLING KINDERSLEY LIMITED
Senior Editor Janet Mohun
Senior Art Editor Vicky Short
Editor Anna Fischel
US Editors Anja Schmidt, Charles Wills
Design Assistants Clare Joyce, Loan Nguyen
Production Editors Sharon McGoldrick, Clare McLean
Production Controller Shane Higgins
Creative Technical Support Adam Walker
Picture Library Claire Bowers, Lucy Claxton
Managing Editors Julie Oughton, Angela Wilkes
Managing Art Editor Christine Keilty
Art Director Bryn Walls
Publisher Jonathan Metcalf

THE PRICE GUIDE COMPANY LIMITED
Publishing Manager Julie Brooke
Assistant editors Jessica Bishop, Sara Sturgess
Editorial assistants Carolyn Malarkey, Louisa Wheeler

CONTRIBUTORS
Jill Bace
Mark Hill
Alycen Mitchell
Anna Southgate
John Wainwright

The Price Guide Company (UK) Ltd
info@thepriceguidecompany.com

First American Edition 2007
First paperback edition 2009

Published in the United States by
DK Publishing
375 Hudson Street
New York, New York 10014

09 10 11   10 9 8 7 6 5 4 3 2 1

TD222—June 2009

Published in Great Britain by Dorling Kindersley Limited

A CIP catalog record for this book is available from the
Library of Congress

ISBN: 978-0-7566-5097-1 (paperback)

DK books are available at special discounts when purchased in bulk
for sales promotions, premiums, fund-raising, or educational use.
For details, contact: DK Publishing Special Markets, 375 Hudson
Street, New York, New York 10014 or SpecialSales@dk.com

Color reproduction by Colourscan, Singapore and DK, India
Printed and bound in China by
Hung Hing Offset Printing Company Limited

Discover more at
www.dk.com

Foreword

Like many people I grew up in a home without any antiques or art. My parents were part of the 1950s "Formica generation" who wanted everything to be "new" and modern. Not only did my mother get rid of all my grandparents' possessions—she proudly paid people to come and take them away.

However, I became fascinated by "old things" and during my student days in Edinburgh in the 1960s I began collecting pretty plates I found in junk shops for a penny each. I knew that they were old but where they came from and when they were made was a mystery both to me and to the shopkeepers I bought them from. With no one to tell me what to look out for I simply bought what I liked and could afford (always a good rule for the beginner).

But, when I started going to auctions a few years later, life became a lot more confusing. Why did the dealers take drawers out and turn them over? Why were they biting pieces of porcelain?

What did they see when they held glass up to the light? Why did they breathe on silver marks? Why did they upset a doll's hairstyle to examine her neck?

I needed to find a way in to this secret world but where should I begin? I needed to become an antiques investigator.

There were no books for the beginner in those days and so I copied what the dealers did, and asked questions of antiques dealers I had got to know, to help me to understand the strange behaviour I had seen. Little by little I pieced together the evidence needed to find the clues and identify my suspects.

Now there are many books, magazines, and TV programs about antiques and collecting. However, anyone starting out in the field needs a trusted companion to help them solve any antiques case. I hope that this book becomes just that.

Judith Miller.

Contents

Metalware

Collectibles

Composite photos

Resources

Introduction

THE WORLD OF ANTIQUES has always been full of mystery and intrigue. My aim is to guide you past the false trails and show you how to conduct a thorough inspection and sound assessment of the evidence—in short, to teach you to be an antiques investigator.

There are no shortcuts to becoming a real expert but, trust me, the journey is an enjoyable one. This book will teach you the systematic methods of looking at pieces.

"The briefing" pages explain how to go about examining chairs, tables, storage furniture, ceramics, glass, and metalware. You need a starting point of basic principles: How was a piece constructed? How was it decorated? Was it hand-made or machined? Once you have this skill, you can compare pieces, and "The interrogation" pages do just that. Sometimes the comparison is between similar pieces from different countries; other times the examples are high-quality and inferior, so you can see exactly why the price tags differ. While "The interrogation" pages look at two examples in great detail, "The prime suspects" pages enlarge the picture with a few more suspicious characters. "The lineup" parades a whole string of accomplices. And the "Composite photos" section near the end of the book helps you to piece together the evidence of furniture handles, legs, and feet; ceramic, metal, and glass marks; and decorative motifs.

Potential antique heaven
Whenever I open a cupboard door I get a thrill of anticipation—I never know what I might find. Will there be an 18th-century Meissen dinner service? Or an Art Deco figure? That's the joy of being an antiques investigator.

Look and learn

Would you have known that this blue and white double gourd vase, lined up on page 90, is worth over $5 million? The initiated will spot the clues:

• The body is painted in underglaze cobalt blue and the overall glaze has a distinct blue/gray tinge.
• The painting has a strong rhythm to it and is bold.
• The piece is thickly potted.
• The base is unglazed with a shallow-cut broad foot-rim.
• There are rusty iron oxide markings on the unglazed area of the foot rim.

We have all heard the stories of people who have been staggered to discover that something they used daily was

Seven-figure value
Once you are an antiques investigator you will understand why this Chinese vase commands such a high value. Gauge its credentials on page 90.

Ming bowl
Today this piece of Chinese porcelain, used daily as a dog's water bowl, would be valued at $20,000–24,000. It was made about 400 years ago.

Building up the clues
This commode provides plenty of clues: the gently curving shape, vibrant ormolu mounts used in combination with a marble top, and the *chinoiserie* decoration all point to French Louis XV.

in fact a priceless antique. Take the lady whose spaniel had a favorite water bowl, which she later learned was late Ming (see below left).

Gathering the evidence

Handling antiques is the way to get your eye in—to recognize when something is not quite right or alternatively a real gem. When you have inspected something in detail—gathered your clues—stand back and look at the piece as a whole. Inspect the potential crime scene in context. What looks out of place? What doesn't fit with the statement? What could not have been there when it pretends to be? Take nothing at face value. Learn to identify honest wear and tear and signs of age. Make

TOOLS FOR INVESTIGATIVE WORK

- Magnifying glass and "loop" to examine details on silver, ceramics, and glass
- Flashlight—to check out those dark corners
- Tape measure
- Notebook
- Camera
- Duster
- Distilled water—to gently clean (but check with the owner first!)
- For attending auctions, a cushion and thermos flask
- For attending flea markets and yard sales, waterproof jacket, and—for the optimistic!—comfy shoes, and thermals/sunscreen

Genuine Gallé
I have seen rows of so-called "Lalique" and "Gallé" vases lying in fields at antiques and collectibles shows all over the world. Given how expensive the real deal is, is it likely that I would find wonderful pieces of art glass like the one above lying in a field?

good use of the antiques investigator's prime clue—patination (that glorious surface color of a real antique), created by years of dust and sweat.

Look at good examples. Cultivate friendly dealers and go to museums, collections and, above all, auctions. Auctions allow you to handle the pieces and hear expert opinions as to what the object is, how old it is, where it was made, and an estimate of what it will make on the day.

Assessing marks

What's in a mark? Most people think a mark or a signature is an authenticating factor. But this is not always the case, and marks can deceive.

For example, François Linke (1855–1946) was an eminent French furniture-maker who combined the flamboyant French Neoclassical with the naturalistic Art Nouveau. He signed his pieces. But his signature has been copied by less talented craftsmen. The antiques investigator must assess the whole piece. Does it exhibit the quality of the Linke piece below?

In the case of silverware, check that each part of a multi-part silver piece, for example a teapot, is separately marked. Watch out for patched-on hallmarks. You can

Silver hallmarks
Genuine hallmarks are your friend and help you pinpoint the maker, date, and place of origin. But be alert for fake marks that lead you to think something is more valuable than it really is.

often see the joins when you breathe on a piece. Also check that the patination is consistent. Many fakers overdo the "aging" process. Natural aging on a piece of silver should show small scratches and marks of different depths. Large gouges going in the same direction are unusual.

With ceramics, treat marks with suspicion—many are fakes. Many makers copied the mark of the most successful factory of the period, be it Meissen, Sèvres, or Worcester. As an antiques investigator, all you can do is look at the other evidence. What is the quality of the painting and the gilding? Is the modeling up to standard?

Fakes and copies

Do you know there are more Elizabethan oak refectory tables around the world than there were houses in 16th-century England? Herbert Cescinsky wrote in the 1920s in his book *The Gentle Art of Faking Furniture* (still worth a read) that: "There is more English antique furniture exported to America and Europe in one year than could have been made in the whole of the 18th century."

Terminology is all-important when considering the authenticity of a piece, and you need to be aware of the differences in meaning of these terms. Genuine or period means that the piece is original, of the correct date, and authentic. Something that is "reproduction" is an imitation, a copy. A fake, on the other hand, is a piece that has been deliberately copied with the intention of being passed off as a genuine, more valuable piece.

Even the innocent Carltonware Guinness toucan (above right) can be faked. Fakes generally have bright white necks and the head of beer is too white. The red and orange on the beak is often over-delineated or smudged.

Marriage or divorce?

Many pieces were made to copy popular and desirable wares. They were created or adapted with no thought of fraud. Furniture cut down to fit a smaller room is a perfect example. In the 19th and early 20th centuries many two-pieces such as bookcases and chests-on-chests were

The genuine article
Look at the proportions, the gently splaying legs, and use of the veneers. This is indeed the work of the master, François Linke, whose signature (right) has been much copied.

Beware fakes
The real McCoy—or toucan—has the correct Carltonware marks. It also has a creamy rather than bright white head of beer and neck.

Unhappy marriage
Look at the variation in color and figuration in the base of this chest-on-stand—your first clue that all is not as it should be.

"divorced" later. A marriage is where two otherwise unrelated pieces are joined in an unholy alliance, because the pieces are more saleable as a chest-on-chest or highboy. You should always look carefully at any two-part piece of furniture to check that the carcase wood, veneer, and color match. Different styles of construction and uncomfortable proportions indicate a marriage.

Finally, once you have gathered the evidence, interrogated the main suspects, checked the alibis, heard the testimonies, and come to a decision on the case in

hand, remember that learning about antiques is an ongoing process.

We all make mistakes. An old dealer once said that if you pay $400 for a piece and later find it is only worth $200, the other $200 is experience. You won't forget and you'll check the clues a little more thoroughly next time. And, most important, enjoy being an antiques investigator.

KEY CLUES ON CERAMICS

- Many marks are workmen's marks or gilders' marks.
- Early marks were applied by hand, so no two are identical.
- Pattern numbers on a piece tend to be after 1805 but are usually much later.
- Limited or Ltd. is unlikely before 1860 and is much more common after 1885.
- An impressed Trade Mark is after 1862.
- The word Royal is late 19th century.
- If you find the name of a country: for example "France", on the bottom of a piece, it was probably made after 1891. If you find "Made in France" it is probably after 1921—but it could be much later than that.

KEY CLUES ON FURNITURE

- Is the wood used right for the period? There are general time spans for the three main woods:
  Oak Period up to c1670
  Walnut Period c1670–1735
  Early Mahogany Period c1735–70
  Late Mahogany Period c1770–1810
  Exotic timbers are predominantly 19th century.
- Is evidence of wear on arms, stretchers, legs, and handles convincing?
- There should be patches of discoloration around the heads of screws, nails, handles, escutcheons (keyhole plates), and in corners.
- Is the carving original? Early carving stands proud of the surrounding area.

KEY CLUES ON GLASS

- The foot of an 18th-century wine glass should be wider than the rim.
- Up to c1860, colored glass tended to be restricted to tumblers, decanters, and bottles and was not that common.
- Old engraving shows gray when backed by white cardboard; new engraving is white and has a powdery appearance.

KEY CLUES ON SILVER

- Patina (due to oxidation and handling) should be overall with no obvious imperfections.
- Over-cleaning makes the piece look too white.
- Marks should follow the shape of a piece: in a circle if the bottom is round and in a line if the bottom is square.

Style guide
Baroque

THE ELABORATELY DECORATED and complicated shapes that define Baroque (c1620–c1700) were initially inspired by Italian painting, sculpture, and architecture in the early 17th century. Buildings and monuments commissioned by the Vatican inspired architects and designers and their wealthy patrons to recreate the style in their own countries. Baroque furniture incorporated architectural and sculptural elements and molding, carving, gilding, and floral marquetry. The 17th century saw an increase in trade between China and the West, which led to a demand for blue and white porcelain, lacquerwork panels, and furniture decorated with *chinoiserie*.

In France, craftsmen created masterpieces for Louis XIV and his court. The French style spread throughout Europe following the publication of engravings by designers such as Jean Le Pautre, and the emigration of Huguenot craftsmen.

KEY CLUES

- Heavy, sculptural shapes, usually curved and bulbous.
- Formal, symmetrical decoration, including swags, double scrolls, acanthus leaves, masks, cornucopia, lion's-paw feet, chinoiserie, and finely modeled figures.
- Materials were luxurious and included velvet, brocade, and damask upholstery; semi-precious stones and ivory.
- Marquetry, boullework, japanning.
- Decorated glass, gilt gesso, ormolu (gilded brass) mounts, carved and turned wood.

Carved angel
Painting and gilding were often used to embellish finely carved figures such as this Austrian angel. The angel's posture and drapery are typically detailed.

Back splat set with carved rosettes

Side rails carved with rosettes flanked by husks

Bambocci chest
Architectural style and cartouches are typical features of Italian Baroque "Bambocci" chests.

Carved figures cover the chest

William and Mary salon chair
The carved decoration on this chair features Baroque motifs. It was based on a design by the Huguenot craftsman Daniel Marot.

Rococo

BY THE 1730s, European taste was moving away from the heavy and formal Baroque style toward the lighter Rococo taste that originated in France. The golden period spanned from c1720 to c1760. It was a time of relative peace in Europe. The aristocracy became wealthier and the middle classes grew in numbers, resulting in a greater demand for fashionable goods.

The classical symmetry that typified early Baroque was embellished with delicate repeating patterns of scallop shells and light scrolls. By the mid-18th century, the style became more extravagant, exotic, and asymmetrical. It was at this time that rocaille work—the shell and rock decoration that gives the style its name—became popular. Craftsmen combined scrolls, leaves, *chinoiserie*, *rocaille* work, cartouches (ornamental scrolls), monkeys, and Indian, Turkish, and allegorical figures to create exuberant works of art in porcelain, silver, and wood.

Asymmetry was a key feature of Rococo design

Carved shell on apron

Cabriole leg carved with scroll and acanthus leaf

Extravagant scrolls are typical of the period

Console table
Silver paint and gilt have been used to highlight the carved frame of this marble-topped Italian table.

Louis XV clock
Scrolls, naturalistic flowers, a crowing rooster, and cupid are all hallmarks of Rococo excess on this Swiss clock.

Birds are a common theme in Rococo decoration

The shell-like shape is a key Rococo style

KEY CLUES

- Curvaceous and asymmetrical shapes; elaborate combinations of C- and S-scrolls; cabriole legs.
- Shell and rock shapes, naturalistic flowers and foliage, "grotesques," and *chinoiserie* decoration. Latticework and the use of small, repeated patterns.
- Decoration included theatrical and pastoral figures.
- Typical techniques included gilding; light, bright enamels; ormolu mounts; marquetry; and carving.

Vauxhall cream boat
This porcelain cream boat is embellished with the bright colors and gilded highlights typical of the Rococo style.

Early Neoclassical

TOWARD THE END OF the 18th century, designers moved away from the exuberance of Rococo and, instead, took inspiration from Classical antiquity. The early Neoclassical period extended from the mid to the end of the 18th century. Designers and patrons alike were impressed by publications documenting archaeological finds at the recently discovered ancient Roman sites of Herculaneum and Pompeii. From this fascination, a Neoclassical style developed, which borrowed motifs from ancient Greek and Roman architecture. Shapes became rectilinear and were decorated with fluted columns, Vitruvian scrolls (wave pattern), husks, or garlands. The Roman urn shape was everywhere. Ceramicists and glass-makers tried to recreate the look of ancient materials.

Early examples of this refined style could be seen in the *goût grec* style of Louis XVI's France and the work of architect Robert Adam in Britain. The style spread throughout Europe. A lighter version was adopted in the US, where it was known as the Federal style.

Garlands

Sèvres vase

This French vase bears a number of early Neoclassical features: elegant tapering sides; bands of color with gilded foliate motifs; and a romantic, Classical-style landscape.

KEY CLUES

- Shapes were generally geometric and symmetrical, with architectural features; urns were popular.
- Motifs included paterae, husks, garlands, Vitruvian scrolls, columns, and Classical landscapes.
- New materials included mahogany and European porcelain.
- Some carving and decoration tended to be light and restrained.

Adam period chair

This oval-backed chair is typical of Adam-style furniture, much of which was painted and gilded to complement the decoration of the room.

Paterae

Fluted leg

Philadelphia urn

The urn was represented throughout the Neoclassical period, from silver sugar urns or coffee pots to motifs in decorative panels to finials crowning furniture.

Late Neoclassical

Eagle on plinth is flanked by foliage and acorns

BY THE TURN of the 19th century, the Neoclassical style began to reflect the imperial taste of Napoleon. Under his direction, and that of his architects Percier and Fontaine, a new look emerged in France—the Empire style. It was adopted in much of Europe.

The fashion grew for emulating Roman and Greek designs and forms with greater accuracy. In furniture, rectilinear forms were even more exaggerated, with huge pediments or deep plinths. Motifs began to represent ideas of military campaigns: laurel wreaths, medallions, and eagles were commonplace. There was also a trend for Egyptian imagery such as hieroglyphs, scarabs, and lotus leaves.

In Britain, the similar late Neoclassical look was called Regency, while Empire was the current style of Sweden, Germany, and Austria. Empire influenced the American late Federal style, which was characterized by motifs such as eagles, bellflowers, and thunderbolts.

Empire urn

Finial

This silver urn is typical of the late Neoclassical style, with its vase shape, lion-shaped finial and lion's mask motif, and tripod stand.

Federal giltwood girandole

The round shape of the convex mirror in this girandole (candle holder) was common in the first half of the 19th century.

KEY CLUES

- X-frames and tripod forms were popular; sabre (out-turned) legs on furniture.
- Motifs included the eagle, laurel leaves, medallions.
- Typical materials included mahogany, satinwood, rosewood, damask, and thin-sheet silver.
- Brass inlay, fluting, and cut glass were common.

Swedish console table

Mythological figures were popular, as in the carved and gilt griffins that form the front supports of this large-scale Swedish Empire side table.

19th-century revivals

FROM THE MIDDLE OF THE 19th century, there was an air of nationalism in Europe that was punctuated by the unification of Italy in 1861, and of Germany 10 years later. Here, as well as in Britain and France, architects, designers, and craftsmen looked back to bygone eras for inspiration. Helped by innovations in manufacturing techniques, they were able to create a wide range of furniture, ceramics, glass, and metalware that reflected dominant styles from the previous 500 years. In some cases, direct replicas of extant pieces were made, while, in others, details from a number of styles might be combined in one piece.

Architectural elements taken from medieval churches and cathedrals

Quatrefoil panel

Gothic Revival chair
This pitch pine dining chair has typical Gothic features, including the pointed-arch chair back, quatrefoil-carved panel, and the oak-leaf details. c1880

Gothic Revival

Popular in Britain, France, and, later, the US, the Gothic Revival style took inspiration from the architecture of the 14th and 15th centuries. Designers of furniture, in particular, used many architectural motifs in recreating the style, including latticework, pointed arches, quatrefoils, and heraldic motifs. There was a preference for dark woods such as oak, and heavy, solid forms.

Early on, Gothic devices were applied to contemporary forms. As the century progressed, however, a number of designers such as AWN Pugin in Britain sought to produce close renditions of existing medieval pieces. Predominantly masculine in feel, the style was also applied to ceramics, textiles, and silverware, where Gothic motifs were used as decoration.

Renaissance Revival

A number of 19th-century designers looked to the Renaissance for inspiration. German and Italian furniture designers sought to recreate the massive, architectural pieces of 15th- and 16th-century Europe. Using predominantly oak and walnut, which were well suited to prolific carving, they produced a number of large-scale, deep-carved pieces in the Renaissance style. Typical motifs included rows of fine spindles, strapwork, molded cornices, and arched doors.

In France, where the style was known as "Henri II" (after the 16th-century French monarch, married to Catherine de' Medici), ceramicists recreated the naturalistic works of Bernard Palissy. The Renaissance also influenced the design of ceramics at Meissen and Sèvres, where gray and white porcelain decorated with Classical figures, grotesques, and swags was made.

Gadrooning

Italian library table
Large, deep-carved pieces were typical of the Renaissance Revival. This Italian library table borrows motifs from Classical Rome: gadroons, acanthus leaves, urn-shaped supports, and lions' masks. Mid-19th century

Baroque Revival

The rich, elaborate style of the 17th century provided inspiration for designers across Europe. In furniture, typical features included heavy, foliate-carved pieces with elements from Classical architecture—pediments, sculptural figures, volutes (spiral scrolls), and acanthus leaves. In Britain, there was a revival of Elizabethan style. Various techniques were revived, including the Boullework of Louis XIV's Versailles, Dutch floral marquetry, and *pietra dura* (inlaid marble). In Italy, glassmakers sought to recreate elaborate Venetian and *façon de Venise* (Venetian-style) pieces. Masculine in appearance, the style tended to be more exaggerated than it had been in the 17th century, and pieces generally larger.

German cabinet
This German side cabinet epitomizes the style of the Baroque Revival, with its high-relief carving depicting playful *putti* (cherubs) and grotesques. The shaped, pierced back is also a characteristic. Mid-19th century

Rococo Revival

The exuberance of early 18th-century style, epitomized by asymmetrical, naturalistic forms and scrollwork, also found renewed favor. Ceramicists looked to manufacturers such as Meissen to produce pieces with elaborate floral ornament and gilded or enameled detail. In Britain, many factories made majolica—rich-glazed wares based on Italian maiolica (see p74). Furniture designers created light, feminine pieces with carved S- and C-scrolls and rich gilding, championed in the US by John Henry Belter, who produced exquisitely carved pieces from laminated rosewood.

Meissen water jug
A fine example of Rococo Revival porcelain, this painted and gilded Meissen jug depicting one of the four elements is elaborately decorated with applied Classical figures and leaping horses. c1840

Historicism

In Germany and Italy, influenced by the prevailing mood of nationalism that accompanied their respective unifications, craftsmen and designers pillaged the creative history of their countries for inspiration. The Nymphenburg porcelain factory in Germany, for example, produced a range of *Walzenkrug*-type tankards decorated with medieval motifs.

Glassmakers—in particular the Bohemian manufacturers Counts Buquoy and Harrach—turned to traditional styles such as the *Pokal*, or lidded beaker, decorated with spurious coats of arms and Renaissance-style motifs.

Bohemian painted and gilded vase
Known in Germany as *Milchglass* (milk glass), this opaque glass was made by a number of European manufacturers. Late 19th century

Style guide
Arts & Crafts

THE ARTS & CRAFTS movement took root in Britain and the US toward the end of the 19th century. It sought to revive the skills of medieval craftsmen in producing hand-crafted furniture, textiles, ceramics, and glassware.

At the heart of the movement were the socialist views of writer and art critic John Ruskin and designer William Morris. They were openly critical of the inferior goods of mass production. In a bid to further their ideals, craftsmen's guilds were established on the medieval model.

Designers used traditional methods to make simple, functional pieces. Ornament was sparse to show off the natural beauty of raw materials. Furniture, designed by William Morris and Charles Voysey in England and Gustav Stickley in the US, tended to be solid oak. The Roycrofters in the US hand-hammered copperware; Englishman Charles Robert Ashbee made silverware set with stones; and the Grueby Faience Co. handmade earthenware pots.

KEY CLUES

- Simple, handcrafted furniture, often influenced by country pieces.
- Motifs based on medieval imagery including repeated patterns of stylized flowers and birds; heart shapes.
- Oak for furniture, often fumed or stained to give it "age"; other period materials were inexpensive metals like brass and copper.
- Techniques include exposed construction of joints in furniture.

Stoneware bird
The London-based Martin Brothers created some of the most original Arts & Crafts wares—fanciful salt-glazed stoneware birds and animals with human features.

Stickley armchair
This American armchair epitomizes Arts & Crafts furniture: simple in shape, it is made from solid oak and has exposed tenons.

"Greenery" tapestry
William Morris was renowned for his textiles. This medieval woodland scene is woven in wool and mohair—the colors typical of Morris.

Art Nouveau

TAKING INSPIRATION FROM the Rococo style of early 18th-century Europe (see p11), Art Nouveau was epitomized by its flowing, asymmetrical lines and a pervasive interest in nature. Designers began to produce furniture, ceramics, glass, and metalware of elegance and high quality. Pieces were inherently feminine in character, with the female figure itself a popular motif, often represented with long, flowing hair and billowing robes.

Furniture designers made use of exotic veneers and applied carvings; glassmakers experimented with layered techniques and lustrous finishes; metalware, including jewelry, incorporated enameled embellishments and semi-precious stones. Natural motifs included stylized leaves and flowers and winged insects—particularly the dragonfly.

Art Nouveau started in France and Belgium—its name derived from the Maison de l'Art Nouveau gallery, opened by Samuel Bing in Paris in 1895. It was popular in Germany and Austria, where it was known as Jugendstil, and in Spain, Italy, and the US.

French designers associated with Art Nouveau include Emile Gallé for his innovative work with glass; Louis Majorelle for his exquisite furniture; and René Lalique for his jewelry. A more austere, geometric version can be seen in the work of Charles Rennie Mackintosh and the Glasgow School in Scotland, and Josef Hoffmann and the Wiener Werkstätte in Austria.

KEY CLUES

- Fluid, organic (based on nature), and asymmetrical forms.
- Motifs include whiplash curves; stylized nature; beautiful maidens, sometimes turning into flowers (*femme-fleurs*).
- Common materials of the period include exotic woods; iridescent glass; semi-precious stones.
- Techniques include veneering; applied decoration; enameling.

Gilt-bronze lamp
Loïe Fuller was the dancer who inspired this large, sculptural lamp. The female figure was a popular motif throughout the period, often depicted in swirling robes.

Tiffany "Laburnum" lamp
American Louis Comfort Tiffany was as innovative with glass as Emile Gallé. All of Tiffany's lamps were handmade, so no two are identical.

Majorelle writing desk
Typical of the Art Nouveau style are the sinuous, tapering legs, the kidney shape of the desk top, and the exotic-wood floral inlay.

Style guide
Art Deco

"ART DECO" IS A 1960s term used to describe the innovative style that dominated international design from the 1920s to the 1940s. The style takes its name from the *Exposition Internationale des Arts Décoratifs et Industriels Modernes* held in Paris in 1925, which showcased the latest advances in materials and techniques. Caught up in the Machine Age, Art Deco is known for its luxury materials, streamlined shapes, strong geometric lines, and stylized decoration. Influences included the vivid colors of the Ballet Russes (Russian Ballet) backdrops and costumes, African tribal art, and the stepped pyramids of South America.

Furniture styles ranged from lavish ivory-inlaid ebony suites to angular, lacquered "Skyscraper" furniture. Ceramics varied from the boldly colored geometric patterns of Clarice Cliff to the stylized Classical figures of Jean Mayodon. Glassmakers such as René Lalique (pp134–35) pioneered the use of hot-metal molds to mass produce glass, often with repeated geometric motifs.

1930s armchair
The reversed C-shape armrests, short sabre legs, and striking geometric upholstery are typical of Art Deco.

KEY CLUES

- Forms are angular, geometric, and streamlined.
- Chevrons, frozen fountains, and sunbursts are recurrent motifs.
- Exotic woods, sharkskin, Bakelite, lacquerware, and pressed glass are favored materials.
- Acid-etching, chroming, and lithography occur.

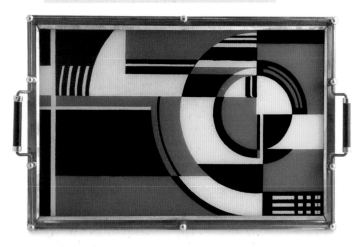

Glass and chrome tray
The geometric glass design reflects the Art Deco fascination with speed. Chrome was one of the new materials that helped to define the era. 1930s

Clarice Cliff vase
This brightly colored vase has a stepped, graduated square form. The latona tree with geometric leaves is one of 2,000 patterns designed by Clarice Cliff. 1930s

Modernism

WITH ITS ROOTS in the Machine Age of the 1920s and 1930s and the German Bauhaus school of design, Modernism paved the way for much 20th-century design. Modernist designers, including Le Corbusier and Walter Gropius, advocated the function of a design over its decorative detail. They used materials such as tubular steel and glass to produce works that were starkly geometric and devoid of ornamentation. As the century progressed, innovations in plastics, in particular, encouraged designers to experiment, resulting in more sculptural and organic forms.

New materials transformed furniture techniques and design in the 20th century. Finnish designer Alvar Aalto pioneered the use of bent plywood, producing a wide range of lightweight stools and chairs. Marcel Breuer used chrome-plated tubular steel to make the first cantilever chair. Charles and Ray Eames and Verner Panton explored new plastics such as fiberglass and polyurethane.

Swedish studio bowl by Stig Lindberg
The organic design—a stylized leaf shape—and colors are typical of the more sculptural style of the 1950s.

Georg Jensen pitcher
This water pitcher was designed by sculptor Henning Koppel. Known affectionately as the "pregnant duck," it epitomizes Koppel's sculptural style, which is known for its strong, fluid lines and sinuous curves. c1950s

Charles Eames chair
The fiberglass shell sits on a black metal cat's cradle base with birch runners. c1950

KEY CLUES

- Forms may be cantilever (in chairs), rectilinear, organic, or sculptural.
- Materials include tubular steel, bent plywood, polythene, fiberglass, and leather.
- Techniques include steam-bending laminates and exposed construction.

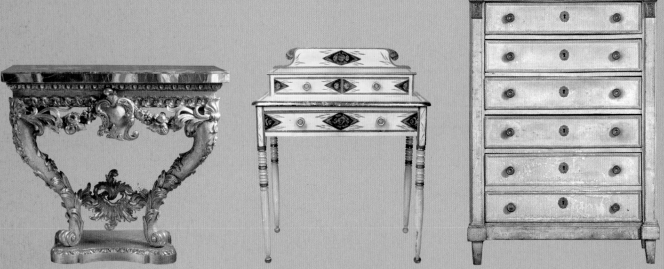

FURM

ITURE

CHAIRS AND SOFAS

Until the 17th century, the chair was a symbol of status, used to show a person's power and influence. But as society changed, and the wealthy began to expect comfort when they entertained, more equal seating arrangements were introduced.

CHAIRS HAVE BEEN MADE since ancient Egyptian times. Before the late 15th century, only the master of the house or very important guests used a chair. Other members of the household sat on stools or benches. All seats, whether stools or chairs, were made of solid, local woods.

By the early 17th century, cabinet-makers started to lengthen the back legs of the stool to create the frame for a chair back—and so the earliest side or dining chairs (without arms) were made. In France, lighter chairs with caned or upholstered backs and upholstered seats evolved. The fashion for these spread across Europe.

Sitting in comfort

From around 1700, suites of side chairs were placed around the edge of a room to emphasize its architectural features. By the middle of the 18th century, women began

Oak joint stool

This style has been in common use since the 16th century. This example has a molded rectangular seat above ring-turned legs and blocked feet.

Ring turning

Stretcher

Blocked foot

to entertain more and the armchair, or *fauteuil*, was made to suit the fashion for intimacy and conversation. Upholstery became more generous and chairs more comfortable, with flowing lines and shaped, cabriole legs. The result was an armchair with upholstered sides, known as a *bergère* in France and an easy chair in England. French chairs were widely copied throughout Europe from the 18th century onward.

By the 1760s, the enduring style of Thomas Chippendale was produced in workshops in Britain and the US. His

Acanthus leaf terminal

A cornucopia is a horn-shaped container filled with fruit, vegetables, or, as here, leaves

Carved mahogany sofa

This upholstered Classical sofa was made in Philadelphia around 1820. The arching rolled crest is carved with acanthus terminals and the legs with leaf-filled cornucopia.

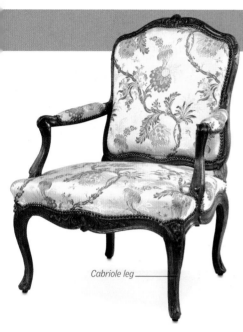

Louis XV fauteuil
The frame of this armchair (c1760) has been carved with flowers along the top rail, arms, and cabriole legs. The style was widely copied throughout Europe.

Cabriole leg

Slatted side

Arts and Crafts chair
This A. L. & J. G. Stickley Morris chair has short slats and long corbels under flat arms. Its drop-in spring seat and back cushion are upholstered in vinyl.

Corbel acts like a bracket

legacy can be seen in the intricate Gothic-, Rococo-, and Chinese-inspired chair backs associated with mid-18th-century furniture. As Chippendale's designs were taking hold so the Neoclassical style emerged and was evident in the light and elegant chairs of the late 18th century. In Britain, it was interpreted by George Hepplewhite and Thomas Sheraton. Their designs also found favor in the US where they inspired the Federal style.

French influence

In early 19th-century France, Neoclassical elements were embellished with decorative motifs from ancient Rome and Egypt, which celebrated Napoleon's successes. This Empire style was exported to the US, Sweden, Russia, and Germany. In Britain it was called the Regency style. Common to both Empire and Regency was the fashion for sets of dining chairs, which included a pair of armchairs.

In the 1820s, the development of coiled upholstery springs, used in button-back chairs among others, increased comfort. The 19th-century passion for style revivals—from Renaissance to Rococo—saw little innovation in chair construction. The Arts and Crafts movement in Britain and the US at the end of the 19th century also based its designs on the British country and American Mission styles of the past. There was one exception—Austrian

Modern easy chair
This "Tank" chair, designed by Alvar Aalto in 1936, has bent laminated birch sides and original tiger-skin fabric upholstery.

Michael Thonet's bentwood furniture, first seen at a trade show in 1841. His method of steam-bending led to the mass-produced bent-ply chairs made by Charles and Ray Eames a century later.

In the 1920s, Art Deco designers used new materials such as Bakelite and aluminum. Chair design began to change. Designers such as Marcel Breuer at the Bauhaus in Germany, Le Corbusier in France, and Alvar Aalto in Finland used chrome-plated tubular steel and bent plywood. Their cantilevered frames revolutionized chair design in the mid-20th century. By the 1950s, designers were using laminated wood, new plastics, fiberglass, and foam padding to make affordable and comfortable chairs that suited the new informality.

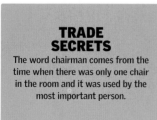

TRADE SECRETS
The word chairman comes from the time when there was only one chair in the room and it was used by the most important person.

The briefing
Looking at chairs

THE WAY A CHAIR WAS constructed gives valuable information about when and where it was made. The earliest chairs had pegged joints, while screws, pins, and glue came later. The amount of carving, especially where it required extra, detailed work from the craftsman, is a sign of quality. Always look at the style of a chair and the motifs it is decorated with, as these will help with identification. Look for honest wear and damage.

WATCH OUT!
Never lift an antique chair by its arms as this puts an unnecessary strain on its weakest points.

Top rail

Splat

Side rail

Shoe bar

Knee

Front rail or apron

George I burr walnut side chair
A gently curving top rail is carved with a central shell and the tops of the side rails curve round to join the top of the wide, veneered splat. Carvings on the front rail and knees are a sign of quality. The cabriole front legs terminate in claw-and-ball feet. c1720

Closer inspection
Examine the chair carefully, paying particular attention to the underside where all sorts of clues may have been left by the maker.

Construction

The way in which a chair was constructed will provide many clues to its date. The underside of the chair, which is not visible when the chair is in use, will not be as well finished and so you may be able to see many of the original elements of the chair. Look underneath the chair to see the type of joints, whether the wood was hand- or machine-cut, and how any decoration was done.

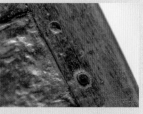

Joints
Examine the joints. Are they held together by pegs, screws, or glue? Pegs were the earliest method used to reinforce a joint.

Under the seat
Check under the seat. Is the seat drop-in or over-stuffed? Is any part of the decoration an integral part of the frame or has it been attached afterward?

Manufacturing marks
Clues to construction may be seen in marks on the wood. Circular marks suggest a machine saw. Hand-worked marks are irregular.

What to look at

Top rail

This is often a good place to look at the wood for clues to quality and age. Is the wood veneered? If so, what color is it and how thick is it? Does the thickness vary? Is any detail carved from the wood? Is it flat or raised to the touch? *See p215 for checking wood types.*

Shoe bar

The shoe bar attaches the back to the seat. The way that the back section is attached to the shoe piece can give a clue to age. Has it been left plain or is there carved or other decoration?

Chair back

The shape of the seat back can give you clues to identity. Look at how it is decorated. Is it painted or gilded? Is it upholstered? Is it veneered? If there's a back splat, is it solid or pierced? What shape is the splat? Is it carved? *See p209 for chair back shapes.*

Arms

The arms should follow the style and shape of the rest of the chair. Look for signs of early construction such as pegged joints. Shapes that were difficult to carve—such as shepherd's crooks—are an indication of quality.

Leg shape

Look at front and back legs. What is the shape? How are the legs decorated? Do they match the style of the chair? Check the sweep of the legs and see how they are joined. Are there signs of repair? *See p213 for leg shapes.*

Carvings

Does the carving stand proud (greatly elevated) from the wood? Is it well executed? What is the style of the carving? What sort of motifs have been used?

Knees

What is the shape? Have they been decorated? What is the quality of any carving? Use the thumb test—how raised is it? Is there one simple motif or have other elements been added?

Feet

Look at the shape and decoration, if any. Do they match the style of the chair? Is the wood darker in areas hard to dust (a sign of "honest" ageing)? Do signs of age match normal usage? *See p210 for foot shapes.*

Early 18th-century chairs

THE 18TH-CENTURY STYLE of chair inspired by Dutch high-backed designs that emerged towards the end of the 1600s is widely referred to as Queen Anne. These chairs have a straight, narrow back with rounded shoulders. Early examples feature a solid vase- or baluster-shaped splat, round or balloon-shaped drop-in seats, and legs joined by flat or turned stretchers. As the 1700s progressed, chair backs developed serpentine crests rails and wider, more ornate splats. The introduction of corner blocks to the interior edges of the chair frame made stretchers unnecessary, leading to widespread use of the curvaceous cabriole leg terminating with claw-and-ball feet.

English chair

This side chair, dating from around 1720, is shorter and wider than its later American counterpart. It is made from burr walnut, which is typical of chairs of this period. Walnut was often used as a hand-cut veneer over oak for the frame, while the legs were made of solid walnut, although elm and oak occur in vernacular pieces. The balloon-shaped seat is covered in *gros* and *petit point* needlework. The eye is drawn to the ornate carving of the crest rail, a stark contrast to the wide, flat back splat, and echoed in the carving to the seat rail and on the knees.

TRADE SECRETS

Look out for 19th-century alterations to these chairs. Quite often, on English chairs, shaped corner brackets might have been screwed and glued to the seat frame to offer additional support for the seat. This is less common on American chairs, where the original seat frame had a more substantial, rectangular support. Some examples might also have a metal brace added to the back of the chair, strengthening the area where the horizontal top rail joins the upright stile.

Back splat
It was not uncommon to have scrolled ears on the back splat, just below where it joins the crest rail.

Crest rail is ornately carved

Carved back splat

Balloon-shaped seat

Foot
The solid walnut leg terminates in a well-carved claw-and-ball foot, popular from 1725.

Cabriole leg
The knees are carved with a single shell motif, flanked on either side by volutes.

George I side chair
One of a pair, this chair is short and heavy with an emphasis on the horizontal.
c1720; $100,000–150,000 (the pair)

CLAW-AND-BALL FEET

Good: The claws around the ball, from a George I walnut card table, c1720, are well defined, but while they are nicely carved there is little fine detail.

Better: The carving of the claws from a George II mahogany concertina action tea table is more defined and the claws are separate from the ball.

Best: The high-quality carving shows plenty of details such as the hairs and sinews of the claw. This example is from a George II wing armchair c1750.

American chair

The Queen Anne style developed in the colonies from 1720 to 1750. Philadelphia produced some of the finest chairs. Made from walnut and sometimes mahogany, chairs tended to be carved from solid wood, not veneered. Form usually followed English examples, with balloon-shaped seats and solid, vase-shaped slats. Chairs were often taller and more slender. The claw-and-ball foot developed around 1740 in the US. Pad or slipper feet lingered well into the second half of the century.

Ornament was more restrained, but carved scallop shells were still popular in the US as well as in England

Philadelphia side chair
This solid walnut chair is taller and more slender than English examples. c1760; $20,000–25,000

Crest rail
The chair has a more pronounced, serpentine crest rail, often seen on later examples, with a simple, carved shell motif.

Back splat
The flat, unornamented splat emphasizes the inherent beauty in the grain of the wood.

Cabriole leg
The shell-carved knees are considerably less ornate than the English example.

Foot
Elegant cabriole legs terminate in intaglio-carved slipper feet—in use for longer than in England.

Mid-18th century armchairs

IN THE 18TH CENTURY, the French trend for salons—where the wealthy could gather to enjoy conversation—was led by women. The latest fashions for hooped skirts (from 1720) and high, elaborate hairstyles led to changes in chair design. Arms were shortened and backs lowered to make chairs more comfortable. The relative informality of the salons also meant that elegant, less formal furniture was required. The *fauteuil* was an upholstered armchair with open sides, while a *bergère* had upholstered panels between the arms and seat. These new forms were copied throughout Europe, and interpretations of the *fauteuil* became the chair of choice in fashionable homes.

French chairs

The new *fauteuils* were lighter and more refined than chairs from the 17th century, reflecting the fashion for feminine furnishings. They were often decorated in the same style as the other furniture in the room.

The sitter's comfort was assured by an upholstered seat, back, and arm rests, and the arms were set back from the front of the chair to accommodate ladies' skirts. The Rococo decoration and cabriole legs gave *fauteuils* an elegant, graceful style.

KEY CLUES

- Arms set back about a quarter of the length of the side rail.
- Asymmetrical Rococo decoration incorporating shells and *rocaille* (rockwork).
- Curved frame featuring cabriole legs.
- Painted pale blue, green, or yellow with gilding to emphasize the shape and carved detail.

White-painted frame is highlighted with gilding

Upholstery is in fabric typical of the period

Gilding emphasizes the carved shellwork

French bergère

The new chairs had to be comfortable. Here, a further seat and back cushion have been made to supplement the upholstered back and seat. c1780

Reeded leg

Toupie foot

French fauteuil

As the century progressed, Neoclassical elements were incorporated, seen here in turned and reeded legs that terminate in *toupie* feet. c1780; $1,000–1,500

French fauteuil

The elegant proportions and gentle curves are typical of French *fauteuils*. The shell motifs carved on the crest rail and knees indicate the date. c1750

TRADE SECRETS

In the 18th century, French cabinet-makers worked within a strict guild system. Between 1743 and 1751, they had to stamp their initials followed by the letters JME (*juré des menuisiers et ébénistes*) on their work. As a result, much French furniture from Louis XV's reign (1724–74) can be attributed to a maker.

German chairs

Chairs were heavier in style than their French and Italian equivalents. Bavarian and Rococo decoration were popular and often resulted in swirling gilded frames. German cabinet-makers followed the French style by choosing pale upholstery that complemented the frame of the chair.

KEY CLUES

- Heavier, more ornately carved frame.
- Frames gilded or painted white with gilt highlights.
- As in France, upholstery chosen to reflect the décor of the room.
- Carved with Rococo motifs.
- Cabriole legs.

*Accentuated curves
are German in style*

*Cabriole legs
are typical
of the period*

German fauteuil
The ornate *rocaille* carving and heavy gilding are evidence of the chair's German heritage. c1745

English chairs

Designers such as Thomas Chippendale and Giles Grendey were inspired by the new French forms and the European fashion for Rococo. The result was an armchair that followed the French Rococo shape but was decorated with Classically inspired details such as palmettes and paterae.

KEY CLUES

- French in shape with rounded back, inset arms, and upholstery.
- Legs may be straight or gently curved into cabriole shape.
- Frames heavily gilded with Classical rather than Rococo decoration.

*Neoclassical decoration
such as scrolls suggests
a later chair*

English armchair
Although French in style, the square, tapering legs point to a date later in the 18th century. c1775

Italian chairs

The design of Italian chairs was influenced by French Rococo but styles differed from region to region. Craftsmen in Piedmont and Liguria were heavily influenced by pieces from neighboring France, while in Venice, the style was more exaggerated. *Fauteuils* had higher, rounder backs, which were ornately carved and often gilded.

KEY CLUES

- Higher backs more often oval or fan-shaped than French counterparts.
- Intricate carving picked out with gilt.
- Chair frames carved all over rather than in highlighted sections.
- Elegant, feminine style set off with colorful paintwork.

Intricate leaf carving

JARGON BUSTER

Cabriole Furniture leg popular in the first half of the 18th century. It curves out at the top and tapers to an inward curve.

*Elegant curved
arms are
ornately gilded*

*Carving covers
most of the
frame*

Italian armchair
Italian craftsmen copied the pastel paint and coordinating upholstery favored by the French. c1750

Louis XVI and Gustavian chairs

IN THE YEARS before the French Revolution, the ill-fated king Louis XVI and his Austrian bride Marie Antoinette filled their palaces with sumptuous furniture. Chairs from early in their reign (1774–89) are often referred to as Transitional, as they feature both Rococo and Neoclassical elements. Later examples tend to be more Neoclassical.

Whatever the style favored by the royal couple, their taste was copied by other wealthy French households and the ruling classes elsewhere in Europe, who were keen to follow the latest fashions. Gustavian chairs from Sweden follow a similar style to the Louis XVI chairs and were inspired by King Gustav III's visit to Italy and Versaillles in 1771.

Louis XVI chairs

During Louis XVI's reign, chairs in France became less rounded and more rectilinear in shape. Oval and shield-shaped chair backs had been common since 1760 and this continued during the Transitional period, to be replaced by squarer backs later. Chair frames were carved with Classical motifs such as Vitruvian scrolls. They may be painted but are usually gilded.

Fabrics used for upholstery were usually pale, feminine silks, which complemented the gilded frame.

KEY CLUES

- Substantial, heavy frame, with plenty of complex carved overall ornamentation.
- Wood is covered with gilding.
- Neoclassical motifs such as repeating patterns copied from friezes of ancient Greek temples.
- Turned, tapering legs with further carving.

Finial

Top rail is carved and pierced with ribbons and flowers

Vitruvian scroll is like a series of waves

Fluted legs are half painted, half gilded

Louis XVI fauteuil
This painted and gilded chair has an oval back and carved top rail, finials, arms, seat rail, and legs. c1785

Guilloche pattern comes from Classical architecture

Carved sphinx

Louis XVI bergère
Popular motifs include carved guilloche on the back and sphinxes on square, fluted pedestals that support the arms. c1785

Louis XVI fauteuil
Patterned blue silk upholstery on the arm rests, oval back, and shaped seat was designed to match the décor of the room. c1775

Louis XVI fauteuil
The elegant proportions of the rectangular back with its slightly arched top rail and cut-out corners are typically French. c1780

JARGON BUSTER
Finial Decorative knob applied to furniture or lids of silver, ceramic, or glass containers. A finial is often shaped like an acorn or urn.

GUSTAV III OF SWEDEN

Gustav III visited Versailles before his coronation in 1771 and fell in love with the French Neoclassical style. When he returned home, he turned Sweden into the "Paris of the North" by introducing a cultural and architectural sophistication that had not been seen before.

Gustav invited French cabinet-makers to Sweden to make furniture in the latest designs. When he was unable to pay them they went back to France, leaving their work behind. Local craftsmen imitated the costly materials used in France and Italy. However, they substituted native pine for walnut or imported mahogany. They painted the wood to look like marble and the grain of exotic trees.

King Gustav III The monarch brought French Neoclassical style to Sweden.

Gustavian chairs

Early Swedish chairs were often carved from walnut, but later pieces were usually made from local, cheaper woods such as pine and schubirch. The wood was whitewashed or painted gray, as the Swedish nobility could not afford the gilding popular at court. The carving was lighter and simpler than on French chairs.

Some Gustavian chairs show a British influence with motifs such as urns. Upholstery tended to be the pale silks that were also favoured by the French.

KEY CLUES

- Local woods rather than mahogany.
- Painted not gilded frame, although there may be occasional gilt highlights.
- A light and elegant interpretation of French style.
- Simple, reeded legs.
- Decoration more restrained.

The frame is carved with Neoclassical motifs

Reeded legs

Gustavian armchair
The white-painted frame is typical of Gustavian furniture. The upholstery features a Neoclassical design. c1790; $2,500–3,500

Pierced splat of stylized intertwined "Gs"

Gustavian armchair
Painted white with gilt highlights, the pierced splat is in the form of entwined "Gs" in homage to Gustav III. c1780; $3,000–3,500

Late Gustavian fauteuil
More austere than earlier examples, this gilded, upholstered chair has restrained carving and fluted legs. c1810; $2,000–2,500

Baluster spindles

Gustavian chair
The chair back, made by Erik Öhrmark of Stockholm, has baluster-shaped spindles, a Swedish feature. c1815; $1,500–2,000

Gustavian armchair
This hat-backed chair has a typically Swedish painted frame, with turned, tapered legs and gilt highlights. c1790; $3,000–4,000

The lineup
18th-century chairs

THE MANY CHAIR DESIGNS in the 18th century reflect the many changes in style and politics of that time. In the first decades, the Baroque style continued to be influential. But as the European upper classes adopted the French fashion for informal entertaining, they copied French Rococo styles of the *fauteuil* (open-sided armchair) and *bergère* (closed-sided armchair).

In England, the war with France at the beginning of the century led to a move away from French influences and new British styles developed. At first, Queen Anne style was popular, but the publication of Thomas Chippendale's *The Gentleman and Cabinet-Maker's Director* in 1754 introduced a new style that remained popular for over 100 years. Cabinet-makers in the American colonies interpreted both Queen Anne and Chippendale styles. In the mid- to late 18th century, the Neoclassical style took root. Chairs were squarer and straighter with turned, tapered legs rather than cabriole. At first, chairs were made singly but, from the mid-century, sets of furniture (suites) became popular.

Cartouche

Shell motif on shaped knees

Burr walnut chair. c1720

George I chairs

This style of chair, with solid, inverted, baluster-shaped back splat and cabriole front legs, was copied throughout Europe and the American colonies.

- S-scroll uprights frame the back splat.
- The crest rail and shaped knees were carved with shells and the center of the seat rail with a carouche.
- Cabriole legs end in animal details such as claw-and-ball feet or hooves.

CHINESE CARVED BLACKWOOD

By the late 18th century, Chinese craftsmen were combining European motifs with their traditional forms. In this example of a blackwood chair, the back splat takes a Chinese shape, while the rest of the chair echoes contemporary European styles. However, the 19th century saw the strict rectilinear designs of the past softened by curves. Native hardwoods were particularly suited to carved decoration.

Chinese chair
Curves round off the corners.
c1850;
$500–700

Shell carving

Marquetry decoration used in Dutch pieces was no longer fashionable in Britain

Shepherd's crook arms

Claw-and-ball foot

George II walnut elbow chair. c1740; $3,500–5,000

Dutch chairs

Dutch cabinet-makers imitated British designs of the period.

- British-influenced features include shell-carved crests and knees, solid vase-shaped splats, drop-in seats, and cabriole legs with claw-and-ball feet.
- Seat rails are more serpentine (wavy) and sometimes have a shaped lower section.

Giltwood

Molding on legs matches arms and back

Fauteuil à la reine by N blanchard. c1755

Louis XVI chairs

The French fashion for relaxed entertaining led to the development of more informal chairs.

- Back and seat rails are shaped, carved, and molded, while cabriole legs were tapering, carved, and molded.
- Frames tend to be gilded.
- Upholstery is silk or needlework.
- Cabinet-makers had to mark their work.

Shell decoration suggests influence of French Rococo

Massive proportions matched by ornately carved frame

Asymmetrical French Rococo-style decoration

Solid vase-shaped splat in British style

Gilt frame side chair. 18th century; $1,500–2,000

German chairs

In the early part of the century, cabinet-makers favored gilded, carved wood frames. Chair shapes and decorations took their inspiration from England and France.

- Heavily carved, gilded, or painted frames.
- Chairs from the north derive from Dutch or English styles such as Chippendale.

Late Baroque chair. c1795; $5,000–10,000

Italian Baroque chairs

The influence of 17th-century Baroque can be seen in the bold carving on the seat frame.

- Chair backs usually have a pronounced outward curve.
- Flaring arms and overall proportions are more exaggerated than the French and English chairs that served as inspiration.

Painted and gilded chair. c1780; $1,000–1,500

Swedish Rococo chairs

Chairs from early in the century were painted and had cabriole legs and a solid back splat.

- The shell carving in the crest rail is often accompanied by a "keyhole" pierced through the upper section of the back splat.
- Carved areas may be highlighted with gilding.
- Variety of styles; design tends to be conservative.

Large-scale shell motif is in the manner of London cabinet-maker Giles Grendey

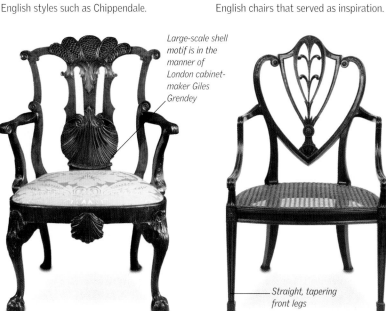

Shield back has a pierced and carved splat inspired by Hepplewhite

Straight, tapering front legs

Mahogany chair. c1740

George II chairs

From the early 1730s, mahogany imported from colonies in the West Indies and Honduras became the wood of choice in Britain.

- The hard wood allowed deep carving, different from French carving.
- Mahogany was also strong—heavy chairs were influenced by the furnishings of architect-designer William Kent.

Carved mahogany chair. c1780; $250,000–350,000

Hepplewhite designs

Hepplewhite's work is known through *The Cabinet-Maker and Upholsterer's Guide* (1788), but no furniture can be attributed to him.

- Designs feature shield-, oval-, and heart-shaped backs with carved and pierced splats in the shape of urns, festoons, and drapery.
- Legs are round or square, straight or tapering, and with leaf ornament.

Mahogany side chair. c1800; $1,500–2,000

American Federal chairs

American Neoclassical was inspired by British designers Adam, Hepplewhite, and Sheraton.

- The shield back typically has a pierced and carved splat and square, tapering legs.
- Early pieces are restrained in form and show great attention to detail.
- Later examples take inspiration directly from ancient Greek and Roman sources.

Chippendale chairs

WORKING IN LONDON from the mid-18th century, Thomas Chippendale (1718–79) has become synonymous with furniture design from this period. He is seen as one of the best designers of his era. Little extant furniture can be attributed directly to Chippendale, yet his style has endured, thanks largely to his book *The Gentleman and* *Cabinet-Maker's Director* (see box, opposite). The designs were copied by furniture-makers in Britain, the US, and the colonies. They are testimony to Chippendale's skill at interpreting Rococo and Neoclassical styles, and also to his interest in *chinoiserie* and the Gothic revival that flourished from the middle of the century.

English Chippendale chair

The Chippendale chair is the epitome of Chippendale's furniture: more than 60 variations appear in the *Director*. Despite the different stylistic influences, the basic shape remains the same. With an emphasis on the horizontal, English chairs are wide and low. The backs are carved and pierced, often with interlaced splats and scrollwork. A serpentine crest rail rests on inward-curving stiles. Most chairs have square or trapezoid drop-in seats. Front legs reflect the fashion for Rococo cabriole legs with carved knees and claw-and-ball feet. Mahogany is the wood of choice, allowing for deep-cut, detailed carving, though walnut and fruitwood are also used.

Knee
The legs are deep carved with the fashionable acanthus motif from thigh to knee.

Crest rail
The crest rail is carved along its entire length, with a central shell motif and leaf-carved ears.

Foot
The cabriole legs terminate in well-rounded claw-and-ball feet.

Back splat
The chair has an elegant, vase-shaped, carved and pierced splat.

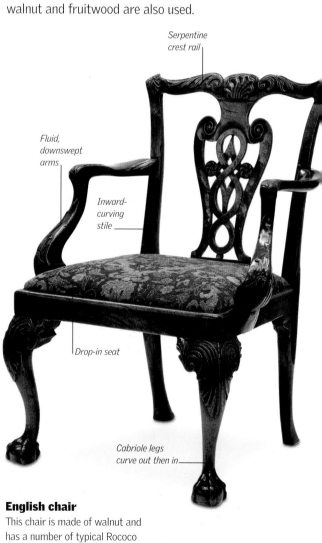

Serpentine crest rail

Fluid, downswept arms

Inward-curving stile

Drop-in seat

Cabriole legs curve out then in

English chair
This chair is made of walnut and has a number of typical Rococo features. c1760; $30,000–35,000

THE GENTLEMAN AND CABINET-MAKER'S DIRECTOR

The Gentleman and Cabinet-Maker's Director, produced by Chippendale in 1754, is a primary reason for the longevity of his designs. Although he is most famous today for his chairs, the book featured designs for everything from desks and tables to commodes and mirrors.

Chippendale published the book as a way to cultivate the patronage of the aristocracy, although the instructions were meant for the cabinet-makers who recreated the designs for their wealthy clients.

His designs included fanciful Oriental styles inspired by *chinoiserie*, French Rococo, Gothic, and Classical motifs.

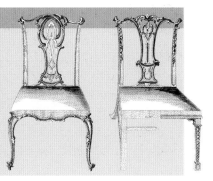

Designs from Chippendale's Director
Cabinet-makers and their clients could choose from a number of styles.

American Chippendale chair

An influx of immigrant craftsmen and the availability of the *Director* meant that Chippendale became the style of choice in the US from the middle of the 18th century. Furniture-makers in the cities—primarily Philadelphia, Boston, and New York—and their rural communities embraced the style. Local and recent immigrant cabinet-makers produced pieces so close to the English originals that in the past they were often confused. But with an emphasis on the vertical, US designs tend to have tall, slender legs and a high shoe in the back splat. Carving, often of acanthus or shell, is usually more restrained. Woods of choice include mahogany, walnut, and maple.

The carved shell serves as an accent

Elegant flat back

High shoe

Raked rear legs

American chair
This chair is made of mahogany and is lighter and more slender than the English example. c1770; $3,500–5,000

Crest rail
The crest rail has a central shell motif and terminates in well-carved ears.

Back splat
An emphasis on the vertical is endorsed by the deep shoe at the base of the splat.

Knee
The knee has a carved shell motif – less common for this period than acanthus or volutes (spiral scrolls).

Foot
The claw-and-ball feet have well-turned ankles and are slightly squared (a New York feature) with straight-lined talons.

The lineup
Neoclassical sofas

THE SOFA EMERGED as a form during the early 18th century. It developed at a rapid pace during the Neoclassical era (c1760–c1830) to meet the demand for greater comfort in the home. Early forms were based on the designs of contemporary side chairs and had carved backs and upholstered seats. By the end of the century, most also had upholstered backs and sides and were covered in luxurious fabrics such as silk, damask, velvet, and chintz. This style is early Neoclassical: pieces were rectilinear, having exposed mahogany frames with little or restrained ornament and elegant, tapered legs. Typical motifs included carved acanthus leaves, guilloche bands, and rosettes.

With the turn of the century came the Empire style in France, interpreted across Europe and in the US. Forms were generally heavier and reflected an attempt to copy typical Classical forms more closely. Sofa frames were more ornately shaped, often with scrolling back rails and outscrolled arms, and stood on sabre legs or lion's paw feet. Carving was more prominent, with sphinx and mummy motifs from ancient Egypt as well as military motifs from ancient Rome, such as medallions, laurel wreaths, and fasces.

Sphinx

Lion's paw foot

Empire canapé. c1800; W: 62in (157cm)

Empire, French

French Empire style dominated Europe in the early 19th century. Dictated, to some extent, by the personal tastes of Napoleon, this was a more heavily masculine version of the Neoclassical style.

- Designers attempted to copy the furniture of ancient Rome accurately.
- Mahogany was the prevalent wood, with carved decoration becoming more prominent.
- Ancient Egyptian motifs were common.

Biedermeier sofa. c1825; L: 85in (215cm); $2,000–2,500

Biedermeier, Germany

This style developed alongside Empire in Germany, Austria, Sweden, and Norway. Empire was popular with the nobility, while Biedermeier tended to furnish the homes of the middle classes.

- Symmetrical, geometric forms prevail.
- Woods include imported mahogany, but also less expensive native walnut, cherry, and birch.
- Emphasis on grain of wood, accentuated with partial ebonizing.

Pine cone finial

Carved ribbon bows

Provincial Louis XVI sofa. c1780; $1,500–2,000

Louis XVI, France

The reign of Louis XVI saw the beginnings of the Neoclassical style, with rectilinear shapes taking over from curved Rococo ones.

- Light, simple rectangular frame, often open to the back and arms.
- Elegant, tapering, reeded legs.
- Restrained carved ornament bearing Neoclassical motifs.
- Provincial pieces not necessarily marked.

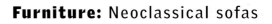

Russian Empire sofa.
L: 80in (200cm); $1,000–1,500

Gustavian sofa. c1800;
L: 74in (185cm); $1,700–2,500

Russian

Russian Neoclassical furniture reflected fashions in France, although many designs were introduced to Russia by architects Thomas de Thomon (Swiss) and Carlo Rossi (Italian).

- Rectilinear frames are heavy and looked less refined than contemporary French examples.
- Often made from mahogany and heavily carved with Neoclassical motifs.

Gustavian, Sweden

Gustavian was the Swedish interpretation of Neoclassical style, named after Gustav III of Sweden, who championed the style.

- Generally a lighter, more conservative, version of the French Neoclassical style.
- Inferiority of native woods, typically pine, meant that many pieces were painted to match the interior design of a room.
- Restrained use of ornament.

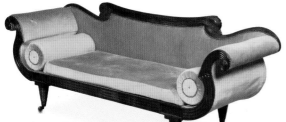

Regency mahogany sofa.
L: 85in (215cm); $2,500–3,500

Federal mahogany sofa. c1830;
L: 74½in (186cm); $1,700–2,500

Regency, UK

Influenced by the exuberant tastes of the Prince Regent (later George IV), the Regency period in Britain (c1800–c1830) saw a more flamboyant expression of the French Empire style.

- Richly upholstered in bright-colored silk or damask, sofas were the ultimate in comfort and luxury.
- Elaborately scrolled back rail and outscrolled arms echo Classical styles of ancient Rome.

Federal, US

A more understated Neoclassical style developed in the US in the early 19th century, with many pieces based on designs produced by Sheraton, Hepplewhite, and Adam.

- Simple, rectilinear frames with silk or satin upholstery.
- Gently scrolled and carved back rails with minimal decoration.
- Reeded or fluted tapering legs.

Classical carved sofa. c1825;
$2,500–3,500

American Empire sofa. Mid-19th century;
W: 88in (220cm); $1,000–1,500

Classical, US

More akin to British Regency designs, the American Classical style evolved from the Federal style from c1815 and is particularly associated with New York city.

- Mahogany was the wood of choice and is often deep-carved with Neoclassical motifs.
- Some pieces have a hint of British exoticism.
- Fashion for scrolled, carved arms in the Regency style.

Empire, US

From c1830, American designers were influenced by the French Empire style that dominated contemporary Europe. They took the earlier, delicate Federal style and made it bigger, bulkier, and more ornate.

- Scroll-end sofas and settees are typical forms.
- Sofas usually have sabre or X-shaped legs.

TABLES

Over the last 800 years, the table has evolved from the simple wooden trestle to the range of metal, glass, plastic, and wooden dining, occasional, and coffee tables that we know today. Its development is closely tied to the social changes during this time.

IN THE MIDDLE AGES, two types of table prevailed. The trestle table had a horizontal frame supporting a rectangular, plank-type top. The refectory table was a large, heavy affair, used among settled communities such as monks. Both types were made of wood, usually oak, and designed for seating a large number of people in a big hall.

Refectory table
The design of this 17th-century oak table is simple: a rectangular planked top on ring-turned supports, joined by stretchers.

Smaller tables

A move from the large hall to smaller dining parlors in the 17th century made large tables unnecessary. Instead, households preferred the gateleg table, which remained popular well into the 18th century. This had a round or oval tabletop, often with hinged flaps, supported on a gateleg base. The table could be carried and made smaller or larger to suit the occasion. Generally made of oak, these tables had turned legs joined by stretchers. It was around this time that small round-topped tables came in as candle stands. Console tables could be found in formal reception

18th-century console table
Console tables were for show, the preserve of the weathiest residences, as is suggested by the elaborate carving, and expensive gilding and marble top.

Bureau plat

Introduced in France during the early 18th century, the *bureau plat* was used by men for writing. It often had a working drawer on one side with a dummy drawer on the opposite side.

Regency breakfast table

This mahogany table with brass inlay is typical of the early 19th century. The top is raised on a single stem supported by four splayed legs.

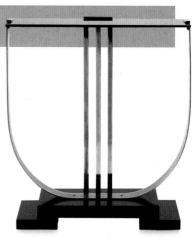

Art Deco console table

Paul Frankl designed this 1920s table with roots in ancient Rome, but used contemporary materials —chrome, lacquer, and glass—and techniques.

rooms. When placed against the wall of a room, these tables had little practical use, but were part of the architectural vocabulary of the room. They were based on designs in the Baroque style fashionable in Italy: heavy, often marble, rectangular tops supported on carved, gilt legs.

Home entertaining

The 18th century witnessed many changes in social life, primarily a demand for greater comfort and entertaining in the home. This shift gave rise to all manner of additional tables. Smaller tables were designed for a range of purposes—playing cards, taking tea, writing letters, and needlework. Many of these tables had drop leaves or tilt tops and drawers, making them more versatile. Kept to the side of a room when not in use, most were mounted on casters to make them easier to move. The *bureau plat* was first seen during the first half of the century. Often housed in the bedchamber, these large tables with drawers in the apron were used as men's writing tables.

Until the 17th century the wealthy tended to eat in large communal halls around long refectory tables. These were gradually replaced by intimate parlors where small groups ate together around circular gateleg tables, which encouraged conversation. However, new forms of dining table emerged in the mid-18th century. Like the gateleg

tables that preceded them, these could be made larger or smaller by adding or removing leaves or folding down flaps. From the 1750s, these tables often consisted of a central, rectangular gateleg table with two D-shaped ends, which could be added to make it longer. When the ends were not required they were often used as pier tables.

The Pembroke table appeared toward the end of the century. This was a small, decorative rectangular table with drop leaves to the long sides. As well as dining, it was used as a games and work table, as its owner required. As it was small, and on casters, the Pembroke table had the added benefit of being easy to move around the room.

The fashion for extravagant meals in the mid-19th century led to the re-emergence of the dedicated dining room and single, large dining tables. Major developments in the 19th century included two-tier tables, and nests of tables, where three or four sizes of the same occasional table were stacked one above the other when not in use.

20th-century dynamism

It was during the 20th century that table design benefited from new materials and techniques. Although the purposes remained the same—dining, writing, display, playing games—tables began to look different. Many incorporated such diverse materials as mirror, bent ply, tubular steel, and chrome during the early 1900s, and new-age plastics and recycled cardboard from mid-century. The coffee table was introduced in the 1950s and can lay claim to being the most recent true innovation.

The briefing
Looking at tables

Although construction methods have become more sophisticated the basic components of a table top and base have changed little. Whether a drop-leaf, gateleg, pedestal, or tripod construction, the clues to the table's date lie in the evidence of craftsmanship, proportion, wood used, the type of carving or veneer, and the complexity of any mechanism. Look underneath the table and inside any drawers to see how they are made as well as studying the table top and legs.

WATCH OUT!
Check that a table top and base match—they are made from the same wood or veneers. Check the underside of the top—there should be no unexplained marks.

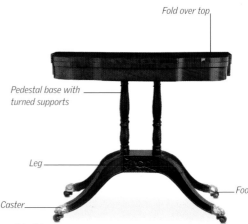

Fold over top

Pedestal base with turned supports

Leg

Caster

Foot

Card table
An American Classical mahogany card table,with acanthus carving and reeded columns and radiating fan veneered top. c1815 H: 36in (91.5cm)

Close inspection
This table opens out to become a card table, with a green baize lining. When not in use it can be folded up and pushed to the side of the room.

Veneers

A veneer is a thin layer of expensive wood glued to a cheaper carcase. Early veneers—from the 17th and early 18th centuries—were hand-cut and of uneven thickness (about $1/8$in/3mm). Later, machine-cut veneers are paper thin and of standard thickness. Woods used include mahogany, satinwood, rosewood, and maple.

Quarter veneer Four sheets of veneer from the same piece of wood are arranged diagonally in pairs so the grain creates an X pattern. Quarter veneers are suited to strong-grained timbers such as walnut, burr walnut, mahogany, tulipwood, kingwood, and laburnum.

Oyster veneer Circular slices of a thin branch are arranged one on top of the other to create the effect of a pile of oysters or logs of wood. Oyster veneers were first used in the 17th century. Woods used include walnut, kingwood, laburnum, and mahogany.

Crossbanding and stringing Strips of veneer set at right angles to the main veneer (crossbanding) are framed with a thin strip (string) of contrasting wood or metal. Early examples used the same wood; later ones use contrasting and exotic woods.

Herringbone veneer This refined crossbanding was also used to frame edges, often on the finest British 18th-century furniture. Two strips are cut on the diagonal from a piece of straight-grained wood. They are placed side by side so one mirrors the other.

What to look at

The table top

Look to see whether the top is solid or veneered. You can tell if there is a veneer by examining the edge of the table top. If the top is a solid piece, is it made from a single plank or interlocking planks? If it is veneered, try to identify the type of wood used as this helps to tell you where the piece was made and its age. Notice whether the veneer is machine or hand cut as this is also a good clue to age. *See box opposite for more on veneers and p215 for checking wood types.*

The shape of the top

The top may be straight or shaped. Identify the shape: *demi-lune* (half-moon or semi-circle), serpentine or, as here, more elaborate. Shaped edges require skill to make and are a sign of quality.

The underside

A period table should have a lighter underside, with none of the patination found on the top. Patination is the surface color caused by years of wear, dust, sweat from hands, and polishing. That doesn't happen to the underside.

Fixture of top to base

Check underneath to see whether the top is permanently fixed to the base. If it tilts or turns, this will give you a good clue as to the table's purpose. Tables with adjustable tops were usually designed for occasional use. The tops would be dropped down and the table moved when not in use.

Decoration

Look at any decoration, such as painting, gilding, mounts, or carving. The style may help indicate the period, and is also a good way of assessing quality. The panel between the legs is carved on this table. The carving, of acanthus leaves, is typical of the Neoclassical designs popular early in the 19th century. *See pp206–209 for more on motifs.*

The legs

Check the leg formation. They may be at the corners, perhaps joined by stretchers. Alternatively, there may be a central stem with three or four legs. The shape of the legs is a good style indicator. So, too, is the decoration: legs may be square, turned, fluted, reeded, and/or painted.

Refectory table Early tables had four legs with a plank top. Turned legs were a refinement.

Gateleg Popular in the 17th century, one leg swings out to support the drop leaf top.

Feet

Look at the feet. They may have an animal theme such as lion's paws or claw-and-ball or end in a pad or spade. Or they may be blocked, shaped like a bracket, or splayed. The shape and style of the feet will help you to trace the table to its origins. This table has brass paw feet and casters, a typical feature of Neoclassical furniture from the early 19th century. Casters made it easier to move the table around the room. *See pp202–205 for more on legs and feet.*

Tripod table 18th-century portable tables had a single column, three legs, and drop top.

Pedestal table From the early 19th century tables had a pedestal base and splayed legs.

Rococo tables

The Rococo style was dominant in Paris during the reign of Louis XV (1723–74), spreading to the rest of France and much of Europe by the mid-18th century. The style is one of utter exuberance, and is exemplified in furniture made for the Parisian aristocracy. Here, all furniture was integral to the interior design of a room, with motifs in carved wall panels repeated in mirror, chair, and table frames. Extravagant and asymmetrical, designs relied on the curve, resulting in tables with serpentine edges, ornate scrollwork, and S-shaped cabriole legs. Many designs were based on sculptor and architect Nicolas Pineau's published designs for carved decoration, known throughout Europe.

French Rococo table

The console table is a seminal Rococo piece. Made from softwood such as pine, the bases were a mass of exquisite carving, which was gessoed (covered in white plaster) and gilded. Many examples had heavy marble-slab tops, yet the fluidly carved cabriole legs gave an impression of lightness. Deliberately asymmetrical, features included an openwork frieze carved with shells, rocks, leaves, and flowers and a central cartouche; scrollwork to the legs; scrolled or ogee bracket feet; and ornate stretchers. Many examples had just two legs, as console tables were often fixed to walls.

Typically lavish ornament, based on natural motifs such as leaves

Shapes were exaggerated with C- and S-scrolls

Louis XV table
This excellent example of a console table has typical Rococo liveliness. The airy pierced carving of the support lightens the solidity of the marble top. 1730

Carved giltwood frame based on curves

Carved giltwood
The carved softwood was often incised before gilding to give greater definition to the carving.

Marble slab
The finest examples of console tables have solid marble tops imported from Italy.

Stretcher
The central stretcher on this example has an elaborately carved scene featuring dogs and birds.

> **TRADE SECRETS**
> Gilded furniture was a feature of the early 18th century. Softwoods such as pine, beech, and lime were ideal for carved designs, which were then covered in gesso and gilded so their snaking shapes gleamed brilliantly in candlelit salons. In Italy and Scandinavia, where native woods were often inferior in quality, pieces might also be gessoed and gilded.

ROCOCO MOTIFS

In the early to mid-18th century, Rococo carvers had a large number of decorative motifs to call on. In 1736, Gaetamo Brunetti published *Sixty Different Sorts of Ornament*, which included shell- and flower-bedecked tables and numerous animal and mask carvings. At the Francophile court of Frederick II (1740–84) the French style became more exaggerated and was called *Friederizianisches Rokoko*. Its zenith was from 1740 to 1760. This German table gains its inspiration from the earlier work of the great French ébéniste André-Charles Boulle (1642–1732).

German giltwood table The deep frieze is carved with intricate fine-scale ornament, and the apron with Rococo flames and swags of flowers. c1750; W: 49in (124.5cm); £45,000–55,000

English Rococo table

The French high-Rococo style found favor in much of Europe, particularly in Italy. Elaborate designs emanating from Venice—Italian capital of fashion and luxury—often rivaled those of Paris. In some countries, including England, the style was too flamboyant for domestic taste.

Although carved and gilt pieces like the example shown here did exist, they were the exception—pioneered by designers and craftsmen like Matthias Lock and Batty Langley. As such, the the overall design is more restrained and asymmetrical than French and Italian examples.

Alabaster-veneered tabletop

The legs, carved with shells, palm fronds, trailing husks, and flowers, help to make the table as elegant as contemporary French pieces

George II table
This carved giltwood console table is in the French style, with cabriole legs and naturalistic motifs.

Carving the textured ground required a high level of skill and is evidence of exceptional quality

The table stands on a shaped plinth

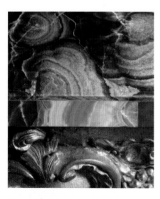

Carving
The table base features typical Rococo motifs—fruit and flowers, shells, and *rocaille* (rockwork).

Stretcher
The legs are joined by a pierced stretcher expertly carved with acanthus leaves.

Cartouche
An asymmetrical blank cartouche with suspended swags of flowers and fruit is the center of the frieze.

Cabriole leg
The two sinuous legs have trailing husks and flowers running down their fronts and sides.

18th-century tables

THE 18TH CENTURY was a time of great social change. The rising middle classes wanted less formal living arrangements and this desire, coupled with novel trends such as tea drinking, gave rise to informal salons for dining and entertaining. Innovative furniture, not least tables, was in demand to fill these rooms. The stalwarts of the more formal rooms—the heavy center table and narrow console table—continued to be made and occupied permanent positions in a room. Now, however, a range of smaller, more portable, tables emerged as well. Side tables appeared in dining rooms; in the less formal salons tea tables and card tables were neatly stored at the edge of the room and moved to the center of activity for use.

In Spain and Portugal, the Baroque style remained popular into the early 18th century. Elsewhere, the Rococo style that dominated the first half of the century was replaced by the more restrained Neoclassical style. Tables were more rectilinear, balanced, and symmetrical. The cabriole leg gave way to tapering, reeded or fluted legs, and florid Rococo ornament was replaced with Classical motifs.

Relatively narrow tabletop

Neoclassical urn motif

George III mahogany side table, one of a pair. c1775; W: 50in (117cm)

George III tables

The Neoclassical style that developed in Britain was influenced by a number of cabinet-makers who published pattern books of their designs, among them Adam, Hepplewhite, and Sheraton.

- Symmetry in form and design was paramount.
- Early mahogany tables with pronounced carving gave way to pieces with wood inlay in satinwood and sycamore.

TRADE SECRETS

Beware of 19th-century copies. There was a succession of revival styles in Europe during the 19th century, and Neoclassical pieces were reproduced, but the forms and decoration tend to be exaggerated rather than exact copies.

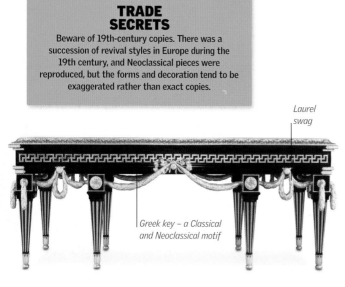

Laurel swag

Greek key – a Classical and Neoclassical motif

Louis XV center table. c1755; L: 80in (200cm)

French tables

The French were the first to develop a Neoclassical style—early designs were known as *goût grec*. Table design became more architectural in the 18th century, with striking symmetry.

- Rectilinear forms with tapering, reeded or fluted legs.
- Exquisite use of marquetry and parquetry.

Inferior quality wood painted to match a room's interior

Laurel swags

Fluted legs typically Neoclassical

Gustavian painted table. Late 18th century; W: 34³/₄in (88.25cm); $5,000–7,000

Gustavian tables

Gustavian furniture was the Swedish interpretation of the French Neoclassical style, adopted by Gustav III, who had admired the style when at Versailles.

- Lighter, more elegant forms than the French.
- Native Swedish woods such as pine were often painted.

Heavy walnut tabletop and frieze are typical

Baluster-turned legs

Box stretchers

Spanish walnut table. Early 18th century; L: 66½in (166cm); $4,000–6,000

Spanish tables

The Baroque style, which started in the 17th century, dominated Spanish furniture throughout the 18th century.

- Elaborate carving, heavy, turned columnar legs, and the use of inlays and marquetry were characteristic.
- Tables designed to stand in the center of a room often had faux drawers to the rear.

Silver mounts

Exquisite turning to legs and stretcher

Portuguese writing table. W: 55in (132cm)

Portuguese tables

Portuguese furniture reflected a range of influences, including British and French, but also Italian and its colonies in Brazil. Many pieces were made from imported woods, such as mahogany and jacaranda.

- Turned, spiral legs are unique to Portuguese furniture from this period.
- A fashion for elaborate carving endured well into the 18th century.

Walnut altar table. c1750; L: 72½in (184cm); $700–1,000

Chinese tables

Chinese furniture of this period was not influenced by Europe, but instead tended to look back to Chinese historical example.

- Prolific use of hardwoods such as walnut, rosewood, and ebony.
- Tables were of simple construction with little or no ornament.
- The function of a piece was paramount.

Lion's mask

Frieze faced with glass panels, back-painted to simulate onyx

Sicilian side table. Late 18th century; W: 45in (126cm)

Italian tables

Italian furniture designers took their lead from France, but were also influenced by the contemporary discovery of ancient sites in Italy.

- Tabletops were often made from marble or *pietra dura*.
- Low-relief carving to legs and frieze, often painted and gilded.
- Popular Neoclassical motifs included lions' masks and laurel leaves.

Philadelphia mahogany card table. W: 36in (90cm); $14,000–17,000

US tables

The influx of immigrant craftsmen to Boston, New York, and Philadelphia meant that fashions mirrored those of Britain, with a slight delay.

- Widespread influence of British pattern books, in particular Chippendale, Sheraton, and Hepplewhite.
- Increased use of mahogany alongside native walnut, maple, and cherry.

Dutch walnut card table. 18th century; H: 28¾in (73cm); $6,000–8,000

Dutch tables

Designs in the Low Countries were inspired by and in return inspired British furniture design, including the innovative card and games tables.

- Features included cabriole legs, shell-carved ornament, and the use of walnut.
- Marquetry continued to flourish during this period.

JARGON BUSTER

Goût grec French term for early Neoclassical furniture, meaning "Greek taste." The German equivalent is *Zopfstil*—"braid style," from the Classical swag motif.

The interrogation
Tilt-top tables

THE INVENTION OF tilt-top tables coincided with the popular pastime of drinking tea in early 18th-century England. Composed of three parts—the tabletop, birdcage, and columnar support with base—the form was a versatile one. The birdcage mechanism operated in such a way that the tabletop could be tilted upright and stored flat against a wall. This was a great space-saving device, but also meant that the table could double as a firescreen. Finer examples had a raised edge around the tabletop, so preventing precious porcelain cups from falling off when entertaining. The form proved popular in both England and the US colonies, and was made well into the 19th century.

American table

Tilt-top tables were made in the US from the mid-18th century, where the birdcage mechanism was more popular than in England. The example below was made in Philadelphia and is of exceptional quality. The top is made from a single piece of figured mahogany and has a fine, scalloped edge. It sits above a simple, uncarved column and a tripod base with claw-and-ball feet. Furniture made in Philadelphia is considered among the best made in the US. With the finest examples made of mahogany, it is not always easy to tell them apart from English ones.

Scalloped edge
While many tilt-top tables had flat surfaces, the better examples have a dished top with a slightly raised edge or, as here, a piecrust edge.

Locking mechanism
The top of the column is carved with a peg, which slots into this hole in the base of the birdcage, ready for securing.

Scalloped edge

Tripod base
Each of the three legs terminates in a claw-and-ball foot. The slightly flattened shape of the bulbous ball is a typical feature of Pennsylvania furniture.

Securing the column
Once the column and birdcage have been assembled, the wedge is inserted through a slot cut just below the peg at the top of the column.

Elegant tripod base

Philadelphia tilt-top table
This exceptional, well-proportioned example is in the Chippendale style. c1765; H: 48in (122cm); D: 35in (89cm); $150,000–200,000

TEA DRINKING

Tea had been imported since the establishment of the first trade links with the Far East during the 17th century. Tea drinking became a fashionable pastime throughout Europe, with Britain leading the way. By the middle of the 18th century, the British East India Company was importing some 4,500,000lb (2,000,000kg) a year. Such was the extent of the fad that a whole industry was built on tea-drinking ceremonies. Entire services were made in the finest porcelain, silversmiths created all manner of tea-related wares, and there was a wealth of additional paraphernalia, including caddies and caddy spoons.

Berlin cabaret set in case A cabaret, or tête-à-tête, usually consisted of two cups and saucers, a small teapot, a tray, tea canister, *sucrier*, milk jug, and spoons. c1770

English table

Although small tables like the one below were originally conceived for serving tea, by the end of the 18th century and into the 19th century, larger versions were used for breakfast and dinner. This solid mahogany table has a tapering gun-barrel supporting shaft and a tripod base.

The unusual legs are carved in human form with shod feet, typical of pieces from, or relating to, the Isle of Man, off the coast of Lancashire. Unlike the American example, the tabletop does not have a raised edge, but the quality of the mahogany and carving suggest that it is still a fine piece.

Tabletop in upright position

The table has a locking mechanism on the underside consisting of a brass "snap catch". This catch fits into a slot in the center of the birdcage (see below) to secure the lowered tabletop in place

Tabletop
Like the American example, the tabletop is made of a single piece of mahogany and is of a fine color with beautiful figuring.

Well-carved tripod base

English tilt-top table
This elegant table has good color and patina (surface sheen). c1770; D: 33in (84cm); $25,000–35,000

Birdcage
This ingenious birdcage mechanism consists of two platforms joined by four pillars. It takes its name from its birdcage-like appearance.

Tripod base
Each of the three distinctly shaped legs has been skillfully carved from a solid piece of mahogany and terminates in an exquisite buckled shoe.

The interrogation
Arts & Crafts tables

ARTS & CRAFTS designers were inspired by traditional pieces that helped inspire their belief that furniture should be made from solid, honest materials and—most important—be functional. William Morris, who pioneered the movement, believed that everything should be handcrafted. However, this meant few people could afford it. American designers such as the Stickley brothers, Limbert, and others, who combined Arts & Crafts integrity with machine manufacture, reached a far wider audience. The traditional aspect of Arts & Crafts furniture in England can be seen in the handmade pieces from the Yorkshire workshops of Robert "Mouseman" Thompson.

Stickley brothers

In 1891, brothers John, George, and Albert started Stickley Bros. in Grand Rapids, Michigan. Furniture was usually plain oak or mahogany and relied on construction elements as decoration. Later pieces were inspired by furniture from England and Scotland and often had more decoration. They are usually labeled "Quaint Furniture."

Top is made from quarter-sawn oak planks

Square-section legs are joined by a flat under-tier

Sides are simply decorated with three plain spindles

Oak side table
This simple design is typical of the Stickley Brothers. 1900–15; W: 30in (76cm); $5,000–10,000

Gustav Stickley

The most successful of the five Stickley brothers, Gustav (1858–1942) favored simple, geometric lines and heavy, solid oak with a dark "fumed" finish. He used as decoration construction elements such as mortise-and-tenon joints, dovetails, chamfered boards, and long arched corbels. Pieces are usually signed "Als Ik Kan" (Flemish for "As I can") within a joiner's compass.

Gustav Stickley occasional table
The circular oak top sits on square-section legs. H: 35³⁄₄in (91cm); $2,000–3,000

Stretchers attached to legs using through-tenon joints

Acorn finial

Stacked, arched cross-stretcher

Mortise-and-tenon joint
The joint between the stretcher and the legs are fixed with a wooden peg and forms part of the decoration.

Tenon joint
The stretcher tenons protrude through the legs. This construction feature was amalgamated into the design.

X-frame stretcher
The stacked, arched cross-stretchers are topped by an acorn finial.

HARVEY ELLIS

Architect and designer Harvey Ellis provided an antidote to Gustav Stickley's plain, heavy furniture when he joined The Craftsman Workshops in 1903. His lighter style included pieces embellished with small, inlaid motifs featuring flowers or Art Nouveau motifs. He used

various materials, including metals such as copper, pewter, and nickel, as well as various stained woods. This furniture tends to be smaller and made from oak and usually has a pale brown patina.

Ellis died after only seven months in Stickley's employ but

his more subtle and elegant approach can be seen in later designs by Gustav Stickley.

Harvey Ellis inlay The inlay of a sailing ship is surrounded by an Art Nouveau-style border in copper, pewter, and stained woods.

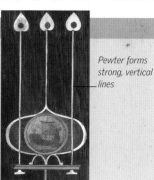

Pewter forms strong, vertical lines

William Morris

London firm Morris, Marshall, Faulkner & Co., founded by William Morris (1834–96) and others, used natural materials and traditional techniques. They used mahogany with satinwood inlay, although later favored timbers

associated with country furniture such as oak and ash. Joints and hinges were used as a form of decoration. Many copies were made but most authentic pieces bear the "Morris & Co." stamp.

Large mahogany dining table

This table was designed by Philip Webb, who favoured simple, turned, and carved elements. Authentic pieces bear the Morris & Co stamp. 1860s; L: 70½in (176cm); $50,000–70,000

Detail
Here, the legs and stretchers are decorated with ring turning.

Oval top has an incised edge

Outer supports united by horizontal rods

Plain central support holds six radiating ring-turned spokes

Mouseman

Robert "Mouseman" Thompson (1876–1955) was inspired by medieval carvings in cathedrals as well as 17th-century designs. Furniture is usually oak but may incorporate wrought iron or cowhide. He used an adze (ax-like tool) to shape the timber, resulting in uneven, rippled surfaces.

The planks are not smooth, as they were worked with an adze

Detail
The signature "Mouseman" mouse appears on every piece.

Refectory table

Made of oak, the top comprises three planks joined by dowels (wooden pegs). It sits on two chamfered supports. c1910

Chamfered supports have flattened corners

Block feet are joined by a plain stretcher

STORAGE FURNITURE

The earliest form of storage—the chest—dates back to ancient Egypt, where it was used for household linen and valuables. By the Middle Ages, chests doubled up as tables or benches.

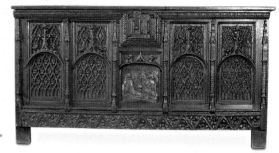

French 15th-century chest
Typically, this early chest is simply made but lavishly decorated. It has a hinged lid, carved panels, and block feet.

IN MEDIEVAL TIMES, the rich tended to travel between their homes and so the chest was the most important piece of household furniture. Chests were simple in construction—a hinged, lidded box or a frame with a number of panels—and usually made from oak. Many were elaborately carved in high relief and raised on bun feet. All sorts of belongings were kept in the chest. To make items easier to find, designs from the middle of the 17th century incorporated a single drawer at the bottom of the chest. During the 17th century, many households began to use an *armoire* or linen press. Designed for storing linen, linen presses were large case pieces, often made from walnut. Common examples had an upper section with two doors and a shelved interior, and a lower section with a drawer. Of huge proportions, linen presses were based on architectural forms, with carved panels and bun feet.

> **JARGON BUSTER**
> *Bombé* A French term to describe the fashion around 1700 for "pot-bellied" case pieces, with fronts and sides that bulged outward.

Chests of drawers

The chest of drawers as we know it today appeared toward the end of the 17th century, making the lidded chest all but redundant. Early versions were based on French examples, and were of *bombé* form with two or three drawers raised on cabriole legs.

As the century progressed, and with the emergence of the Neoclassical style, these chests became more rectilinear in shape and stood on shorter, often tapering legs. Variations on the chest of drawers emerged throughout the 18th century, and included the cupboard-on-chest and the chest-on-chest, which offered an alternative to the linen press of the previous century. The tallboy, a chest on top of a table-type base—also with drawers— was particularly popular in

Louis XV commode
In France, chests of drawers were called commodes. It was fashionable for the decoration to ignore the division between the drawers, treating the front of the chest as a single surface instead.

American Sheraton sideboard
The *demi-lune* (half moon) sideboard offers an elegant storage solution for the dining room. Some versions incorporated a cellaret drawer for bottles of wine.

the US, where it was known as a highboy. Such pieces reflected a family's wealth and were status symbols.

Another form toward the end of the 18th century was the fall-front desk, which offered an adaptable alternative to the *bureau plat* (see p41). These tall, flat-fronted cabinets had a hinged upper section, which opened to reveal a leather-lined writing surface, and a lower section with either cupboards or drawers for storage.

Later innovations

Inventions in the 19th century included the sideboard. Designed for the dining room, early examples were low and rectangular with cupboards at either end separated by drawers. The side cabinet and *chiffonier* were similar, and often had doors with silk-backed brass grilles.

An additional piece to the dining room, as the century progressed, was the buffet, which began to replace the earlier court cupboard. This imposing structure often comprised an open, shelved upper section above drawers and a lower section with cupboards. The buffet combined storage space and a display area for china or silverware. Such pieces were popular well into the 20th century, when the upper section might also be glazed.

In the 20th century, a host of innovative materials and techniques enabled designers to experiment. Although there were no new forms as such, there was a fashion for modular wall storage, where a number of units could be arranged to suit the user, and for integral pieces, which combined sideboard, drawers, and shelving all in one.

George I chest-on-chest
This 18th-century piece comprises two sections, each with a number of drawers. The bottom drawer of the top section has a fall-front, which opens to provide a writing surface.

Eames cabinet
Reflecting the mid-20th century fashion for all-in-one wall units, this cabinet combines open shelving with cupboards and drawers. It is made from contemporary materials—steel rods and fiberglass.

The briefing
Looking at storage furniture

TO INVESTIGATE A LARGE PIECE of storage furniture, you need to study a large number of elements. Whether it is a simple chest of drawers, a bureau, or a glazed cabinet or bookcase, you carry out the same basic investigation. You can learn much from the carcase and the construction. Check inside the drawers, the base, and the backboards. Check all over for unexplained holes or signs of damage. Always stand back from the piece, too, and assess its proportions.

JARGON BUSTER

Dovetail During the 17th century, iron-nailed joints were slowly replaced by dovetails. Dovetails are triangular-shaped wedges that interlock.

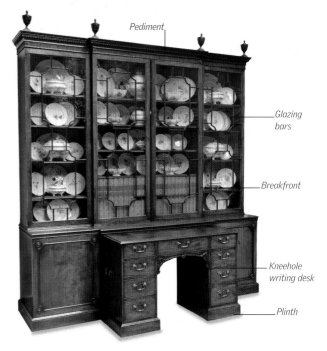

Pediment

Glazing bars

Breakfront

Kneehole writing desk

Plinth

George III mahogany library breakfront bookcase
This vast bookcase is centred below by a pedestal library writing table. c1770; H: 106in (269cm)

Closer inspection
The construction of the drawers, and any changes made to them, can reveal a lot about the age of a piece of furniture.

Glazing

Until the 19th century the technology did not exist to make large sheets of glass. Glazed areas on furniture were made up of small panes held together by semi-circular glazing bars. Early glass such as this has a slightly rippled surface and impurities in the glass will be visible as flecks and bubbles.

From the 19th century, large sheets of glass were used. Astragals (lightweight wooden moldings) were used to create the same decorative effect as glazing bars, although they had no practical purpose as they sit on the surface of the glass rather than hold pieces of it in place. As a result, astragals may be arranged in complex patterns.

Pre-19th century glass
Early glass has a rippled surface and was made in small panes set in a frame of glazing bars.

19th century and later
Later glass appears completely smooth and the large pane is decorated with astragals.

What to look at

Type of wood

The show-wood is a useful indicator of quality. It can also help with where the piece was made and when. Is it solid wood or veneered? If veneered, is it hand- or machine-cut? How thick is it? The thickness of the veneer can give a clue to age. What type of wood is the piece made from? Remember that woods may appear to be different colors depending on age, and whether they have been stained or polished. Is it decorated with marquetry, parquetry, or lacquer? *See pp186–87.*

Check all internal fittings

Pull out the drawers (if any) and examine them from all sides. Check that the internal fittings correspond to the age of the rest of the piece.

Drawer construction

Check the drawers. Are there channels down the sides so they can run on bars or runners attached to the carcase? If so, the piece is probably 17th century. If the runners are beneath the drawer it's likely to be after c1680. Check dovetails, if present, match. Machine-made dovetails are post-1880s.

Handles and handle plates

The shape of handles is a clue to age, but they are often replaced. If replaced, you will see the marks on the front and plugged holes where they were removed on the back. *See pp190–93.*

Pediment and top of piece

Look at the top of the piece and see whether it has a pediment. Pediments can often give a clue to style. Does the pediment conform to stylistic type such as Neoclassical or Gothic? Is it intact or broken? Does it have a molded top or a molded cornice? Does the top overhang? Is the form architectural? *See pp188–89 for pediment types.*

Carvings and decoration

Look at any decorative features such as carvings. This is a good stage to check for authentic age clues. Are there darker areas where it is difficult to dust?

Leather skiver

A skiver is a thin, soft, tanned leather inset panel on a desk or bureau, which is often gilt-tooled. The leather provided a comfortable surface to write on and helped to protect the wood from ink and scratches.

High chests

HIGH CHESTS—COMMONLY CALLED chests-on-stands in England and highboys in the US—were a development of the chest of drawers and originated in Holland. High chests first appeared in England from the late 17th century and were made well into the 18th century. They were popular in the US where they were first made at the beginning of the 18th century. The trend continued until the late 18th century. High chests are usually made in two pieces: a base or stand and a top section. The two pieces should be a perfect match. The most elaborate examples were made in the US in the Chippendale style. The most extravagant feature bonnet tops and carved aprons.

English chest-on-stand

English chests-on-stands from the early 18th century are typically veneered with walnut. Sometimes only the front is veneered, while the sides are stained pine. The top usually consists of a series of short drawers over three or four long ones, while the stand usually has three or four drawers. When compared with an American example, an English chest-on-stand tends to appear shorter, with little to the apron, and wider—emphasising the horizontal rather than the vertical. English cabinet-makers also used restrained decoration and less complex shaping, so examples may look severe when compared to their American counterparts.

Cockbeading *Featherbanding*

Edge of veneer

Restrained molding

The proportions of the top and base and the matching veneers are evidence that the two halves were made to go together

Decoration
Featherbanding and cockbeading along the edges of the drawers complement the carving of the cornice. Cockbeading hides the join between the veneer and the wood.

Veneers
At the edges of the chest, it is possible to see the cut edge of the walnut veneer where it is joined to the carcase. The color has faded.

Carved apron
The simple shape of the carved apron is typically English and adds to the chest-on-stand's relatively squat proportions.

Original cabriole legs
Elegantly shaped legs terminate in pointed feet, a style of the early 18th century. All legs are liable to rotting, woodworm, and breaking.

George I walnut veneered chest-on-stand
The color of the pale walnut veneer is typical of the period. c1715; H: 63in (160cm); $35,000–40,000

LOWBOYS

Highboys were often made with matching dressing tables known as a lowboys. This piece of furniture, which resembles the base of a highboy, was made in a similar style. A portable mirror would have been placed on the top while the user dressed their hair or applied toiletries. A lowboy should be a fifth to a quarter smaller in width and depth than a comparable highboy base.

Pennsylvania Queen Anne walnut lowboy The case has fluted corners and a shaped skirt on cabriole legs with shell carved knees and trifid feet. H: 28½in (72.5cm); $5,000–10,000

American highboy

Highboys are considered to be among the most spectacular pieces of American furniture. They are often more than 80in (2m) tall and appear to sacrifice practicality for elegance, as the only way to reach the top drawers is to stand on a stool. This vertical emphasis is a hallmark of American high chests. Pieces made in the

Queen Anne style may have a simple cornice or high bonnet with carved finials, shaped apron with turned drops, and cabriole legs. Those with a flat top are decorated with more restrained carving than bonnet top pieces. They were usually made from solid walnut, mahogany, cherry, or maple rather than decorated with veneers.

Cornice is simply designed

The top fits into the overlap on the bottom

Original batwing brass handles and escutcheons

Pennsylvania walnut highboy
The drawers are carved with lip molding and the crest with plain cove molding. c1755–60; H: 77in (196cm); $18,000–20,000

Decoration
The side edges are carved with a Neoclassical fluted column known as a reeded pilaster.

WATCH OUT!
A seemingly authentic Chippendale highboy can be made using other pieces of furniture such as the top half of a chest-on-chest on a highboy base. Check the proportions, and make sure the drawers in both sections were made in the same way and that both sections are of the same wood.

Cabriole leg
The knees of the cabriole legs are carved with shells—a form of decoration favoured by American craftsmen.

Apron
The shaped, scalloped apron is a typical American feature and adds to the impression of height.

18th-century commodes

THE COMMODE—French or French-style chest of drawers —became a seminal piece of the 18th century. Early commodes were made in France with a sweeping, *bombé* (convex) form and cabriole legs. They were typically wider than they were tall, had two or three drawers, ormolu (gilt-bronze) mounts, and parquetry or lacquerware panels.

As the century went on, more restrained forms emerged, reflecting the Neoclassical style. Influenced by Classical architecture, commode shapes became squarer and more geometric. They were less ornate, with simple molding instead of mounts, elegant metal fittings for handles and escutcheons (keyhole plates), and veneers.

French Louis XV commode

This two-drawer commode is also referred to as the "Cressent commode," after Charles Cressent, the French cabinet-maker most associated with its design. The piece is typical of the dominant Rococo style of the early 1700s, with its *bombé* form, serpentine top, and cabriole legs. The

parquetry design to the front of the example below is designed as a single decorative unit, ignoring the division between the drawers, and is ornamented with ormolu mounts. The marble top was probably chosen to match the marble of the room's fireplace, as was the current fashion.

Rococo style
Asymmetry was key to much Rococo styling—achieved in this example through the applied cartouche and escutcheons.

Mounts
Ornamental mounts were a decorative feature, but also served to protect the piece from knocks and scrapes.

Parquetry
Geometric marquetry—here in kingwood—was a popular form of decoration in early commodes.

The sans traverse decoration ignores the division between the drawers

Splayed legs
The feet are protected by decorative ormolu *sabots* in a foliage design.

Escutcheon

Ormolu mounts frame the wavy-edged ornamental panel, called a cartouche

Louis XV commode
This commode has parquetry panels, ormolu mounts, and *sans traverse* front. c1745; W: 57in (145cm); $300,000–400,000

MARQUETRY AND PARQUETRY

The fashion for marquetry coincided with the import of exotic woods such as ebony, amaranth, and kingwood. *Ébénistes* (cabinet-makers specializing in veneers) developed skills that made much of the rich colors of these new veneers. Early 18th-century cabinet-makers designed pieces with exquisite parquetry, where the different colored woods were arranged to form geometric patterns. The large panels of repeating cubes, lozenges, or trellises were a striking contrast to the swirling, scrolling gilt-bronze mounts. From the middle of the century, a trend developed for marquetry panels featuring motifs. The urn was popular, as were renditions of Classical figures, all within fine roundels or ovals, often framed within delicate ribbon-tied swags or garlands. Woods of choice were light and golden in color such as satinwood and sycamore.

Marquetry
Veneers are made into motifs.

Parquetry
Veneers are laid in geometric patterns.

English Neoclassical commode

This commode is typical of the Neoclassical designs that dominated the second half of the 18th century. The overall shape is more restrained and rectilinear, although it still has a slightly curvaceous form and curved, outswept legs. Standing taller than earlier commodes, it has four drawers. Despite its apparent simplicity, the complex decoration and molding show the work of an accomplished cabinet-maker. The dramatic appearance is achieved with contrasting veneers—satinwood with purplewood and sycamore—and simple metal hardware.

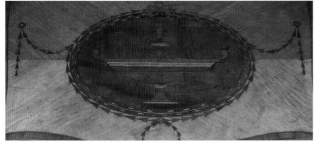

The top
The urn, a ubiquitous Neoclassical motif, is central to the marquetry design on the top of the commode.

Delicate details
Intricate ribbon-tied flower chains frame the oval marquetry panel to the top of the commode.

Drawer pulls
Elegant metal ovals and ring-pull handles repeat the marquetry urn motif.

George III commode
This shaped and molded commode has marquetry panels and graduated drawers. c1760–c1770; W: 41½in (105.5cm); $200,000–250,000

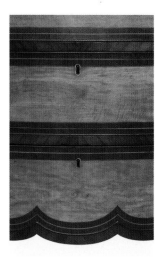

Molding
The top and front have restrained molded edges, which would have been complex to carve.

The prime suspects
Painted chests

PAINTED CHESTS were common in Central Europe and Scandinavia, especially in the mid-18th century. Immigrants took the tradition to North America, where it was popular in rural communities into the 20th century. Most of the chests made by rural craftsmen were not decorated with carving, so painting allowed the maker to put his own mark on it or decorate it to suit the person who commissioned it. The paint also disguised inexpensive wood and helped protect it. Chests were usually decorated by itinerant specialists, but some pieces were painted by amateurs. It is pieces by itinerant painters whose work can be identified that command a premium today.

European chests

By the late 18th century, the fashion for painted furniture reached its height in Europe. Each country or region had its own distinct style such as the *rosmålning* (rose painting) popular in Norway from the early 18th to the early 20th century.

Pieces were often made as wedding or betrothal gifts (dower chests), and many were passed on to other newly wed couples at a later date. New paint that has been added to take in this change of ownership will not affect value but restoration may—collectors place a high importance on an untouched paint surface. While finding a piece with its original paint is rare, a dry, worn surface with flaking and faded paint is acceptable.

The border is painted in an effect known as "Farmer's marble"

German farmer's chest
This carved and painted chest is decorated with vases of flowers and a knight riding a horse. It has a secret compartment. 1781; $2,500–3,500

KEY CLUES

- Painted decoration often tells a story such as a scene from a traditional folk tale, or features a local or imaginary view.
- Blue was an expensive pigment and hard to use, so pieces painted with this color command a premium.
- Chests may be carved as well as painted.

Spanish colonial dower chest
This pine chest has a domed lid and is decorated with landscapes, inscriptions, and heraldic motifs. 19th century; $700–1,000

Tyrolean farmer's chest
While the top has been left plain, architectural moldings frame painted vases of flowers on the front and legs. 18th century; $7,000–9,000

Eastern European marriage chest
This pine chest is decorated with urns of flowers in red and green on a gold ground within yellow borders. 19th century; $600–800

MINIATURE WORKS OF ART

Like their European counterparts, American craftsmen created items for every room of the house and every purpose and, like decorated chests, these miniature versions are popular with collectors today.

Exceptional pieces such as this candlebox show the vibrant colors used by 18th-century artists. Made with similar hinges and hasps to larger boxes from the Lancaster County region of Pennsylvania, the front is decorated with urns of tulips and birds, with a white column on each side painted with botehs (stylized cypress leaves—paisley pattern). Such European motifs suggest a nostalgia for the Old World.

The lid has a series of arches and dots. It slides off by pushing a grooved, indented thumbpiece.

Pennsylvanian candlebox At auction in 2005 this chest sold for the equivalent of $70,000. Late 18th century; L: 12¼in (31cm)

American chests

In the 18th century, many Central European immigrants lived on isolated farms where the influence of the outside world was rarely felt. As a result, traditional European styles continued to be used long after they had been replaced elsewhere.

Many young girls preparing for marriage had a dower chest, which they used to store household items such as linen and needlework they were collecting for use in their married life.

Today, the simpler, naïve style of painting from itinerant decorators in the New World is more popular than traditional European landscapes or religious themes.

Front has a central heart inscribed "Maria Stohlern 1788"

Molded lift lid decorated with a central cartouche in black, red, and white with a tulip and geometric border

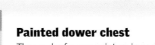

Tombstone panels with tulips and star

Painted dower chest
The work of some painters is so distinct it can be identified—even if the name of the artist cannot. This chest was painted by an artist known as the Embroidery Artist. 1788; $50,000–90,000

KEY CLUES

- Painted with European motifs such as hearts, tulips, and birds and, later, with symbols of the new democracy such as eagles and American animals like the wild turkey.
- A central panel was often used to record the bride's name and the date of her wedding.
- Usually 3–4ft (90–120cm) long.

Painted pine blanket chest
The lid, attributed to David Ellinger, is painted with stylized hearts; the front panels with tulips. Mid-20th century; $14,000–20,000

Pennsylvanian dower chest
The Federal style can be seen in the spread-winged eagle, with shield and banner, painted on the front. 19th century; $10,000–14,000

Berks County tulip chest
The tombstone panels on the front lend an architectural element to the tulip, sawtooth, and heart decoration. c1800; $35,000–50,000

The lineup
Painted furniture

IN FASHIONABLE CIRCLES, the trend for furniture with painted decoration was popular from the mid-18th to the early 20th century. Designers in France and England—including Robert Adam—produced furniture that was painted to match walls and ceilings, often in light colors. A little later, from the late 18th to the mid-19th century, wealthier American families decorated their homes with painted "fancy" furniture.

There has been a tradition of painted furniture in rural communities throughout Europe since medieval times. The skills were taken to the US by settlers from the 18th century and practiced there, as in Europe, into the 20th century. These folk pieces were often painted to imitate high-style designs or to satisfy a nostalgia for the Old World. Furniture was also painted to disguise poor-quality native woods or to protect them.

WATCH OUT! It wasn't unusual to repaint furniture to reflect changing fashion. But watch out for furniture that has been repainted and distressed to make it appear old. Genuine "old paint" commands a premium. Look for authentic layers of paint with signs of dirt between them.

Restored paint can reduce value by half

Neoclassical motifs include swag-hung paterae and bellflower borders

Demi-lune commode, with restoration. c1790; W: 48in (122cm); $7,000–10,000

English commode
The discoveries of Roman remains at Pompeii and Herculaneum helped inspire new styles of furniture painted in the Neoclassical style. Paint was often used in the place of marquetry.
- Painted in rich colors.
- Artists able to create more precise details than with marquetry, more in keeping with the decorative scheme of the room.

Original ocher wood grain decoration

Late 18th-century painted Kas, Lancaster County, Pennsylvania. H: 87in (221cm); $7,000–9,000

American Kas
A Kas is a type of European Baroque cupboard, a traditional storage form continued by Central European settlers to the US. As the main storage place for a family's belongings it took pride of place in the home.
- Kas were often painted with floral motifs or a solid color such as dark red or brown.

"Farmer's cupboard" painted wardrobe. Late 18th century; H: 73in (186cm); $15,000–20,000

Austrian wardrobe
Many late 18th-century country pieces imitated furniture shapes from earlier in the century.
- Painted decoration replaced original carving.
- Pieces often made from pine and the entire surface painted with colorful designs.
- Typical decoration included flowers, landscapes, and religious motifs.

Curvaceous scroll-fronte[d] drawers

Painted pine chest. Early 19th century; W: 41in (103.5cm); $2,000–2,500

Central European chest
During the 19th century, country furniture-makers drew on Rococo asymmetry in their painted decoration.
- Bold, contrasting colors.
- Floral decoration recalled earlier marquetry.
- Many such pieces have been later decorated, so beware of overly bright colors.

Ribbon-tied foliate swags and scrolling foliage were popular Neoclassical motifs

Satinwood bureau. c1800; H: 42½in (106cm); $7,000–9,000

English bureau

Neoclassical motifs such as delicate swags of flowers were ideal to paint onto furniture.

- Painted detail allowed for lighter rendering of contemporary marquetry designs.
- Drawer pulls and escutcheons could be incorporated into the design.

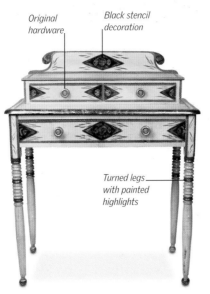

Original hardware

Black stencil decoration

Turned legs with painted highlights

Double-tiered maple and pine dressing table. c1840; W: 35in (89cm); $7,000–9,000

American "fancy" dressing table

Many pieces were based on Neoclassical shapes by designers such as Sheraton or Hepplewhite.

- The most elaborate furniture was painted in Baltimore, Maryland.
- Painted Neoclassical motifs or landscapes often combined with gilt highlights.

Original painted decoration

Typical geometric simplicity of Directoire style

Directoire semainier. c1810; W: 41in (104cm); $10,000–12,000

French semainier

The French Directoire style (c1795–c1800) remained popular into the 19th century. Sophisticated semainiers usually have seven drawers, one for each day of the week but country examples (as above) may have only six.

- Light, pastel tints on Neoclassical forms with simple molding.
- Other decoration rare.

Painted "farmer's" or "rider's" cupboard. Late 18th century; H: 83½in (212cm); $10,000–15,000

Austrian cupboard

Painted portraits and landscapes were often combined with wood grain and marble effects to imitate more expensive furniture.

- They often contained secret compartments and were equipped with a lock and key.
- Elaborate examples may combine veneers and applied ornament with painted detail.

Hanging cupboard. H: 27½in (69.5cm); $1,000–1,500

German hanging cupboard

Hanging cupboards provided essential storage space and paint helped brighten the interior.

- Simple box shape with door; more elaborate forms included drawers and display shelves.
- Decoration included wood grain effects imitating more expensive woods such as mahogany, floral motifs, and landscapes.
- Restoration dramatically reduces value.

Painted panels depict the Ages of Man

Rare, high-quality, dated marriage cupboard. 1780; W: 80½in (204cm); $35,000–45,000

Central European cupboard

Marriage cupboards were often given as wedding presents in rural communities. In Norway, itinerant painters learned their skills at special schools. At the beginning of the 19th century, many emigrated to the US.

- Usually dated, but sometimes re-dated and passed on to the next generation.

CER

AMICS

CERAMICS

The term ceramics covers pottery (earthenware and stoneware) and porcelain. While pottery has been made since Neolithic times, the landmark was the Chinese discovery that by adding kaolin (china stone) to the batch they could create porcelain.

Rookwood Art Nouveau vase
This silver-overlaid vase was designed by Japanese artist Kataro Shirayamadani in 1898.

Meissen Rococo Revival figure
This personification of Autumn exemplifies the Rococo Revival style of the 19th century with its gilded *rocaille* feet and the rustic garland of corn in the figure's hair.

Earthenware is porous and needs to be covered with a glaze. Stoneware was produced in China during the Shang period (c1600–1050BCE) with glazes first used c1000BC. Europeans did not use lead glazes until after the 8th century when Arab forces invaded Spain and brought glazing techniques with them. The Arabs added oxides, among them tin, which gives an opaque, white glaze.

Tin-glazed earthenware

The tradition for tin-glazed earthenware, or maiolica, began in Italy during the 13th century. Several centers emerged over the next 200 years, particularly Gubbio, Urbino, and Faenza. From here the fashion spread to the rest of Europe during the 16th and 17th centuries, thanks to immigrant Italian craftsmen. It was known as faïence in France, fayence in Germany, Delft in the Netherlands (after the main production center), and delftware in Britain.

Decorative styles varied. Italian and early French examples often depicted Biblical or mythological scenes, painted in yellows, blues, and greens. German and later French examples favoured landscapes, birds, and animals, while many Dutch and English potters made blue and white designs based on porcelain imports from China.

Typical pieces included plates, tankards such as the German *Walzenkrug*, chemists' jars, tiles, and vases. Among the most striking were the Delft tulip vases—towering blue and white pyramids for displaying flowers.

The introduction of creamware, developed by the Staffordshire potteries around 1740, led to the decline of tin-glazed wares. However, a fashion for revival styles in

Chinese porcelain bowl

Most Chinese export porcelain was blue and white until 1700, after which more varied color schemes were introduced. This *famille rose* bowl is named for its opaque pink enamel.

Sèvres cup and saucer

Sèvres was renowned for the brilliance of its colors, such as the *bleu celeste* ground of this cup and saucer. The colors were particularly well married with delicately tooled gilding.

the mid-19th century saw some British and American factories producing brightly colored lead-glazed pieces known as majolica—inspired by Italian maiolica.

Porcelain

The Chinese discovered a porcellaneous ceramic as early as the 7th century, by combining china stone and china clay. By the Ming Dynasty, they were making a strong, white, translucent material suited to molding and painting. By the 16th century, quantities were exported.

Trade with China fostered a European interest in all things Chinese and this included a passion for porcelain. So great was the demand that European potters sought to produce it themselves. A method for producing hard-paste porcelain eluded European makers until the start of the 18th century, when German alchemist Böttger created a formula. By 1710, the first European hard-paste porcelain factory was founded at Meissen. Over the next 50 years, factories were established in other cities. Vincennes and Chantilly in France and Worcester and Derby in England made a soft-paste porcelain because they lacked the formula, or the ingredients, needed for hard paste.

Vincennes moved to Sèvres following the acquisition of a hard-paste formula in 1768 and, along with Meissen, led the field. Meissen and Sèvres dominated the porcelain scene for over 100 years, creating exquisite services for wealthy patrons.

JARGON BUSTER

Maiolica Italian tin-glazed earthenware, not to be confused with 19th-century majolica, which has thick, bright, usually lead, glazes.

Art Deco platter

This platter was designed as a limited edition for the Primavera Design studio at the Au Printemps department store in Paris.

Early pieces were in the flamboyant Rococo styles that dominated Europe. The two factories turned to Neoclassicism toward the end of the 18th century, and well into the 19th. They inspired a growing number of porcelain producers throughout Europe, who scrambled to copy their wares. From the mid-19th century, factories responded to the trend for revivals, enjoying particular success with Rococo-style pieces based on early Meissen.

20th-century ceramics

Developments in manufacturing enabled factories throughout Europe and the US to mass produce. Numerous wares reflected changing styles such as Art Nouveau and Art Deco, many designed by leading contemporaries, including Henry van de Velde for Meissen, Suzanne Lalique for Sèvres, Clarice Cliff for A. J. Wilkinson and, more recently, Jasper Conran for Wedgwood.

The resistance to mechanization expressed by followers of the Arts & Crafts movement gave rise to a tradition for studio, or art, pottery from the late 19th century. Artists preferred to make and finish pieces by hand. Of note are the Martin Brothers in England and Rookwood in the US.

Looking at ceramics

CERAMICS ARE KNOWN to have been made for thousands of years: they are arguably mankind's oldest achievement. To make the ceramic body, different types of clay or stone are ground and mixed with water to produce a paste. The paste is then fired in a kiln to fuse the particles and produce a ceramic. Ceramics are surprisingly durable and have been made by all civilizations. So the quantity of Oriental, Islamic, Asiatic, European, Oceanic, and North and South American ceramics is vast. With the added diversity of decoration and styles the task facing the antiques detective can at first seem overwhelming. But there are some clues to point the way.

Rectangular with shaped corners

Although the design relates to similar Dutch Delft dishes, these fish look more exotic than herrings

Rim

Qianlong blue and white export ware

The dish imitates Dutch Delft herring dishes. It has some rim fritting. c1775; W: 10½in (24cm)

Pottery or porcelain?

There are two types of pottery: earthenware and stoneware; and two types of porcelain: hard paste and soft paste. Look at the body (fired clay) to determine its color and characteristics.

Earthenware, such as terracotta, is fired at a relatively low temperature and will not hold water unless it is given a protective glaze. The fired body is opaque and may be red-brown, buff, white, or gray, depending on the clay it was made from.

Stoneware is fired at a higher temperature and does not need a glaze to make it watertight. It is usually opaque. Stoneware is strong and hard wearing and may be thinly potted with detail or rough and grainy. It can be polished to a silky smooth surface. The fired body can be darkish, grayish, red, white, or sand colored.

Hard-paste porcelain can become translucent during its second, glaze firing. It contains kaolin, which refines it. As the body and glaze fuse it can be hard to see that the glaze was originally separate. The white body, with its hard, glittery glaze, tends to feel cold. When hard-paste porcelain chips it leaves a break similar to a chipped flint or glass.

Soft-paste porcelain does not contain kaolin. It vitrifies at its first firing and so the second, glaze, firing is at a lower temperature. As a result the layer of glaze sits on the surface. The glaze is also prone to pooling and crazing and early examples may have discolored. It feels slightly warm.

The term china traditionally meant porcelain made in China or in the Chinese style. Today it is best used to define bone china, a white, translucent, English porcelain developed c1794.

Earthenware
The body exposed by the chips in the white tin glaze is typically a buff color. Tin-glazed earthenware chips easily.

Hard-paste porcelain
Very white paste and crisp modeling are signs of hard paste. Its texture resembles the icing on a cake. The glaze is glassy or thin.

Soft-paste porcelain
It is more brittle and has a more grainy texture and the color ranges from pure white to gray.

Hold the piece up to a strong light
If it is translucent then it is definitely porcelain; if it is not then it could be a thickly potted or not very translucent porcelain, or it could be a piece of pottery.

How to look at ceramics

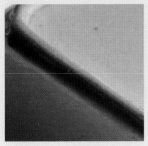

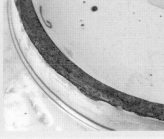

Rim

Tap the rim – a dull thud could indicate restoration. A perfect piece will give a pleasing ring.

Base

The first step to identifying a ceramic is to investigate the paste (the unglazed "body"—the mixture of clay and flux ingredients). The only place you find the unglazed body is on the base. Is the base completely smooth? This could hint at a later date. Is there evidence of some dirt or frit marks? This could be a clue for an early date. Are marks scattered over the whole base? This could point at early Oriental ceramics.

Damage and chips

The best way to learn how to tell the difference between pottery and porcelain is to handle as many pieces as you can—especially broken or chipped examples that allow you to see the body under the glaze. Also buy damaged examples of hard- and soft-paste porcelain to hold in your hand to feel the differing temperatures.

Decoration

This could be the proverbial red (or blue!) herring! The form of decoration or the style of dress worn by figures is no clue to the origin or date of the piece.

Glaze

Take a magnifying glass and look carefully at the glaze. Glaze is a covering of glass (silica) that has been fused to a ceramic body (such as clay). The glaze will either be shiny or matte.

Marks

Many ceramics have fake marks that copy those of the most successful companies. So always satisfy yourself about the factory, quality of body, decoration, and age before you look at the mark. Meissen is the most copied mark. Many inferior-quality Dresden, and other minor European factories, copied the crossed swords mark.

Crazing

This surface shows signs of crazing, which is a defect in the glaze.

Matte

This is a matte glaze much favored by American Arts & Crafts potters.

Tin glaze

This typical tin glaze has a gray-blue tinge indicating lead.

Check if the mark shows its country of origin such as France, Germany or, as here, England, as this probably denotes a date after 1891. Also check for any recognizable factory marks. *See p224 for pottery and porcelain marks.*

If the mark shows "Made in" a country, this probably denotes a date after 1921 but could be much later. Look for telltale clues like decoration style. The designer/artist, here Keith Murray, may also add to the value considerably.

Identifying ceramic decoration

OVER THE CENTURIES, CERAMICS HAVE been decorated with an almost unparalleled variety of techniques and designs. Artists all over the world have skilfully embellished every type of ceramic, from functional earthenware pots to ornate porcelain sculptures, using glazes, enamels, and gold. In the mid-18th century, technological innovations such as printing processes revolutionized the ceramics industry and opened up further possibilities for decoration. The names of many of the painters, artists, and gilders employed by the great porcelain and pottery factories are unrecorded and yet these decorators have left us a rich legacy of techniques.

Hand-painted

Expensive and time consuming to make, hand-painted wares dominated the ceramics market before printing was invented. Ancient functional ceramics had simple geometrical designs in slip and natural pigments. As ceramic production emerged as a commercial enterprise, painting became highly skilled and designs more complex.

Transfer-printed

Introduced in the mid-18th century, transfer printing involves inking an engraved copper plate and transferring the design onto a sheet ("bat") of tacky glue. The design is then pressed onto the surface of the object using oil. The whole is dusted with colored powdered oxides, often in blue, and fixed by firing.

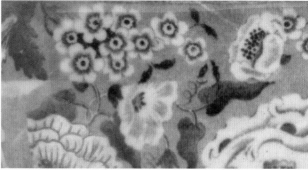

Gilding

Ceramic, usually porcelain, surfaces can be decorated with a thin layer of gold, either in the form of gold leaf or a fine powder that is applied with a brush. It is then fired at a low temperature. Sometimes the gold is mixed with mercury to give a bright metallic finish or with honey to create a dull but rich effect.

Luster

First used in the Middle East around the 7th century CE, the luster technique involves dissolving oxides of metals such as gold, silver, and copper in acid and combining them with an oil medium. The mixture is then applied to the surface of an object and fired to create a metallic or iridescent shimmering finish.

FLOW BLUE

Flow Blue describes 19th-century and early 20th-century white or cream earthenwares decorated with underglaze blue transfer patterns. The blue flowed out of the sharp outline of the design, creating a blurred effect. At first it happened by mistake, but the effect proved so popular that the potteries had to work out how to recreate the error to meet demand. The advantage to them was that the blurred design also covered errors in the earthenware blank or the transfer pattern. Flow Blue was primarily made in Staffordshire, England and exported to the US from the 1830s onward.

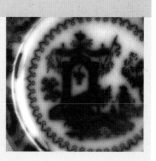

Early Victorian plate Chinese patterns and landscapes were popular in the Early Victorian period c1835–60.

Underglaze color

Finely powdered oxide is mixed with water or oil and applied to an unglazed surface. Cobalt blue is the most common color, but copper green, manganese purple, antimony yellow, and iron red are also often found. The object needs firing only once, making the technique less expensive than other forms of decoration.

Overglaze color

Known as "enamels," colors painted over the glaze require firing at low temperatures to fix them to the body. Metallic compounds are combined with a flux and ground into a powder. They are then mixed with oils and painted onto the surface of an object. Multiple firings are sometimes needed.

En camaïeu

The French term *en camaïeu* refers to a style of decoration that involves painting the surface of an object in two or three tones of a single color. Similar to the *grisaille* technique of painting in shades and tints of gray, *en camaïeu* can result in a detailed, three-dimensional appearance.

Applied decoration

Raised up in low relief, applied decoration can be used to create designs ranging from the simple to the sophisticated. Slip can be daubed onto a surface in naïve patterns, or can be built up to create fine *pâte-sur-pâte* decoration. Separately molded elements can also be used, in a technique known as sprigging.

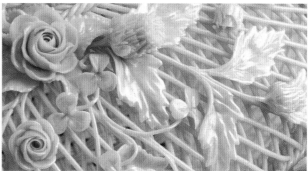

Delftware

Tin-glazed earthenware was first produced in the Low Countries at the beginning of the 16th century by immigrant Italian potters. It has a soft earthenware body covered with a lead glaze made white and opaque by the addition of tin oxide. One of the main centers of production was the Dutch town of Delft. British delftware was also inspired by the blue and white porcelain flooding the market from the early 17th century. War interrupted the trade in 1647, and potters in the Low Countries and Britain immediately sought to fill the gap by copying the much-coveted products. The decoration was later inspired by the brightly colored wares from China and Japan.

Dutch Delft

Dutch Delft is finely potted and the glazed surface is often pitted (known as peppering). This effect is caused by air bubbles trapped by the glaze exploding during firing. Dutch Delft was painted with a strong, bright indigo blue, often outlined in manganese purple—a technique known as trekking. Much Dutch Delft is a direct copy of Chinese pieces.

Central panel shows a bowl of flowers

Stylized, compartmentalized border panels

KEY CLUES

- Body is a warm yellow-buff color; the texture is like grains of sand.
- Thickish white glaze.
- Firing flaws are common.
- Known for fine detailed brushwork, with bright colors.
- Foot-rims tend to be thick.

Pale blue decoration is typical of 20th-century Delft

Dutch Delft dish
The dish is decorated in typical *kraak* style, named after the Portuguese ships called "carracks," which carried the porcelain. D: 14in (35cm); $1,500–2,000

Tulip vase
Intended to display tulips, this heart-shaped vase has a romantic scene. c1920; H: 9¼in 23. (5cm); $350–500

Posset pot
This pot has strong blue decoration and thick white glaze. 18th century; H: 5½in (14cm); $700–900

Painted cows
These cows were inspired by the Butcher's Guild of Delft's flower-bedecked cows on feast days. 19th century; $350–500

WATCH OUT!
Tin-glazed earthenware is extremely prone to damage, particularly chipping on the rim and foot. If you find a piece purporting to be from the 18th century that is very smooth and unchipped be suspicious, be very suspici

DELFT QUALITY

Good... The naïve *chinoiserie* scene of a young boy chasing a butterfly has vibrancy and charm. c1760; D: 9¼in (23.5cm); $700–1,000

Better... The addition of the polychrome palette, well-painted scene, border swags, and particularly the hot-air balloon make this superior. c1785; D: 8¾in (22.5cm); $2,500–3,000

Best... The detailed, dated, and named ship painting and the border decorated with cherubs as the Four Winds ticks all the boxes. 1765; D: 8¾in (22.5cm), $10,000–15,000

English delftware

English delftware is more thickly potted than Dutch Delft, with a coarse and hard body. Colors are more muted— particularly the blue, but also the distinctive sage green. The colors used to decorate English delftware sink into the glaze—with the exception of red, which sits proud. The factories are particularly known for polychrome designs with portraits of monarchs, bold flowers, and oak leaves.

KEY CLUES

- The smooth glaze has a blue (more rarely pink) tinge.
- Decoration often clumsy and crude but with appealing naivety.
- *Chinoiserie* designs popular.
- Foot-rims tend to be quite thin and often flared.

Blue tinge to glaze

Lambeth chinoiserie charger
This charger is painted in typical iron red, yellow, green, and cobalt blue. c1765; D: 13½in (34.5cm), $3,000–4,000

Blue dash border is characteristic

King William III dish
Paintings of monarchs are typically English. They often had a distinctive blue-dash border. Late 17th century; D: 13¾in (35cm); $24,000–28,000

Puzzle jug, Lambeth
Made in England from medieval times, this puzzle jug has a verse and floral motifs. Mid-18th century; H: 6¾in (17cm); $1,500–2,000

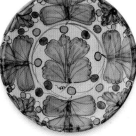

Oak-leaf charger
Patterns are quite primitive, with simple repeating patterns like the oak leaves on this charger. c1700; D: 13in (33cm); $7,000–9,000

English delftware is rarely marked but this commemorative piece bears a date and the initials "EIP"

Posset pot
The blue tinge in the glaze and the imprecise brushwork of this pot are English characteristics. 1689; D: 10in (25cm); $5,000–7,000

The prime suspects
Maiolica

MAIOLICA IS THE NAME given to tin-glazed earthenware made in Italy. During the 15th century, Italian pottery became more refined and by the 16th century, Renaissance potters were producing work of great artistic merit. The dishes and jars they made were often decorated with *istoriato*—or narrative—paintings that told stories from the Bible, mythology, or history. The originals were reproduced as woodcuts, engravings, and book illustrations, which were used for inspiration. In the 19th century, the fashion for Renaissance styles led to many of these works being copied—some of which were of a very high quality, but many were pale imitations of the originals.

16th-century maiolica

Skilled Renaissance artists decorated maiolica with bold, colorful designs. The designs featured plenty of fine detail such as muscular bodies, expressions on faces, as well as leaves on trees and ripples in water. Tiny, precise brushstrokes were used to build up shading. Pin holes in the glaze show where air that was trapped under it burst through during firing in the kiln. Any inscriptions will be simple and in a fluid 16th-century Italian script.

KEY CLUES

- High-quality painting contains lots of detail.
- Strong, bright colors used with confidence.
- Shading and detail built up using fine, painted lines.
- Genuine 16th-century marks.
- Pin holes in the glaze as a result of firing.
- Bold and ambitious decoration.

Fine brushstrokes were used to create the details in the image

Judgement of Paris
Exceptional details in the painting mark this as the work of Guido Durantino who worked in Urbino. 16th century; D: 18in (45.5cm)

Muscular bodies are painted with movement, and facial expressions are apparent

Bold and ambitious decoration

Italian albarello
This traditional pharmacy jar for storing drugs is boldly decorated and bears an inscription. c16th; H: 8¼in (21cm); $5,000–7,000

Globular jar
The decoration on this Venetian jar features two portraits interspersed with flowers and foliage. c1580; H: 9½in (24cm); $3,500–5,000

Castelli saucer
Views of a shore with ships and figures were inspired by a print by Gabriel Perelle. c1720; D: 7in (18cm); $1,200–1,800

TRADE SECRETS
The shape of 19th-century maiolica (see opposite) bears little resemblance to the pieces from the 16th century, which it aimed to emulate. Later potters frequently used fashionable Rococo Revival shapes, based on 17th-century styles, which would not have been familiar to the craftsmen of the century before.

VICTORIAN MAJOLICA

Italian maiolica was one of the inspirations behind majolica—an elaborately molded earthenware decorated with thick, vivid glazes, developed around 1850 by the British firm Minton. Shown at the Great Exhibition in London in 1851, it quickly became popular throughout Europe and the US. Majolica was used to make domestic wares such as vases, dishes, and jugs, as well as enormous ornamental vases and seats that featured the exaggerated decoration fashionable in the mid- to late 19th century. In the UK majolica was made by such factories as Joseph Holdcroft, Wedgwood, and George Jones & Sons. In the US, the Bennett Pottery in Baltimore, Maryland, and Eureka Pottery in Trenton, New Jersey, were among the best manufacturers.

Elephant jardinière The extravagant molded shape and bold colors are typical of majolica.

19th-century maiolica

The easiest way to tell whether a piece of maiolica is from the 19th century is to look at the painting. Artists used softer and paler colors and were often less accomplished: their figures are often outlined with sharp, black lines and have crudely drawn hands and feet.

Lower-quality production meant that the glaze did not stick to the body and bubbled or "crawled" when it was fired, leaving a surface with lots of holes.

KEY CLUES

- Decorators used a palette of softer, paler colors.
- Painting is less assured, even clumsy in its execution. Details are blurred.
- Pitted glaze is evidence of lower-quality wares.
- Marks may have been removed to deceive potential buyers.
- The foot rims are generally thin and flared.

Classical 19th-century dish
This less realistically painted dish features Apollo with a lyre surrounded by figures from Classical mythology.
19th century, D: 11 1/2in (29cm), $250–350

Figures are crudely painted

Handles are in the shape of a swan's neck

Mask terminals

Spanish flask
A green lizard forms the handle of this maiolica flask decorated with figures of animals. c19th; H: 10 1/4in (26cm); $100–150

Italian footed jardinière
The lustrous colors are typical of 19th-century pieces from Deruta. The jardinière has paw feet. c1900; W: 19in (48.5cm); $400–600

Italian vase
This Rococo shape is typical of 19th-century maiolica. The shell shape is painted with a rural scene. W: 10in (25cm); $100–150

Italian vase
This vase has serpent handles with mask terminals and paintings of *putti* (cherubs). c19th; H: 21 1/2in (55cm); $500–700

The lineup
European faïence

LIKE DELFT AND MAIOLICA, faïence is earthenware coated with a tin glaze, which makes the terracotta body shiny and white like porcelain. Faïence is named after the Italian city of Faenza and was introduced to France in 1512 when Italian potters came to Lyon. At first, French wares imitated Italian pieces, but by the mid-17th century they used native-style bold mythological figures in blue and ocher as decoration. These gave way to blue and white *chinoiserie* motifs, inspired by Chinese imports. The French expanded their range of colors with *petit feu* (low temperature) glaze techniques.

Dutch potters introduced faïence to Germany in the late 1600s. Initially, German wares imitated Dutch pieces, but in the 18th century, they used Germanic figures, coats of arms, and landscapes for decoration.

Lambrequins form a scalloped fringe pattern

Moustiers plate with mythological scene. 18th century; $4,000–6,000

Moustiers, France
Decoration includes mythical creatures, Classical and mythological figures within a medallion, and festoons.
- Grayish body with a creamy gray glaze.
- Potato flower decoration—also called *fleurs de solanée*—is unique to Moustiers.
- Copied Rouen's lacework style of decoration known as *lambrequin rayonnant*.
- Polychrome floral decoration using *petit feu* colors—a wide range including ochre, red and pink—was inspired by Oriental pieces.

Figure symbolizing fame. c1780; H: 12½in (31.5 cm); $2,500–3,500

Niderviller, France
The elegance, refinement, and delicacy of the factory's figures put them almost on a par with similar porcelain pieces from Sèvres and Meissen, on which they were based.
- Niderviller's decorators were among the best at using *petit feu* colors.
- They excelled at a technique known as *en camaïeu*: using different tones of the same color on white.

Chinoiserie designs such as pagodas were often used as decoration

Tureen, c1730; H: 7½in (19cm); $2,500–3,500

Rouen, France
Rouen was a prominent center for faïence production from the end of the 17th century.
- The pottery has a red body.
- Early Baroque wares have motifs resembling lacework (*lambrequins*) and ironwork.
- From around 1710, polychrome wares were produced in *grand feu* (high temperature) colors—cobalt blue, manganese purple, ocher, yellow, green, and iron red.

Plate in Sèvres style. c1770, D: 9in (23cm); $2,500–3,500

Sceaux, France
One of the leading French factories from c1750, Sceaux successfully used *petit feu* colors to imitate the *chinoiserie*, floral, and landscape decoration on the new porcelain wares.
- Successfully imitated the refined, lively Rococo porcelain of Sèvres, Mennecy, Meissen, and Strasbourg.
- The sage green is unique to the factory.

Plaque. c1775; $25,000–35,000

Aprey, France
Early pieces are crude and based on Rouen blue and white wares, but from c1770 to 1781 Aprey became known for decoration by Jacques Jarry and Antonine Mège.
- Decoration includes exotic landscapes and *chinoiseries* in Rococo scrolls, as well as flowers and birds.
- Best pieces are decorated with Jarry's birds and flowers or Mège's birds and landscapes.

The yellow and green palette imitates Chinese famille jaune *(predominantly yellow) porcelain*

Walzenkrug (tankard). c1790; H: 10in (25cm); $2,000–2,500

Schrezheim, Germany
The Schrezheim factory was in operation from 1752 to 1852.

- Native motifs such as stags, landscapes, and double-headed eagles are typical.
- A tin or pewter lid is usual. Earlier tankard forms and motifs were copied in the late 19th and early 20th centuries.
- 18th-century Schrezheim bodies have a pinkish tone where the glaze is thin.

Plate. 18th century; D: 9in (22.5cm); $350–500

Cralsheim, Germany
The Cralsheim pottery started in 1720 and closed around 1830.

- Architectural landscapes were among the late 18th-century designs. Other decorative subject matter included stag- and boar-hunting, coats of arms, and flowers.
- Egg-yolk yellow is a particularly distinctive Cralsheim color.

Ink stand in the shape of a commode, c1780, W: 6in (15cm), $500–900

Kelsterbach, Germany
Kelsterbach started making faïence in 1758. Three years later, they began making porcelain too, directed by C. D. Busch from Meissen.

- Its main output was blue and white household wares, including dishes and tureens in the form of vegetables.
- Refinement and attention to detail shows influence of porcelain workers.

QUIMPER

Faïence has been made in the French Brittany town of Quimper (pronounced camp-air) since the early 18th century. However, its rustic decoration remains so popular that similar pieces have continued to be made ever since. Most pieces on the market date from 1900 or later, but the style of decoration means it is easy to confuse them with earlier ones. Pieces from the 18th century have a creamy body; later copies are whiter and lighter.

Quimper fan vase The vase is decorated in typical naïve style with flowers and a couple wearing Breton dress. c1875; H: 4¾in (12cm); $500–900

Fan plate with lobed border. c1700; D: 13½in (34cm); $500–900

Frankfurt, Germany
Frankfurt was one of the first factories to produce faïence under the influence of Dutch potters around 1660.

- Much early production resembles Delft but its body tends to be a cleaner white.
- Decoration is blue and white and *chinoiserie*.
- Lobed wares can have more than 30 lobes.

Plate. c1767; D: 10½in (26cm); $350–500

Rörstrand, Sweden
Founded around 1725, Rörstrand peaked circa 1755 after designer Jean Eric Rehn introduced French styles and techniques, allowing the factory to start using overglaze polychrome decoration.

- Early blue and white wares resemble Delft.
- From 1744, overglaze polychrome decoration was modeled on French color palettes.
- The Rehn Pattern, from mid-18th century, has a flower or fruit motif in blue or manganese.

Stoneware

STONEWARE IS MADE UP of clay and ground rock and is fired at high temperatures. It is dense and durable and has been used for vases and drinking vessels for centuries. It is water resistant, but can also be thinly potted and elaborately decorated with molded or applied decoration. It was probably first made in China c1200BCE. By the 8th century, stoneware was a highly refined product decorated with a greenish-gray glaze. Stoneware was first made in Europe in the German Rhine valley in the 12th century and had distinctive regional variations. Quantities were imported into Britain in the 17th century. It was known as Rhenish ware and widely copied.

German stoneware

The town of Siegberg is known for its *Schnelle*—tall, tapering tankards decorated with shallow reliefs, which were molded separately and applied to the sides. The refined, off-white body was capable of rendering fine detail. Early examples of German *Schnelle* were extensively copied in the 19th century, often by re-using original molds, which means a date on a piece may not be accurate. The relief panels on early examples were applied carefully to ensure they did not crack in the kiln. Those on 19th-century copies were more carelessly made and often cracked in the heat.

KEY CLUES

- German Renaissance motifs such as strapwork are typical, as are Biblical, allegorical, and heraldic themes.
- On later pieces the body is less refined and may look dirty or have a yellow tinge.
- Most early examples have a base that is gently concave in shape; later bases tend to be flat with a rounded rather than a sharp edge, and they often have a maker's mark.

Strapwork

JARGON BUSTER

Bellarmine A jug named after Cardinal Bellarmino (1542–1621) who was despised in Protestant countries for his hatred of the Reformation. In Germany the jugs were called *Bartmannkrug* and, in England, *Greybeards*.

Strapwork
Decorative interlaced bands, called strapwork, form an intricate part of the decoration.

The central panel features the coat of arms of Jülich-Kleve-Berg

Siegburg cylindrical tankard
This rare, dated Siegburg tankard has a tapering body molded with three vertical panels flanked by two further armorial shields. 1274; 10in (25cm); $4,500–6,000

Bellarmine
This type of jug has a molded mask of a bearded man, often above a coat of arms. Late 17th century; H: 8in (20.5cm); $500–700

Westerwald tankard
The glazed decoration of stags on this metal-lidded tankard is typical of Westerwald. 18th century; H: 10¼in (26cm); $350–500

Creussen tankard
Creussen tankards were often squat. This one is painted with a hunting scene in relief. c1680; H: 8½in (21.5cm); $7,000–9,000

WATCH OUT!
16th- and 17th-century potters used a cheese wire to remove the tankards from the surface they had been made on, leaving curved marks. On reproduction pieces these marks tend to be much straighter.

SALT GLAZING

German potters toward the end of the 15th century discovered salt glaze.

They found that common salt thrown into the kiln when it was at its hottest reacted with silica in the clay to create a thin glaze that had a texture like orange peel.

It was soon copied in England. Around 1720, Staffordshire potters developed a fine, white salt-glazed stoneware, used for table- and teaware until 1900. Staffordshire salt-glazed wares may be decorated with enamel colors or applied textures.

Bear-baiting jug
This salt-glazed jug and cover were covered with clay chippings to simulate fur. Eyes, collar, and paws are picked out in brown. c1760; H: 10in (25.5cm); $5,000–7,000

English and North American stoneware

English tankards from the 18th century can be identified by their gray, gritty body, which is visible if it has chipped. Wares from factories in and around London were sometimes decorated with a two-tone brown glaze. The tradition was continued in the 19th century by the Doulton Lambeth factory. Stoneware was made by the North American colonists, with a boom in production in the 19th century. Used for storage vessels, stoneware was often embellished with a naïve cobalt decoration.

Any chips will reveal the color of the body

KEY CLUES

- Early pieces may be dated and inscribed with names.
- Applied decoration on 18th-century pieces often has sporting or wassailing (drinking festival) themes.
- 19th-century copies may be marked with a pottery or registration mark. They may also have applied panels on a commemorative, hunting, or harvesting theme.

Beer mug
This Vauxhall salt-glazed stoneware beer mug is decorated with a portrait of Queen Anne and motifs. It has a characteristic two-tone brown glaze. c1710; H: 8in (20.5cm); $4,500–5,000

The decoration copies Chinese color schemes and flowers fashionable at the time

New York jug
The unusual cobalt bird and flower decoration of this two-gallon jug adds to its desirability. $9,000–11,000

Staffordshire teapot
This salt-glazed miniature globular teapot and cover are decorated in *famille rose* (mainly pink). c1750; H: 2½in (6.5cm); $400–600

Quebec crock
The cobalt flora decoration was handpainted. The crock is impressed with the maker's mark. c1860; H: 11¼in (29cm); $5,000–7,000

Redware tea kettle
Probably made in Yorkshire, this kettle imitates Chinese Yixing red stoneware. c1775; H: 9in (23cm); $5,000–7,000

Staffordshire figures

IN THE EARLY 19TH CENTURY, porcelain figures made by factories such as Meissen, Derby, and Chelsea in the 18th century were hugely popular. Such porcelain created a huge demand for cheaper imitations from the growing middle classes. Dozens of small Staffordshire potteries started to produce decorative earthenware figures for the mass market. They are rarely marked. Popular subjects included Classical deities, allegorical and Biblical figures, and rustic groups such as children or shepherds. From the 1840s, the potteries began making press-molded "flatback" figures designed for mantelpieces. Decorated on one side only, they were produced in vast numbers.

Early Staffordshire figures

Figures were modeled by hand to create lots of detail. Here, the bocage (flowering tree placed behind the figures), rope around the bear's neck, and performer's stick would have to have been made separately.

The sections were press molded individually by hand, so look underneath the figure for finger and tool marks. They were then assembled and fixed using a thin, watery clay called slip.

KEY CLUES

- Careful modeling with the figure made up of several separate parts with individual limbs.
- Decorated with bold colors and plenty of detail.
- A vent hole was made in the base to prevent the thick clay exploding in the kiln.
- Feels heavy because the hand-pressed clay is relatively thick.

Flowers in the bocage have painted highlights—a sure sign of quality

Bold colors and intricate details bring the figures to life

Pearlware is cream-colored earthenware with a blue tint

Pearlware bear group

The expression on the performer's face, detailed painting on the base, and separate rope and stick all suggest an early figure. 1820–30; H: 9in (23cm); $2,500–3,500

Early figures often feature a square base

Biblical pair

These rare pearlware groups depict the Flight into Egypt and the Return from Egypt. Early 19th century; H: 7³⁄₄in (20cm); $3,500–4,500

"Dandies" group

Bright colors and accurate depictions of 19th-century fashion suggest an early date. c1820; H: 7¹⁄₂in (19.5cm); $2,000–3,000

Prancing fox

This finely modeled fox has separate legs and tail. The tree stump held up the body during firing. c1850; H: 6¹⁄₂in (16.5cm); $1,000–1,500

Staffordshire panther

Exotic beasts such as this panther were unusual subjects, making this example a rarity. c1820; H: 6in (15.5cm); $2,500–3,500

COMFORTER DOGS

Good... This pair are well molded and painted, with details such as shading to the fur and claws. c1860; H: 9½in (24cm); $1,000–1,2000

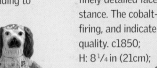

Better... These dogs are well modeled with finely detailed faces and an open-legged stance. The cobalt-blue bases needed an extra firing, and indicate quality. c1850; H: 8¼in (21cm); $4,500–5,000

Best... The detail of the dogs themselves, the children, and the baskets of flowers are evidence of high quality. c1850; H: 10in (25cm); $5,000–6,0000

Late Staffordshire figures

Ever-increasing demand led to factories creating figures from a single mold. Figures with delicate details were at greater risk of breaking during production. As a result, later figures were made as a single piece with as few protrusions or gaps between their limbs as possible. Painted decoration was kept to a minimum, using large areas of less vibrant colors with little detailing. Gilding was poor quality and easily worn away.

The figure lacks detail and the color is applied thickly

The two figures have been molded as one piece

Remains of gilding

The base has minimal decoration

KEY CLUES

- Figure modeled as a single piece with little depth of detail to the molding.
- Painted with few details.
- Relatively light when held because less clay was used.
- Interior will be smooth from mechanized press molding.
- Back may be flat and/or undecorated.

Highland dancers group
Queen Victoria's love of Balmoral inspired a craze for all things Scottish, making Highland dancers a popular theme. c1870; H: 13¾in (35cm); $250–350

By 1850 figures of famous people were in vogue

WATCH OUT! The popularity of Staffordshire figures means they have continued to be made right up until the present day. Newer versions are much lighter and clumsily decorated. They may also have been artificially aged.

Actor David Garrick
This portrait is simply molded with blocks of bright color indicating a poorer quality and later date c1860; H: 9½in (24cm); $400–500

Elephant spill vase
The unusual subject matter is a rare find. Careful painting shows that this is better quality. c1855; H: 6in (15cm); $1,500–2,000

Crimean Admiral
Patriotic characters were made in great quantities in the second half of the 19th century c1854; H: 15¼in (39cm); $350–450

Chinese ceramics

IMITATION IS THE SINCEREST form of flattery, and people have been imitating Chinese ceramics for centuries. European pottery and porcelain factories of the 18th century were in effect copying the Oriental factories that in turn often emulated the best work of their ancestors. This assimilation of style is part and parcel of the history

and development of fine ceramics. The problem comes when articles purport to be older and more valuable then they really are. These are not copies—they are fakes. With knowledge of the techniques and methods of decoration used in certain key areas and periods, you will be able to spot suspect pieces and buy with confidence.

Transitional Period vase

Early in the 17th century, during the long wars that marked the transition from the Ming to the Qing dynasties, the potters of Jingdezhen (the main porcelain center from the 14th century) began to produce fine wares. Mainly for the European market, the ceramics were decorated with lively figures in vibrant tones of blue. It was a period of

artistic freedom, which led to new shapes and decorative motifs. From about 1620 to 1683, these "Transitional" wares were shipped to Holland and were highly prized by Dutch merchants and their wealthy European customers.

The neck, decorated with stylized tulips, shows Islamic influence

The painting is in the "High Transitional" style and includes banana plants, scholars, and rocks

Genuine
Transitional bottle-shaped vase. c1640; H: 14 1/2 in (37cm); $25,000–30,000

TRADE SECRETS

A strong blue color, made from expensive cobalt, suggests a high-quality piece. A similar piece with a paler blue could be worth far less than the vase shown here – perhaps only $10,000. On many Ming and Transitional pieces, the powdered cobalt used was uneven and caused irregular, dark specks in the painting. These burst through the glaze during firing and turned black, creating an effect known as "heaped and piled."

The figures
Careful use of shading in the rich blue tones gives the figures movement and perspective. Grass is depicted using V-shaped marks.

The base
The foot-rim is high and raised. It is unglazed and shows kiln marks—slight imperfections like specks of dirt.

The pattern
The scenic panels are typically separated by clouds (the swirling blue lines). Glaze and body have a blue tinge. As processes improved over time, these became whiter.

FROM CARGO TO COMMODITY

The great age of trade between Europe and the East Indies brought wealth and glory to many, but some were less lucky and whole crews and cargoes were lost at sea. Technological advances have made it possible to salvage these long-lost wrecks, and the Oriental ceramics they contain have been the subject of intense interest from collectors. Most shipwreck porcelain is export blue and white ware, although *blanc de chine* and polychrome

items have also been found. The most famous shipwreck cargo, known as the "Nanking," came from the Dutch ship *Geldermalsen*, which sank in 1752. The 317 tons of tea on board would have netted the owner a profit of 400,000 guilders—a huge sum. The 130,000 pieces of blue and white porcelain in the ship's hold were of minor concern to the paymasters in Holland, yet when this cargo came on the market in 1986 it made $20,000,000.

Late 19th-century fake

Many copies of Chinese porcelain were not made as fakes. They were produced by the Chinese potters to venerate their ancestors and were decorated in an archaic style and given marks of previous dynasties. However, with pieces of early Chinese porcelain making ever higher prices, the buyer must be aware of the unscrupulous faker. One of the major clues that something is not what it seems is the attempt to over-age a piece. The fakers are also often tripped up by the many technological advances in potting techniques. These days it is difficult *not* to attain a brilliant white body and shiny glaze. And artificially created distressing, as in the rim below, is often too regular.

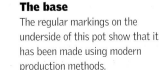

Fake
Blue and white vase. Late
19th century; H: 17in (43cm); $120–140

The border
The painter has given the border an overall wash, covered with haphazard crosshatching.

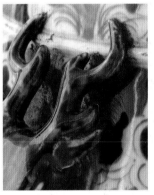

The handle
The dirt introduced behind the stag's head looks applied. The handle bears no relation to the vase's subject matter.

The base
The regular markings on the underside of this pot show that it has been made using modern production methods.

Brushstrokes
The quality of the painting is poor. For example, there are no clear, precise brushstrokes evident in the painting of the flower-heads.

The interrogation
Chinese export porcelain

DURING THE REIGN of the Emperor Wanli (1573–1619), the amount of blue and white porcelain made purely for export increased dramatically. The main center was the ancient kilns at Jingdezhen in Jiangxi province. After the potters lost imperial patronage in 1618, they had to look for expanding markets overseas. During the Transitional Period (1620–83), potters had creative freedom and new shapes and decoration combined with an improved body and glaze. European influence can be seen in shapes such as candlesticks and table salts. The Emperor Kangxi (1662–1722) reorganized the kilns in 1683 and there followed a golden age for Chinese export wares.

Kangxi porcelain

Blue and white wares in this period (1662–1722) are known for their pure white ground, and thin, tightly fitting, glassy glaze. The neatly trimmed foot rims often have an amber tinge. The blue decoration varies from a silvery hue through a pure sapphire brilliance to purple. Decoration includes narrative scenes (some taken from literature) and landscapes, which often feature idealized trees, islands, pagodas, and fishermen in sampans. Flowers and plants growing among rocks, animals, and fish are popular. The decoration seems crowded in comparison to earlier wares.

TRADE SECRETS

Marks on Chinese porcelains are notoriously difficult. Chinese potters venerated their ancestors and often copied the decoration and the earlier dynasty or reign mark. Fakers in the late 19th and early 20th centuries also copied early marks. Sometimes they were caught out, for example, by using a four-character mark of the Emperor Kangxi, which is not found on pieces from the period.

Detail of fish
The painting is of high quality. Each scale has been individually painted and shaded and the waterweeds are separately picked out.

Each fish is different

Detail of back
Orange iron oxide on the foot rim suggests an early date. Molded details are sharply picked out and pleasingly shaped, suggesting a higher-quality early piece.

Detail of mark
The sacred fungus mark, a symbol of good luck, is common on Kangxi porcelain. This also indicates that the piece is finely potted.

The branch on the back is carefully painted using a variety of brush strokes

Kangxi plate
Hand-painted saucer, with decoration of fish; stapled. c1700; D: 5¼in (13.5cm); $150–200

STAPLED WARES

Before the invention of epoxy and polyester resins, ceramic restoration was the work of jewelers and silversmiths. Ceramics were expensive and valued and they were repaired rather than disposed of. The staple method used, also called metal clamp repair, has its origins in the Ancient World. By the 18th century, china menders were active in many towns. Using a small "string" or "bob" hand drill with diamond tips the jeweler would drill two small holes to insert a rivet or wire lace. The repair was only visible from the back and is remarkably strong. Stapling was the preferred method of repair in Europe from the 1600s until well into the 20th century. Stapled wares are now a collectable in their own right.

Stapling Two rivets, or "staples," are used to mend a Kangxi saucer.

Good-quality Kangxi copy

By the late 19th century, many people who owned dinner or tea services produced in the early 18th century needed replacement pieces. They would have the pieces copied in China. Although this is a good example, there is less detail in the painting and the saucer is more cluttered. The glaze is more thickly applied, which means the molded detail is less pronounced. The fish have less individuality.

Decoration
The fish has been painted with a flat wash, then the scales picked out.

Kangxi copy
Hand-painted saucer with fish decoration. Late 19th century; D: 5¼in (13.5cm); $20–40

Poor-quality fake Kangxi

Poor-quality fakes are quite easy to spot. The quality of painting is poor. Dots simplify the waterweed design and some overlap the fish. There is little variation in tone and the overall design is cluttered. There is little definition to the molding to the interior and the overall shape is flatter. The petals to the back are more crude. On the original, a crab is painted in the center, but here the fish is repeated.

The border is a simple repeated pattern with smudging

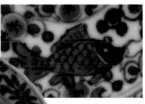

Decoration
The fish is a simple overall wash with little detail on the scales.

Kangxi fake
Hand-painted saucer with fish decoration. Late 19th century; D: 5¼in (13.5cm); $10–20

Kakiemon and imitations

KAKIEMON WARE WAS produced at the kilns at Arita in the Hizen province of Japan using a distinctive palette of soft iron red, deep sky blue, yellow, eggplant, turquoise green, and black. It was named after the celebrated potter Sakaida Kakiemon, who legend credits with introducing enamel decoration on porcelain to Japan in the 1640s. The outstanding quality of Kakiemon decoration was prized in the West, imitated by the new soft-paste porcelain factories that sprang up across Europe in the 18th century, including Chantilly, Mennecy, and Saint Cloud in France, and Chelsea and Worcester in England. Meissen in Germany copied Kakiemon, too, in hard-paste porcelain.

Kakiemon

The hard-paste porcelain, known as *nigoshide*, produced at the Arita potteries typically was painted in an asymmetrical style. Kakiemon decoration features delicate, well-balanced designs. Subject matter includes birds, flying squirrels, the quail and partridge, *prunus* (cherry tree family) blossoms, bamboo—the national flower of Japan—the chrysanthemum, and figure subjects. All decorative enameled elements were sparsely applied to emphasize the fine milky-white porcelain body.

KEY CLUES

- The milky-white porcelain body is hard paste.
- Overglaze enamels include iron red, sky blue, turquoise, yellow, black, and sometimes purple.
- Small dishes, bowls, bottles, and vases were painted with asymmetrical patterns.

JARGON BUSTER

Nigoshide The unique milky-white porcelain body of Japanese porcelain. It was covered with an almost colorless glaze.

The shape copies a traditional ancient Japanese bronze form

Molded handles

Rocks and waves decoration

Kakiemon elephant
Japanese decorators painted porcelain animals in Kakiemon style. From the mid-18th century, these were highly prized by collectors. 17th century; $250,000–300,000

Kakiemon dish
Rocks, *prunus* blossoms, and flowering plants are arranged asymmetrically and colored with the Kakiemon red, blue, and turquoise palette. c1690–1710; D: 5in (12.5cm); $1,500–2,000

Japanese Arita vase
The Kakiemon color palette of iron red, blue, and turquoise enhances the typical Japanese decoration on this vase, featuring chrysanthemums, rocks, and waves. c1660–80; H: 6³⁄₄in (17cm); $25,000–35,000

Chantilly

The magnificent array of Japanese Kakiemon porcelain assembled by the Prince de Condé inspired the founding of the Chantilly factory in France in 1725. It produced useful and decorative wares and figures in the Kakiemon style, faithfully copying many of the originals in his collection.

KEY CLUES

- The soft paste has an opaque, creamy tin glaze.
- Decorative patterns appear flat and linear as the enamels sink into the glaze.
- Black outlines distinguish Chantilly from true Kakiemon and other French factories.

Brushwork is highly detailed

Pair of wine coolers
This pair has the Chantilly mark of a red hunting horn. c1735–40; D: 8in (20cm); $50,000–70,000

Meissen

From 1729, Augustus the Strong commissioned the Meissen factory painters to make copies of his Oriental porcelain. They adapted Japanese Kakiemon designs to create a new style of decoration known as *Indianische Blumen* (Indian flowers).

KEY CLUES

- Thin and glassy creamy-white glaze.
- The palette differs from the Japanese, with clear yellows and a milky grayish-blue turquoise.
- Painted decoration can be extremely close to authentic Kakiemon.

The shapes of bottles and vases were frequently copied from Japanese originals

Meissen vase
The decorative motifs on this double-gourd vase include bamboo, *prunus* blossoms, and a vibrant tiger. c1740; H: 3½in (9cm); $1,500–2,000

Worcester

The popular Kakiemon-painted decoration looked to Meissen for inspiration rather than to Japanese porcelain. Worcester continued to produce Kakiemon-style tea and coffee wares and decorative vases and figures into the 1770s, long after the fashion had faded elsewhere.

KEY CLUES

- The green-tinged body is covered with a greenish or bluish glaze.
- Includes *famille rose* and *famille verte* as well as Kakiemon colors.
- Kakiemon designs often mingled with European decoration.
- Narrow, unglazed margin appears around the interior of the foot-rim.

Waist-shaped vase
A ho-ho bird perched on a pierced rockwork base and flanked by flowering branches decorates this early beaker vase. c1755; H: 5½in (14cm); $15,000–20,000

Chelsea

Made of a milky-white soft paste with impurity specks, Chelsea porcelain looks warm and creamy, in contrast to true hard-paste Kakiemon. Shapes were often inspired by English silver. The foot-rims of hollow vessels were ground down after firing to remove the three porcelain spurs.

KEY CLUES

- Inspired by Meissen designs that used a soft autumnal palette featuring brown, puce, and a distinctive greenish turquoise.
- Rims are edged in dark chocolate brown.
- Japanese shape may be decorated with European pattern.
- Enamel colors sink into the glaze.

Imitates shape found in contemporary silver

Lobed beaker
Painted in the typical Kakiemon palette with a Japanese-inspired bird, rockwork, and flowering branches, this beaker is marked with the Chelsea red anchor. c1750; $4,000–6,000

The interrogation
Satsuma ware

THE TERM SATSUMA has come to mean a fine earthenware with a distinctive cream-colored ground and delicately crazed glaze decorated with overglaze enamel and gilding known in Japan as *Satsuma nishikide*. From the 1870s, Japanese craftsmen were encouraged to sell their wares to the West and Satsuma ware was exhibited at international exhibitions. The exotic export wares created a Western craze for all things Japanese including a demand for more affordable, gaudier Satsuma. The time-consuming skills required to decorate Satsuma ware are now lost. The technical brilliance of pieces from the mid-19th century will never be re-created.

High-quality Satsuma

An exceptional piece dating from the early Meiji period (1868–1912) took months to make, so Satsuma ware was prohibitively expensive at home and abroad. Essentially a painting in miniature, it was carried out by artists who served a long apprenticeship. Most Satsuma artists bought glazed blanks from potters and decorated them freehand with traditional Japanese motifs and patterns such as foliage and flowers (often chrysanthemums, hydrangeas, lotus flowers and leaves, *prunus* blossom, and bamboo); landscapes (dragons, lions, and unicorns); real and mythical birds; and human figures engaged in ceremonial, military, or domestic activities. The scenes are usually surrounded by borders of flowers such as peonies or diaper (chequerwork) or fretwork designs.

Shaped and pierced rim
The rim features images of dragons and human figures over waves. The dragon is an important symbol of imperial power in Japan.

Detail
The finest details were painted using a single rat's hair. This allowed the painter to create lifelike expressions on faces and exquisite detailing on robes.

Marks on base
Two panels (cartouches) describe how the plate was made and are evidence that this is an example of the highest-quality Satsuma ware.

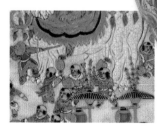

Enamel and gilding
The enamel and gilding is applied on top of the glaze so that it stands proud of the surface. The crazing of the soft, creamy glaze is typical.

Satsuma plate
Procession scenes were popular with Satsuma artists and gave them scope to show their skill as painters. c1870; D: 8¼in (21cm); $20,000–30,000

THE INFLUENCE OF JAPAN

The impact of the Japanese ceramics, metalware, and furniture at international exhibitions in London, Paris, and Philadelphia was so great that designers throughout Europe and the US were soon making pieces in the Japanese style. Often referred to as Japonism or Japonaiserie, it features Japanese-influenced glazes and simple, rectilinear shapes. While some craftsmen applied Japanese motifs to Western forms, others tried to blend Japanese influences with their own. British designer Christopher Dresser traveled to Japan in the early 1880s and on his return published *Japan, Its Architectures, Art and Art Manufactures*. It was a cornerstone of the Aesthetic Movement.

Minton plate Decorator William Mussil combined a Japanese-style scroll-shaped panel with a European painting. 1873; D: 9½in (24cm); $400–500

Poorer-quality Satsuma

Satsuma craftsmen showed examples of their work at exhibitions across Europe and the US from 1862 onward. Although the top Satsuma craftsmen catered for the aristocracy, many began to make pieces for several different markets, while others took the work of the best craftsmen and imitated it, making Satsuma ware available to a wider audience. The result was often inexpensive and decorated with overcrowded designs in garish polychrome enamels and plenty of gilding—a glitzy interpretation of traditional Japanese designs. Western technology such as plaster molds and metal stencils allowed the Japanese to increase production with greater uniformity. Mechanically made pieces tend to be substantially less valuable than the more subtle, hand-decorated wares.

Ovoid Satsuma vase
Decorated with a traditional Japanese scene of figures on a terrace in a river landscape, this vase is designed to appeal to Western tastes. c1890; H: 6¾in (17cm); $300–400

Floral border
A band of flowers decorates the neck of the vase. Flowers such as peonies were popular with Japanese and Western buyers alike.

Gaudy colors
Later mass-produced Satsuma ware features bold colors that were popular with less discerning buyers and far removed from traditional decoration.

Artist's signature
The base of the vase has been signed by the artist but their identity is no longer known. Many were given a standard signature.

WATCH OUT!
Beware any damage to gilding, as this is a serious defect. Look out for poor-quality restoration work: the telltale sign is when the color of the restored gilding does not match the original and it may feel lumpy. This will reduce value by up to 50 percent.

The lineup
Oriental ceramics

CHINA AND JAPAN have one of the longest ceramic traditions, dating back to 7000BCE. Chinese wares had a profound influence over those made throughout the Far East, Middle East, and Europe. They were the first to use glazes in c2000BCE and, by 300CE, were making refined pottery. Fine porcelain was produced by the 14th century and, during the Ming dynasty 100 years later, Chinese potters were making some of the finest wares ever.

By 1650 the Japanese had established a successful market in export blue and white wares with Dutch traders. Later, Kakiemon and Imari porcelain boasted distinctive decoration in colorful enamels.

The fine modeling of the horse's head helps to date the piece

Horse with rider. c234–581CE; H: 15in (38cm); $2,000–2,500

Early Chinese
From the 1st century CE, Chinese ceramics included funerary figures to accompany the deceased into the afterlife.
- Fine, white-bodied earthenware figures are crisply modeled.
- Figures were left unglazed, decorated with pigment or straw-colored glaze, or covered with a three-colored polychrome glaze.

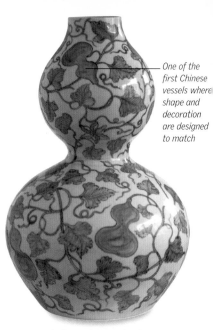

One of the first Chinese vessels where shape and decoration are designed to match

Yuan Dynasty double gourd vase. Mid-14th century; H: 18³⁄₄in (47.5cm); $5,000,000–7,000,000

Ming blue and white
During the Yuan dynasty, Chinese potters used cobalt blue to decorate their wares.
- High-quality blue and white Ming porcelain has a thick glaze with tiny air bubbles.
- Most hollow vessels were made in two parts.
- Early Ming has spacious, balanced designs.
- Marks were used regularly from c1426 and usually comprise four or six characters.

Guandi, or Guan Yu, was a military hero, c300CE

Guandi figure. H: 10in (25.5cm); $20,000–25,000

Kangxi famille verte
The mainly green translucent enamel colors of *famille verte* is dominated by apple green and was introduced in the Qing dynasty (1662–1722).
- Colors resemble wucai, and the glaze can appear to be thin and "glassy."
- The palette includes blue, yellow, eggplant, iron red, and black, as well as gilding.
- Designs include rockscapes and flowers.

The figure is modeled as a European man wearing a wide-brimmed hat

Horseman. 18th century; H: 11¹⁄₂in (29cm); $8,000–14,000

Blanc de chine
Blanc de chine was made from the late Ming dynasty onward.
- Wares include Buddhist deities such as Guanyin, and cups and bottles decorated with plum blossom, magnolia, and pine.
- The unpainted, translucent body is covered in a thick, transparent, cream or ivory glaze.

Pugs are less common than spaniels, and the unclipped ears are rare

One of pair of pugs. c1760; H: 7in (18cm); $35,000–50,000

Chinese export porcelain
Export wares, made from c1500, are decorative but lack the sophistication of Imperial wares.
- From the 17th century, potters began to make pieces to European specifications, using engravings as a guide. This resulted in the development of new shapes and motifs.
- Marks include tripods, lozenges, lotus and artemisia leaves, and earlier reign marks.

Panels of lotus on an iron-red ground

Baluster vase. c1650; H: 11in (28cm); $2,500–3,500

Transitional wucai

Developed in the reign of Jiajing (1522–66), the wucai palette has five colors. It was a less refined version of the 15th-century "doucai" style, and wares were often carelessly painted.

- Decoration is in underglaze blue as an outline or wash, with an overglaze iron red, green, brown, yellow, and black.
- The underglaze blue has a purple tinge.

Decoration is with Dutch canal houses and Baroque swags taken from a Dutch engraving

Vung Tau Cargo Canal House vase. c1690–1700; H: 10¼in (26cm); $800–1,200

Shipwrecked porcelain

In the 17th century, many trade ships returning from China with Oriental porcelain sank, and some cargoes have since been rediscovered. The Chinese saw the porcelain in the ships as little more than ballast. To them, the real value lay in the tea, silk, and spices packed with it.

- A few are decorated with European themes.

Interior painted with a frieze showing huntsmen and hounds encircling a fox

Hunting bowl. c1765; D: 15¾in (40cm); $8,000–12,000

Famille rose wares

In the early 18th century, *famille rose* (mainly pink) enamel colors, made opaque with white and including rose pink, were developed.

- Motifs include branches, rockwork, flowers, birds, landscapes, and interior scenes.
- From the mid-19th century, decoration was sometimes of scenes or motifs set within medallions, surrounded by intricate borders.

Coat of arms painted over banner

Iron-red and gilt scroll border

Armorial charger. c1755; D: 14in (36cm); $5,000–7,000

Armorial wares

In the 18th century, Europeans and North Americans commissioned large dinner services decorated with their crests and coats of arms from Chinese potteries.

- Lavish painting in polychrome enamels embellished with gilding are typical.
- Late examples often incorporate a small crest in blue and white.

Painted chrysanthemum sprays

Molded, shaped rim

Saucer. Early 18th century; D: 7¼in (18.5cm); $250–350

Japanese Imari

Named after the port of Imari near Arita, this porcelain was made from the late 17th century.

- The palette is dark underglaze blue with iron red, gold, yellow, green, and occasionally turquoise and purple.
- Later wares were densely painted.
- Large display pieces were decorated with patterns based on textile designs.

Kutani figure. 19th century; H: 11¾in (30cm); $800–1,400

Japanese Kutani

From the 1880s, the potters of Kutani produced cheap porcelain for export.

- The porcelain is typically eggshell thin with poor-quality molding.
- Most Kutani porcelain is decorated with overglaze colors sometimes dominated by iron red with lavish gilding, or with detailing in black or black and gray.

The lineup
French porcelain

SOFT-PASTE PORCELAIN was first successfully produced in France in the 1690s at the St. Cloud factory near Paris. In the 18th century, several factories, notably Sèvres, produced soft-paste tableware and figures. The sturdier hard-paste porcelain was introduced in 1769 with the discovery of kaolin and, after 1803, the factory ceased production of soft paste. In the 19th century, dozens of factories sprang up in Paris and Limoges, producing hard paste that was heavily influenced by the earlier designs of Sèvres and Meissen.

Border of gilded swags

Plate decorated with flowers. c1780; W: 17¼in (44cm); $1,000–1,500

Tournai

Founded in the Low Countries in 1751, Tournai made soft-paste tableware and figures.
- Plates may have molded basket-weave borders or spiral patterns around the rims.
- Initially off-white with a grayish tinge, later paste is ivory with a soft, translucent glaze.
- Motifs include landscapes and flower sprays.

Bagpipe player. c1760–1780; H: 9in (23cm); $2,500–3,500

Niderviller

Niderviller was making porcelain by 1768. In the late 19th century, the factory used the original molds to copy 18th-century wares.
- Useful tableware and decorative figures adopted the Neoclassical style in the 1770s.
- Best figures include Classical nudes by Lemire and sweet rustic figures by Cyffle after 1780.
- Popular painted decoration includes landscapes and *décor bois*—imitation wood.

Handles are in the form of satyrs' heads

Painted with garlands of flowers and ribbons

Urn-shaped vase. c1800; H: 23in (58cm); $2,000–2,500

Limoges

A factory was established in Limoges in 1771 following the discovery of kaolin (a key ingredient for hard-paste porcelain) nearby. Hundreds of factories around Limoges produced hard-paste tableware, dinner services, tea sets, and decorative objects.
- Styles often lack imagination, copying designs from Sèvres and other French factories.

Painting of the Château de Versailles

Gilt handles with bearded mask terminals

Urn. Early 19th century; H: 14¾in (37.5cm); $2,500–3,500

Paris

Paris had at least 15 factories from the 1780s until the 1840s, working in Renaissance, Rococo, Neoclassical, and Empire revival styles.
- White hard-paste porcelain has a hard glossy glaze impervious to gilding and enameling – the decoration seems to sit on the surface.
- Most porcelain was left unmarked.
- Flower motifs and Classical scenes popular.

The knop is in the shape of a cherry

Floral decoration copied from Vincennes

Custard cup. 1765; H: 3½in (9cm); $500–700

Mennecy

Established in Paris in 1734 under the patronage of the Duc de Villeroy, the soft-paste factory moved to nearby Mennecy in 1748.
- Decoration was Oriental-style or Rococo, in pink, sky blue, turquoise, yellow, and green.
- A creamy white, glassy translucent glaze covers the mellow, ivory-colored porcelain.
- DV mark, for Duc de Villeroy, is usually incised.

Decoration in various tones of one color is known as en camaïeu

Painted with sprigs of flowers

Decoration is in the Kakiemon style

Cane handle. Early 18th century; H: 1½in (4.5cm); $500–700

Lobed plate. 18th century; D: 9in (23cm); $200–250

Reclining figure. c1740; L: 12½in (32cm); $100,000–150,000

St. Cloud

St. Cloud near Paris was the first French factory to produce porcelain commercially.

- Glassy ivory glaze with tiny black flecks covers the grayish-white soft paste.
- Early wares had molded decoration of *prunus* blossoms inspired by Chinese *blanc de chine*, or were painted in underglaze blue with lambrequin borders or with Japanese Kakiemon-style designs (see pp76-77).
- Many pieces have silver or silver-gilt mounts.
- The mark is an incised "St C" over a "T".

Orléans

The *Manufacture Royale de porceleyne de Orléans* was founded in 1753. Other factories operated in the area in the late 18th and early 19th centuries.

- Orléans produced wares in both hard- and soft-paste porcelain.
- Small Mennecy-style figures include Oriental and rustic characters and children.
- It produced mainly floral decorated wares copying Sèvres.

Chantilly

An enthusiastic collector of Kakiemon, the Prince de Condé was the patron of the Chantilly factory, established near Paris around 1725.

- The soft paste has a creamy opaque glaze.
- Wares are in Kakiemon style with flower-based motifs painted in the Japanese palette of iron-red, turquoise, blue, and yellow.
- The factory mark is a small red hunting horn.

SAMSON COPIES

Established in Paris in 1845, Samson et Cie was the most prolific imitator of early ceramics. It copied Oriental and European porcelains, which bear a striking resemblance to the originals. When copying soft paste, Samson cannily added chemicals to the recipe to make their hard paste look creamy.

Blue feuilles-de-choux *(cabbage-leaf) borders surround the flowers*

Gilding is soft, thickly applied, and finely tooled

Potpourri holder. c1750; H: 5½in (14cm); $1,500–2,000

Teapot. 1770; H: 7¼in (18.5cm); $1,700–2,500

Vincennes

The national porcelain factory was established in 1738 at Vincennes near Fontainebleau. It employed accomplished artists and was the leading Rococo porcelain-maker.

- The porcelain is fine, white soft paste covered with a glassy, translucent glaze.
- Decoration is often with delicate flowers and finely detailed bouquets.

Sèvres

The Royal Porcelain Manufactory moved from Vincennes to the village of Sèvres in 1756. It produced hard-paste porcelain from 1769.

- Rococo motifs include flowers and *putti*.
- Brilliant ground colors include *bleu lapis*, green, sky blue, rose pink, and lemon yellow.
- Inside the mark of interlaced "Ls" for Louis XV is a date letter, introduced in 1753.

Sèvres copies Samson wares are marked with an entwined double "S" plus imitation marks of the factory copied. H: 6½in (16cm); $700–1,000

The interrogation
Meissen

THE FIRST EUROPEAN PORCELAIN FACTORY opened at Meissen in 1710 following the discovery of the formula for pure white, hard-paste porcelain by German alchemist Johann Friedrich Böttger. From the 1720s, the factory produced porcelain wares and figures of unsurpassed technical innovation, originality, and artistic skill. Virtuoso modeler Johann Joachim Kändler and Johann Gregor Höroldt, who developed a new palette of polychrome colors, directed operations. They introduced the now well-known mark of blue crossed swords. As time passed, the painted decoration became more European and Rococo and modeling played an increasing role.

18th-century Meissen

Meissen satisfied the demand for tea, coffee, and chocolate wares with finely modeled designs. The porcelain is exquisitely painted in the palette of bright enamel colors developed by the brilliant technician Johann Gregor Höroldt and highlighted with modest gilding. The design shows an Oriental-style garden with architecture, exotic birds and flowers, and figures dressed in flowing robes. These scenes were inspired by motifs found on Chinese and Japanese porcelain. The factory's great patron, Augustus the Strong, enthusiastically collected Oriental wares.

Decoration
Oriental figures and *chinoiserie* scenes were favorite subjects for the decoration of 18th-century Meissen ware that was skillfully painted in a wide range of colors and enhanced with gilding.

Marks
After 1725 the common Meissen mark was the crossed swords painted in underglaze blue, from the Saxony coat of arms. It is occasionally accompanied by a gilder's numeral.

Complex handle
Cup handles are usually simple loops. But the complex construction here shows how advanced technical skills developed at Meissen.

Chocolate cup and saucer
This rare flared cup and saucer is finely painted in enamels in Höroldt style. Much of the body was undecorated to show off the quality of the porcelain. 1739; $15,000–20,000

JOHANN FRIEDRICH BÖTTGER

Imprisoned in the castle laboratory at Dresden, alchemist Böttger was charged by Augustus the Strong (patron of Meissen) with finding the arcanum—the magical compound that would turn base metals into gold. Böttger collaborated with von Tschirnhaus, who longed to unlock the secret of making the pure white, hard-paste porcelain produced in the Orient. By 1708, Böttger and von Tschirnhaus had successfully managed to produce a red stoneware. A year later, Böttger produced his first specimen of glazed white porcelain using a high-firing clay from Colditz to create a white porcelain body. In 1710, he was appointed the first director of the Meissen factory.

Redware Most of the red stoneware and porcelain made under Böttger imitated silver in form and decoration. c1710; H: 4³⁄₄in (12cm); $2,000–2,500

19th-century Meissen

During the 19th century, the reputation of the Meissen factory for porcelain wares and figures of outstanding quality was enhanced by continuous improvements and refinements to both modeling and production processes. This flamboyant piece revives romantic and rustic 18th-century Rococo-style designs. Unlike the delicate and spare decoration of the original Rococo, pieces made in the popular Rococo Revival style are overly ornate. The lavish decoration, expanded color palette, sumptuous gilding, and complex shapes were meant to impress.

The handle is shaped to resemble billowing fabric and decorated with putti

The woman holds a sceptre and crown and sits above a peacock

Molded cloud

Elements jug
Representing "Air," the foot and lip of the jug are decorated with feathers and *putti* (cherubs). 1818–60; H: 26in (65cm); $7,000–10,000

Cherub holding a bird

Faces
Compared to 18th-century Meissen figures, later copies tend to have sweet and rather sentimental faces.

Decoration
Every part is painted and encrusted with richly modeled figures, flowers, birds, and other ornament. The flying birds contribute to the elemental theme of air.

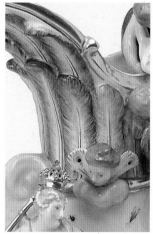

Color
The strong color palette and harsh, shiny gloss gilding used on 19th-century Meissen is much more garish than on earlier examples. Colors are often applied in a haphazard manner.

German porcelain

THE DISCOVERY OF THE FORMULA for producing hard-paste porcelain by Johann Friedrich Böttger in 1709 led to the establishment of the Meissen enterprise near Dresden one year later. Within a few decades, the coveted recipe had spread throughout Europe. By the mid-18th century, a handful of competing porcelain factories had sprung up across Germany, including the prolific Frankenthal, Ludwigsburg, Höchst, and Nymphenburg factories, alongside the less productive works at Fulda and Fürstenberg. Each factory developed a unique style and distinctive hard paste. But they all produced a range of tableware, figures, and ornamental designs that largely took inspiration from the fashionable high-quality Meissen wares and, later, from the French factory at Sèvres. By the late 19th and early 20th centuries, countless porcelain workshops copying the Meissen style had been established around Dresden.

Landscapes and flowers are typical decoration

Bullet-shape teapot and cover. c1770; $1,000–1,500

Fürstenberg

Fürstenberg began making porcelain in 1753.
- Covered with an off-white, glittery glaze, the close-grained hard paste resembles the porcelain body at Meissen and Berlin.
- Palette dominated by dark reddish brown, muddy green, and grayish blue, with lavish brassy gilding.
- Exaggerated C-scroll handles.

Figures were among the most successful Limbach porcelain products

Crisply modeled figures were a speciality

The pot is baluster shaped

Figure of Autumn from a set of the Four Seasons. c1775; H: 6³/₄in (16.5cm); $1,500–2,000

Limbach

Limbach was second in importance to Closter-Veilsdorf. Early wares are in the style of Meissen.
- The early paste has a slightly yellow tinge.
- Charming, naïve figures of peasants, citizens, and royalty in stiff poses are typical.
- A trefoil replaced the early Meissen-style mark of a pair of crossed "Ls" and a star.

Rare Print Seller figure modeled by J.J. Louis. c1766; H: 6in (15cm); $4,000–6,000

Ludwigsburg

Specialities included tableware decorated with birds, fruit, flowers, and landscapes and figures.
- The grayish white, close-grained paste is covered with a smoky glaze.
- Yellow, iron red, and brown with gray-tinged green, puce, and cobalt and gilding is typical.
- Most common mark is a ducal crown above two interlaced "Cs", the cipher of its patron.

Coffee pot. c1770; H: 5³/₄in (14cm); $1,500–2,000

Höchst

Well-painted decorative themes included landscapes and Chinese-inspired designs, along with rustic, battle, and hunting scenes.
- Pure white, hard-paste body covered with a glassy white or creamy glaze resembles a highly refined faience.
- The mark is a wheel, until 1765 painted in overglaze red, puce, or purple and thereafter in a grayish underglaze blue.

The factory was celebrated for the smooth whiteness of its porcelain

Needlecase. c1770; H: 5½in (14cm); $1,100–1,500

Closter-Veilsdorf

Founded in Thuringia in the third quarter of the 18th century, it produced a smooth, milky-white, almost flawless hard-paste porcelain.

- The typical palette includes pale puce, iron red, yellow, green, and grayish blue.
- Popular decorative themes include landscapes, birds, flowers, and figure subjects in the style of Teniers, Boucher, and Watteau.
- The most common factory mark consists of the letters "C" and "V" in underglaze blue.

Painted with sprigs of flowers

Molded basketweave

Molded plate. c1765; D: 9in (23cm); $500–700

Nymphenburg

Nymphenburg produced highly refined wares and figures in the style of Meissen.

- White, close-grained, flawless hard paste with a warm, wet-looking opaque or translucent glaze often with a grayish tint.
- Ocher, puce, sky blue, reddish brown, and yellow are favored, along with ample gilding.
- Decoration includes landscapes with Classical ruins, flower bouquets, birds, Chinese figures, and *Commedia dell'Arte* characters.

Rare pear-shaped jug. c1785; H: 6in (15cm); $2,000–2,500

Fulda

In 1764, Fulda started producing flawless hard-paste porcelain figures and wares.

- Following Meissen, Fulda specialized in landscapes, figures, and scattered naturalistic flower sprays known as *deutsche Blumen*.
- Porcelain is covered in a warm, creamy glaze.
- Colors include green, yellow, brown, orange, iron red, puce, grayish blue, and black highlighted with gilding.

The painted monochrome decoration reflects Rococo taste

Cup and saucer. c1770

Berlin

Elegant tableware, decorative objects, and colorful figures number among the specialities.

- The hard-paste body is grayish white covered with an opaque, blue-tinged glaze.
- Early decoration has Watteau-style figures, landscapes, flowers, and botanical subjects.
- Colors often show small patches of flaking.
- Early mark is a sceptre; after 1832 changes to an orb with "KPM" in underglaze blue.

Indian-style flower painting

Plate. 1758; D: 12¾in (32.5cm); $1,500–2,000

Frankenthal

Hard-paste tableware and figures drew inspiration from silverware and Sèvres.

- Themes include landscapes with Classical ruins, flowers, birds, *chinoiseries*, and figures.
- The glaze is opaque, creamy, slightly gray, and grainy. It absorbs the enamel colors.
- Dominant colors are green and purple, with puce, ultramarine, grayish blue, brown, yellowish green, and gray-tinged yellow.

DRESDEN

During the 19th and early 20th centuries, the area near Meissen around the city of Dresden became a center of porcelain production. More than 40 workshops such as Carl Thieme's factory at Potschappel produced hard-paste wares. They made tea and dinner services in the style of Meissen and Sèvres, as well as vases, candelabra, and mirror frames encrusted with scrolls, shells, or fruit and flower garlands painted in bright enamel colors.

One of pair of jardinières Panels are painted in Watteau style. Late 19th century; W: 14½in (37cm); $2,000–2,500 (pair)

19th-century porcelain plaques

PORCELAIN HAD BEEN MADE by various factories in Berlin since the mid-18th century. From the early 19th century, Berlin became celebrated for superb porcelain decorated with sumptuous portraits and landscapes that imitated oil paintings. Such painted porcelain peaked around 1840 with the development of porcelain plaques.

The rectangular "blanks" were mostly sold to independent decorators known as *Hausmaler*, who initially created copies or details of Old Master paintings in extravagant gilt frames. Later, around 1870, the subject matter included exotic maidens, scantily clad nymphs, and religious topics. The plaques were widely imitated.

Berlin plaques

The Berlin factory pioneered this style of pictorial porcelain. The porcelain is effectively a canvas for painting on, and none of the white body is visible on the finished piece. Examples of Berlin's output are highly sought after. Plaques should be exquisitely painted with natural skin tone and shading. Portraits of attractive young women are the most popular subject matter, and are even more desirable if presented nude or partially clothed.

KEY CLUES

- Look for even skin tone with painstakingly detailed faces, hair, and breasts. Quality of painting is paramount to collectors.
- Folds in clothing and other fabric should be realistic.
- Portraits are more popular than landscapes and religious subjects.
- Berlin plaques are impressed "KPM".

"Solitude" painted by Greiner
The quality of the painting and the female subject make this plaque highly desirable. It was painted by one of the factory's best artists. c1880; 10x7½in (25.5x19cm); $6,000–7,500

Gypsy girl
The finely painted portrait of a girl holding a lute adds to the charm of this KPM porcelain plaque. c1880; H: 13in (32.5cm); $6,000–8,000

Gainsborough lady
Berlin plaques bearing historical portraits inspired by the English painter Gainsborough are currently out of favor. Late 19th century; H: 7in (17.5cm); $1,000–1,500

Young woman
Despite its popular subject matter, the quality of the painting on this KPM Berlin plaque is not as high as others. c1880; H: 9in (23cm); $3,500–5,000

Portrait in profile
This well-executed copy of a work by Asti is signed by Wagner and was painted at the Hutschenreuther factory. c1880; H: 7in (18cm); $3,500–5,000

CHANGING POPULARITY

The Biblical scenes and local landscapes popular with many 19th-century collectors do not strike a chord with buyers today, no matter how well painted. Modern buyers look for attractive female subjects. Static figures and dull colors decrease desirability.

Biblical scene The subject matter of this plaque makes it less popular with collectors today, and this is reflected in the price. It is probably made by KPM Berlin. Late 19th century; 10³/₄x9in (27x22.5cm); $2,500–3,500

City view Washed-out colors and a lack of animation in the figures detract from the appeal of this KPM Berlin plaque. 1908; H: 5¹/₂ in (14 cm); $2,000–2,500

Other European plaques

Many European factories also produced painted porcelain plaques. Some, such as Vienna and the factories in Limoges, France, also decorated the plaques with copies of popular paintings and romanticized folk scenes. In Britain, Royal Worcester used local artists to paint plaques with subjects such as garden scenes. Meanwhile, Royal Crown Derby produced items decorated with a variety of designs, including animals, fruit, and flowers.

KEY CLUES

- Painting varies from competent to excellent and this is reflected in the desirability of each piece.
- Portraits are the most popular subject matter.
- Landscapes command less attention, although Royal Worcester Highland scenes painted by the Stintons are highly collectable.

"Autumn Tints, Berks" painted by R Rushton
The subject of this Royal Worcester plaque has fallen out of favour with collectors. c1924; W: 10¹/₄in (26cm); $2,000–2,500

The painting of a lake beyond trees is less popular with collectors than portraits

Fortune teller
The quality of this Vienna plaque is exceptional. It shows a gypsy in a brightly brocaded skirt reading a boy's palm. c1842; 22³/₄x17¹/₄ in (58x44 cm); $14,000–17,000

Springtime
This French plaque, decorated by M. N. Shearman from a painting by Cot, was made for the 1878 Paris Exhibition. c1878; 15¹/₂x9¹/₂ in (39.5x24cm); $12,000–18,000

Fruit and flowers
Royal Crown Derby plaque painted by Albert Gregory. It has a detailed vignette of fruit and flowers. c1910; W: 5³/₄in (14.5cm); $2,000–2,500

Arts & Crafts vases

ALTHOUGH THE ARTS & CRAFTS movement had its roots in England, it was in the United States that it flourished. American potteries were inspired by the European wares exhibited at the Philadelphia Centennial Exhibition in 1876. The industry saw an opportunity to satisfy the demands of the newly affluent citizens who wanted to decorate their homes in this new style. The New England, Southern, and Californian schools concentrated on handcrafted and modeled wares. The Ohio Valley School, whose most famous and important factories are Rookwood and Roseville, used the vase as a canvas on which to exhibit wonderful painting and complex glazes.

Rookwood pottery

Ceramic production began in earnest in Cincinnati, Ohio, a few years after the Philadelphia Exhibition. Initially importing blanks from Europe, Cincinnati's female potters such as Maria Longman Nichols and Maria McLaughlan began china-painting classes. From this grew Rookwood, arguably the best and most successful American art pottery. Rookwood's first major line was the Standard Brown ware, decorated in browns with bursts of orange, yellow, and gold. The breakthrough came in 1894 with three new lines: Ariel Blue, Sea Green, and Iris. Rookwood anticipated the European Art Nouveau movement with its photo-realistic marine scenes and botanical studies.

Rookwood mark
The flame mark with Rookwood monogram was used from 1886 with an extra flame added each year—by 1900 there were 14 flames. In 1901, the Roman numeral "I" was added below and changed accordingly with each year. Here, "X" is impressed below—1910. "1278C" is the shape number. "LA" is the artist's monogram. The incised "W" is the artist's instruction for white (Iris) glaze.

Smooth tonal transitions
Rookwood is known for the subtle gradations of tone of the background colors.

Paint
The glaze is unsurpassed for the clarity, richness of color, perspective, and depth it imparts to the high-quality painting.

Rookwood Iris glaze bulbous vase
Iris glaze floral studies remain some of the most vibrant of Rookwood's work. This vase is decorated by Lenore Asbury with branches of white hollyhocks. 1910; H: 12in (30cm); $7,000–9,000

Iris glaze was produced until 1912, when the high lead content needed for the very shiny surface was recognized as a health hazard

MASS PRODUCTION

As with many ranges of art pottery this design was mass produced in a mold with embossed decoration that a decorator would then embellish with appropriate colors. What collectors are looking for is crisp definition with good hand painting, as seen in the example of Roseville blue Falline on the right. As the mold was re-used, the definition became "mushy" and the outline indistinct (left).

Two examples of the same vase This example, made from a much-used mold, has poor definition.

Roseville blue Falline vase This example has good, crisply defined outlines.

Roseville

The Roseville factory was built in Zanesville, 150 miles from Cincinnati. It produced art wares from 1898. Although never as successful as Rookwood, Roseville still contributed, with fellow potteries Weller and Owens, to make Zanesville the ceramic capital of the world—in quantity if not quality. Roseville was conscious of what Rookwood was up to. When Rookwood introduced Standard Brown, Roseville countered with Royal Dark and Louwelsa. When Rookwood had success with Iris, Roseville introduced Royal Light, Eocean, and Azurean. Although in Rookwood's shadow, Roseville did tempt English potter Frederick Rhead to Zanesville for a time.

Roseville Azurean bulbous vase
The vase is painted by W Myers. There is some restoration. H: 8in (20cm); $2,000–2,500

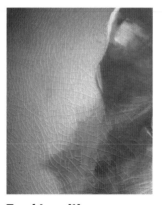

Tonal transitions
The gradations of tone of the background colors are clumsily executed and lack finesse.

Painting quality
The painting has none of the subtlety, depth, and realism of Rookwood. It is one-dimensional.

The glaze is shiny but has no sophistication

Glaze defects
The surface shows crazing and peppering (black dots), which are common with inferior wares.

WATCH OUT!
Unlike Rookwood, Roseville's art pottery is less valuable than its production range. Apart from a few exceptional hand-decorated pieces, the best prices are paid for Roseville's high-quality production ware.

Arts & Crafts ceramics

TOWARD THE END of the 19th century, the Arts & Crafts movement started in Britain and spread to the US. It sought to move the ceramics industry away from mass-produced pottery based on earlier styles to high-quality, handcrafted wares that celebrated the creativity of the individual potter. In the US, factories often employed designers, potters, and artists to work in turn on a range rather than expecting one person to be an expert in all fields.

Cuenca tile. c1905; 6x6in (15x15cm); $3,500–5,000

High-quality matte glaze in silvery green is typical

Tulip-shaped vase. 1903–10; H: 12 in (30cm); $5,000–7,000

Grueby, US

Grueby's Faience Company in Boston, Massachusetts, produced award-winning hand-thrown earthenware vessels.
- Innovative matte green glazes.
- Glazes tend to be thick, opaque, and pitted like a watermelon rind.
- Nature-inspired motifs often hand-carved.
- Also Spanish Cuenca technique—impressed ridges prevent colored glazes intermingling.

Teco, US

The Teco Art Pottery in Illinois produced ceramics in clean, geometric lines championed by the Arts & Crafts style, and looked for inspiration to the Midwest's Prairie School.
- Architectural shapes with thickly potted walls, loop or buttressed handles, and embossed decoration of flowers or foliage.
- Marks are a long-stemmed "T" with the letters "e c o" arranged beneath each other.

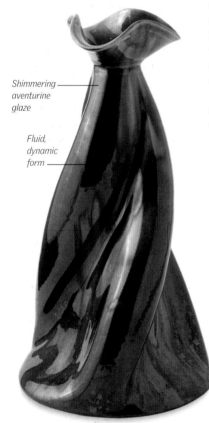

Shimmering aventurine glaze

Fluid, dynamic form

Propeller vase. 1890s; H: 13in (33.5cm); $2,000–2,500

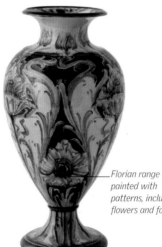

Florian range painted with patterns, including flowers and foliage

Florianware vase. c1900; H: 16in (40.5cm); $2,500–3,500

Stylized designs of plants are typical

Ovoid vase. c1910; H: 7in (18cm); $7,000–10,000

Christopher Dresser for Ault, UK

Ault in Derbyshire was one of a number of companies to employ the multi-talented Christopher Dresser to design art pottery.
- His work took inspiration from many ceramic traditions, including Islam and Japan.
- The impressed facsimile of Dresser's signature appears on the base of his designs.

Moorcroft, UK

The Staffordshire-born ceramicist William Moorcroft created distinctive art pottery.
- Shapes were inspired by Persian, Turkish, Classical Roman, and Far Eastern ceramics.
- Stylized flowers and landscapes painted red, blue, and yellow, often tube-lined for texture.
- Marked "Moorcroft Burslem" and impressed with either "WM" or "W Moorcroft".

Marblehead, US

The Marblehead pottery in Massachusetts specialized in quality handcrafted ceramics.
- Painted or incised stylized flowers, animals, birds, fish, sailing ships, geometric patterns, and Native American motifs.
- Matte glazes in soft, muted colors.
- The mark is the impressed outline of a ship with the initials "MP" in a circle.

Marie De Hoa LeBlanc carved the vase

Imaginative decoration features plants and animals native to the American South

Favorite subjects include finely modeled birds with human features

Vase. c1906; H: 8¹/₂in (21cm); $1,000–1,500

Newcomb, US

Talented female New Orleans students created a range of highly prized American art pottery.

- Shapes inspired by the soft, curvaceous lines found in peasant pottery and Oriental wares.
- Designs include moonlit scenes, tobacco and cotton plants, lizards, and abstract Japanese.
- Marks include the firm's symbol, artist's cipher, potter's mark, and a date.

Vase by Edith Lupton. 1888; H: 12in (30cm); $1,500–2,000

Doulton stoneware, UK

Doulton & Company at Lambeth in south London collaborated with Arts & Crafts designers by establishing an art pottery studio.

- Stoneware in simple, clean shapes decorated by hand with incised, modeled or hand-carved motifs featuring animals, birds, beaded borders, flowers, and leaves.
- Doulton stoneware is signed by the designer and marked by the decorator.

Stoneware bird. c1900; H: 11in (28cm); $38,000–42,000

Martin Brothers, UK

The Arts & Crafts doctrine of individuality found voice with the witty salt-glazed stoneware of the eccentric Martin Brothers. They created a menagerie of fanciful beasts.

- The typical palette has muted hues of cream, gray, brown, blue, and yellow.
- Early mark is "Martin," replaced 1882–1914 with "RW Martin & Brothers London & Southall" with a number and date.

Hand-thrown vessels were pinched and twisted into bizarre sculptural shapes

Speckled owls vase. 1910; H: 11in (28cm); $1,000–1,500

Ruskin, UK

The Ruskin Pottery founded by William Howson Taylor at Smethwick in 1898 relied only on innovative glazing effects for decoration.

- Shapes were influenced by Chinese ceramics.
- Rich palette of vibrant colors.
- Glazing techniques include luster, crystalline, and the Chinese-inspired "blue soufflé" and "flambé": crimson with streaks of turquoise.

Bulbous vase. c1920; H: 12¹/₂in (31cm); $700–1,000

Fulper, US

Fulper in New Jersey added a line of Arts & Crafts ceramics called Vasekraft to its wares. It pioneered various glazing techniques.

- Vasekraft wares have matte, gloss, metallic, or crystalline glazes in subdued colors.
- Combined glaze techniques on single vessels.
- Art ceramics are marked with a vertical impressed or printed "Fulper."

Bulbous vase. 1890s; H: 5¹/₂in (14cm); $5,000–9,000

George Ohr, US

Dubbed the Mad Potter of Biloxi, George E. Ohr made highly original pottery.

- Red earthenware pots tend to be lightweight, potted to eggshell thinness, and brittle.
- Rich lustrous glazes combined with mottled, speckled, metallic, and crystalline effects.
- Impressed "GE Ohr Biloxi Miss" mark replaced with an incised facsimile signature.

Art Deco figures

COLORFUL, ELEGANT, AND DRESSED in the latest fashions, Art Deco figures embody the emancipated women of the time. Hand painted and often finely modeled, they were an up-to-date version of the porcelain figures European factories had been making for 200 years. However, the grand old manufacturers such as Meissen were not the leaders—they preferred to continue to make their perennially popular 18th-century figures. Instead, it was newcomers such as Goldscheider, Rosenthal, and Lenci who made the form their own. Inspired by Flappers, by women now taking part in sports, and by bronze figures, these colorful ceramics were affordable works of art.

Goldscheider

Meticulous attention to detail with elaborate molds and complex arrangements of elements are the hallmarks of a Goldscheider figure. The Austrian company employed leading artists such as Josef Lorenzl and Stefan Dakon to create expressive women in modern or exotic dress. Most pieces were made from a refined earthenware in sections. An integral body and base would have details such as limbs added later, and any imperfections were carefully removed.

KEY CLUES

- Vivid but sympathetic use of color, particularly in detailed areas.
- Pieces modeled by leading designers may have impressed signature on the base.
- Scantily dressed dancers are more common than elegant fashion models.

Figure made from several molded pieces

Serene and elegant pose

Skirt split to the thigh

Creamy-white skin tone

Butterfly wing dress

Woman with borzoi hound

This model by Claire Herczeg (later Weiss) was also made in a red dress. Borzois were a fashionable accessory. H: 17in (43cm); $2,500–3,500

Dancer

A bronze figure by Josef Lorenzl was used to make the mold for this dancer. H: 9¼in (23.5cm); $1,200–1,800

Lady in red

Gracefully posed dancers wearing revealing clothes were a popular Art Deco subject inspired by the Flapper Girls. H: 9in (22.5cm); $1,700–2,000

Lenci

The figures of Italian firm Lenci often lack the flowing form of German makers but were elegant and stylized. The best examples of Lenci figures depict partially dressed young women in "modern" poses: sunbathing or applying make-up.

Rosenthal

The Bavarian firm Rosenthal depicted modern subjects or exotic dancers from tales of *The Arabian Nights* from 1924 until 1939. Modelers included Dorothea Charol and Claire Weiss, who introduced an Art Deco series of Four Seasons in 1932.

Fine white porcelain

Exotic pose and costume

Crown Devon

In the 1930s, scores of British factories made inexpensive Art Deco figures inspired by continental factories. Crown Devon ware was one of the ranges made by the Staffordshire firm of S. Fielding & Co. Many of the figures were modeled by Kathleen Parsons.

Pose gives sense of movement

Alpine walker
The new freedom for women to take part in athletic pursuits such as hiking was celebrated in ceramics. H: 17in (43cm); $2,500–3,500

Snake charmer
The Rosenthal factory produced numerous figures of snake charmers during the 1920s and 30s. H: 10 1/2in (26.5cm); $800–1,200

Rio Rita
Kathleen Parsons's figure celebrates Bebe Daniels's performance in the title role of one of the hit films of 1929. H: 11in (28cm); $1,000–1,500

KEY CLUES

- Figures tend to appear stiff and poses may look "uncomfortable."
- The colors may be less vibrant than on German counterparts or alternatively surprisingly bright.

KEY CLUES

- Modeling and decoration are high quality.
- The base of figurines may feature the molded signature of the modeler.
- Porcelain is either stark white or has an ivory tinge.

KEY CLUES

- Elegant, detailed figures such as Bathing Girl and Beach Girl.
- A series of nude figures by Kathleen Parsons is highly collectable.
- Many pieces are signed by the artist.

Art Deco ceramics

THE CLEAN, ANGULAR LINES, modern geometric shapes, and highly stylized motifs of Art Deco were especially well suited to pottery and porcelain. Championed by the bold, bright designs of Clarice Cliff, the 1920s trend forged a path in Britain that challenged conventional taste. In France, potters such as Jean Mayodon created stylized Classical themes with painterly precision. The popular taste was not lost on factories such as Wedgwood in Staffordshire and Sèvres near Paris, which commissioned celebrated contemporary designers to create wares in the latest fashion. In the United States, factories such as Cowan and Roseville produced limited-edition Art Deco wares conceived by independent designers.

Brushstrokes visible in the glaze

Bizarre Stamford Orange Roof Cottage pattern teapot. H: 5in (12.5cm); $2,500–3,500

Clarice Cliff

Prolific British potter and decorator Clarice Cliff was celebrated for her Art Deco designs.
- Bizarre range uses geometric shapes and bright abstract patterns outlined in black.
- Brightly colored biscuit-fired wares covered with a distinctive honey-colored glaze.
- More than 500 shapes produced.
- Wares often marked with impressed dates, pattern name, and Clarice Cliff's signature.

The leaping deer is a typical Art Deco motif

Earthenware vase, with Leaping Deer pattern, designed by Truda Carter. 1934–37; H: 8¼in (21cm); $1,500–2,000

Poole

In Dorset, the Poole Pottery made a splash in the 1920s and 30s with Art Deco tableware.
- Among the most sought-after designs are stylized female faces by Olive Bourne and the floral and animal patterns of Truda Carter.
- Lavender, pink, and yellow often dominated by blue or used in two-color glazes.
- Angular handles for Studland line; Everest range handles in solid diamond shapes.

Carved with renderings of New York skyscrapers and nightclubs, in Persian Blue and black glaze

Jazz bowl. 1931; H: 8½in (22cm); $60,000–80,000

Cowan

The Cowan Studio was at the forefront of American Art Deco pottery from 1929.
- Earthenware vases, lamps, nut dishes, flower bowls, candlesticks, and compotes in a rich color palette were mass produced.
- Most pieces are marked with an impressed or printed name or monogram of the artist.
- The rare Jazz bowls by Victor Schreckengost are highly collectable

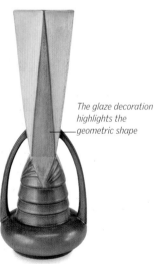

The glaze decoration highlights the geometric shape

Rare Roseville Futura Arches vase. H: 14¼in (36cm); $3,000–4,000

Roseville

By the late 1920s, the company was producing wares in the fashionable Art Deco style.
- Animated and colorful designs, including the decorative Futura range.
- Well-marked examples include angular handles or skyscraper stepping.
- Bright, vividly colored glazes are typical.
- After 1930 the impressed mark of Roseville was used.

Autumnal color palette

Myott fan vase. 1930s; H: 9in (23cm); $600–800

Myott

In the face of competition posed by Clarice Cliff and Susie Cooper, the Stoke-on-Trent factory hand-painted Art Deco wares in the 1930s.
- Geometric vases, jugs with crimped rims, and wall pockets were colored in a palette dominated by orange and brown.
- Designs naïve, and almost crude in execution.
- Marks include Myott's and Myott England.
- Paint flaking and glaze crazing is common.

Symmetrical and frieze patterns are typical

This jug is in the Paris shape

Vase decorated with Adam and Eve with three snakes. 1930s; H: 22³/₄in (57cm); $35,000–50,000

Jean Mayodon

The ceramicist and painter was made Artistic Director of Sèvres in 1941. Mayodon created ornamental wares as well as large fountains, sculptures, and tile panels.

- Decorated in rich colors; designs inspired by Classical antiquity and Hindu motifs.
- Gilding frequently highlights patterns.
- Used a knife to create decorative designs in the thick earthenware paste.

Ovoid faïence vase, decorated with stylized flying pelicans. H: 13³/₄in (34.5cm); $2,500–4,500

Boch Frères

The Keramis factory owned by Boch Frères led the field of Belgian Art Deco ceramics.

- Vase decoration imitates *cloisonné* enamel and includes animals in natural landscapes, stylized flowers, and plants.
- Simple ovoid shapes covered with thick enamel glazes that create a relief pattern.
- Typical palette of turquoise, black, green, and brown on ivory crackle-glazed background.

Moon and Mountains pattern jug. 1928; H: 4³/₄in (12cm); $1,000–1,200

Susie Cooper

British-born Susie Cooper created new shapes, including Kestrel and Wren, decorated with patterns such as Dresden Spray and Nosegay.

- Incised and lithographic decoration as well as hand-painted floral and geometric designs.
- Bright, abstract geometric designs such as polka dots, bands, and exclamation marks.
- Most works marked with a facsimile signature and serial number.

Printed with hieroglyphics in gilt and enamels

Gilding contrasts with mottled vivid blue and green glazed ground

Matte glaze typical of Murray's Modernist Art Deco wares

Tutankhamen pattern tomb jar. 1920s; H: 12¹/₂in (32cm); $7,000–10,000

Carlton

Carlton at Stoke-on-Trent enjoyed its heyday with Art Deco wares in the 1920s and 30s.

- Vases in geometric or Oriental shapes were hand-painted in vivid contrasting colors.
- Lusterware had a pearlized iridescent glaze.
- Enameled decoration and gilding applied after glazing are slightly raised.
- Designs include *chinoiserie*, butterflies, and Egyptian and silver-luster lightning motifs.

Box and cover, with an Odeonesque-style plaque. c1925; D: 6¹/₂in (16.5cm); $1,000–1,500

Sèvres

Sèvres produced some of the finest ceramics in the Art Deco style during the 1920s and 30s, with decoration designed by eminent artists.

- Traditional 18th-century shapes elaborately decorated with striking Art Deco motifs.
- Stylized leaves, flowers, geometric, and Egyptian patterns were favored decoration.
- Motifs are frequently highlighted or outlined with restrained gilding.

Keith Murray for Wedgwood Etruscan white-lined green tall vase. c1934; H:8 in (20.5cm); $600–800

Wedgwood

In the 1920s and 30s, Wedgwood commissioned key artists to design Art Deco wares.

- Futuristic, Modernist wares feature simple patterns such as lathe-turned bands.
- Plain designs by Keith Murray in bold, geometric shapes with celadon, gray, or ivory semi-matte glazes.
- Designer wares have printed signature or name, Wedgwood mark, and letter date.

GLASS

GLASS

Glassmaking is an ancient art, fascinating for the many developments that have shaped its history over the last 2,000 years, from the first glassblowing techniques to the luxury glass of 15th-century Venice and the studio art glass of the modern age.

Cutting and engraving enhance the effect of the colors

Bohemian glass
Early 19th-century Bohemian glassmakers experimented with colored glass, producing a wide range of pieces in the Neoclassical style. This piece by Egermann has multicolored detail. c1835; H: 9¹⁄₂in (24cm)

Roman glass
Early Roman glass has inspired glassmakers down the centuries. Late 18th-century designers sought to re-create the shapes of Roman pieces, while Art Nouveau designers experimented with iridescent finishes. H: 6³⁄₄in (17cm)

THE ANCIENT PHOENICIANS made glass beads as early as 5,000BCE. By 2,000BCE, the Egyptians had started to refine the process, although techniques were rudimentary and involved dipping a molded shape into molten glass and winding glass threads around it. The mold was usually made of a mixture of mud, straw, and clay formed around a metal rod, and produced a crude, hollow vessel.

Having adopted techniques from the Egyptians, the ancient Romans went on to revolutionize the art of glassmaking when they introduced glassblowing techniques in the 1st century BCE. Using a method that remains relatively unchanged to this day, Roman glassblowers inflated a lump of molten glass (the metal), gathered at one end of a long tube (a blowing iron). They could then manipulate the blown glass to form a variety of shapes. Alternatively, they blew the glass into a pre-formed mold. In using these techniques the Romans were able to produce larger vessels, more varied in shape. Not only that, but they could also make glass pieces on an unprecedented scale.

Different types of glass
Glassblowing techniques spread throughout Europe with the growth of the Roman Empire and, depending on the materials available to glassmakers, different types of glass were produced. Glass is made by melting sand and either sodium or potassium at very high temperatures so that they fuse. Soda glass was made predominantly in Egypt

Venetian glass
Among the various revival styles of the late 19th century was an Italian revival of early Venetian pieces. This dolphin pitcher is reminiscent of 17th-century examples. c1890; H: 9$\frac{1}{2}$in (24cm)

Daum brothers cameo glass
Cameo glass was popular during the Art Nouveau era. This piece has applied pink bleeding hearts, or dicentra, decoration. c1905; H: 8in (20.5cm)

Delicate pattern created in the mold

Depression handled dish
Depression glass is so named because it was produced in the US during the Great Depression (1930s). It was molded glass, mass produced at very low cost. 1930s

and Italy, where the sodium element of the mix came from ashes of burned seaweed (sodium carbonate). Potash glass originated in France and Germany, where the potassium element of the mix came from ashes of wood or bracken. This glass was known as *verre de fougère* (fern glass) in France and *Waldglas* (forest glass) in Germany. While soda glass was lightly colored and malleable, potash glass tended to be more green in color and more durable.

Venetian expertise

Glassmaking had become increasingly sophisticated by the beginning of the 15th century, with Venice at the center of all activity. Thanks to the influx of a number of immigrant glassworkers from the Middle East, the island of Murano had been the center of the Venetian luxury glassmaking industry since the 13th century. Glassmakers began to experiment with both new and old techniques, making a breakthrough with the development of *cristallo*, a colorless soda glass that was perfect for making elaborate shapes. The resulting glassware was unrivaled in quality and variety, ranging from colorless glass goblets with applied enamel and gilt decoration to exquisite multicolored *millefiori* (literally,

JARGON BUSTER

Batch The mixture of raw ingredients such as sand, fluxing agents, and coloring agents melted together to make glass.

thousand flowers) vases. Venice dominated the scene for the next 200 years and glass was made in the Venetian style (*façon de Venise*) throughout Europe.

New developments

In 1676, a new type of glass emerged in Britain—lead crystal, developed by George Ravenscroft (1632–83). By adding lead oxide to molten glass, Ravenscroft had a product that was heavier and shinier. It was highly refractive, which meant that it was suited to cutting. A fashion grew for cut glass of all types that lasted well into the 19th century and, to some extent, stole the limelight from Venice. At the same time, Bohemian glassmaker Friedrich Egermann developed lithyalin—an opaque colored glass—in imitation of semi-precious stones.

The end of the 19th century saw a revival of earlier styles from Renaissance to Rococo, and a number of glass manufacturers responded by producing rock crystal ware or pieces in the Venetian style. Mechanization toward the end of the 19th century had a lasting impact, not least in the United States, where the development of press-molding techniques earlier in the century contributed to making glass an everyday item for most households.

Glassmakers in the 20th century produced a wide range of art glass, experimenting with a host of techniques. Innovations included the cameo glass of Emile Gallé, the iridescent glass of Johann Loetz, and the organic forms of mid-century Scandinavian glass.

The briefing
Looking at glass

DECORATIVE AND FUNCTIONAL glass has been made for thousands of years. Since blowing a "gather" (a blob of molten glass) through a hollow iron blowing rod was first discovered by the Romans in the 1st century BCE, the method of production has changed very little. To assess the age and nationality of any glass, it is first necessary to assess the material itself (known, confusingly, as the "metal"), how it has been shaped, how it has been colored, if at all, and how it has been decorated.

WATCH OUT!
Once the main body of glass is formed it is often transferred to a second rod, the pontil rod, for shaping. On early pieces this was snapped off, leaving a rough edge.

Bowl

Collar (where bowl joins knop and stem)

Knop (bulge)

Tear inclusion

Stem

Foot

English heavy baluster goblet
The goblet has a conical bowl, an inverted baluster stem with a large tear inclusion, and a folded conical foot. c1700–10

Closer inspection
To solve the glass case, the detective needs to handle the glass, check for imperfections, work out how it is made, and spot telltale color variations.

Stem shapes

Most glasses are grouped by stem type in a system devised by E. Barrington Haynes in his book *Glass Through the Ages* (Penguin Books). The dates are a guide to periods of popularity.

01 Baluster 1685–1725

02 Molded pedestal 1715–65

03 Balustroid 1725–55

04 Light (Newcastle) 1735–65

05 Composite 1740–70

06 Plain 1740–70

07 Airtwist 1740–70

08 Hollow 1750–60

What to look at

Bowl shape

Check the shape of the bowl of a drinking glass as that can help to date it. (Although remember that every shape has been reproduced later—it is only one clue.) Most early 18th-century bowl shapes were either conical or funnel. By the mid-18th century, there were also bell, thistle, and trumpet shapes. Most plain stem glasses (opposite) have drawn trumpet bowls.

The color

Much can be deduced from slight variations in the color of the glass. Even if it is clear does it have a tinge of gray, green, or amber? Is the glass slightly smoky in tone and does it show "crizzling" (in which the surface of the glass has a network of small cracks)? This could indicate 17th-century Anglo-Dutch glass. A slight greenish tinge could indicate early lead glass. Later lead glass has a bluish tinge under ultraviolet light. Glass that has an amber to brown tinge may well be 20th century.

The stem

Look at the stem to see if it is plain or decorated. If decorated, is it molded or faceted? Can you see thin lines of other glass inside the stem? Are they colored? Does the stem have a decorative knop—a swelling—and is it solid or hollow? *See box opposite for how stem shapes help you to date the glass.*

The feel

Feel and look for any joins to see if the glass has been made in more than one piece. Does the piece have a flat or folded foot—can you feel a ridge at the edge of the foot? Is the base thick or thin? Feel in the center of the foot—is there a rough area that has been broken off? Or is it smooth? Is the piece light or heavy? If the drinking glass has not been made in sections and then joined, it dates from the 20th century.

Flaws and marks

Look and feel for any imperfections in the glass. Imperfections could be one clue to an early glass. Are there bubbles visible in the metal? This could indicate an early glass but be aware that most glasses with numerous bubbles in them date from the 20th century. Most glass that is marked is from the late 19th or 20th century. *See pp214–15 for more on glass marks.*

Identifying glass decoration

Glass has been decorated since it was first made. There is very little new in glassmaking, with most techniques having been practiced for centuries. Decoration can be divided up into effects achieved by "hot" working techniques, executed when the body is still hot and nearly molten, and those achieved by "cold" working techniques, carried out after the body has cooled. Although hot working techniques are practiced all over the world, certain countries have become renowned for specific types of decoration. For instance, Bohemia (now the Czech Republic) is famous for cutting and engraving. Murano in Italy is renowned for its use of applied colour techniques.

Acid etched

A design is first marked out on the surface using an acid-resistant material such as wax, which protects the underlying glass. Then a three-dimensional pattern is created by immersing the glass in acid, which eats it away. The longer the body remains in the acid, the more glass is eaten away, and the deeper the design becomes.

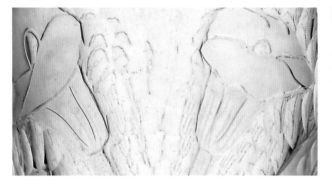

Enameled

Enamel color is made up of metallic oxides and finely ground glass suspended in an oily medium. It is applied to the body with a brush or by transfer. The colors are irrevocably bonded to the surface and solidified in the heat of the kiln. As different colors require different firing temperatures, the process is often time consuming.

Applied

A separate, smaller mass of molten glass is applied to the body when it is still hot and being formed. This mass is then shaped into handles, prunts, rims, or a foot, which may sometimes have patterns impressed into them using a stamp. The molten glass may also be dripped onto the body to form a trail in a pattern.

Gilded

The most common way of applying gold to the inside or outside surfaces is mixing gold leaf or powder with an oily medium and painting it on. It is solidified and fixed to the body through firing. Other methods are using an adhesive to stick gold leaf to the surface, and sandwiching gold leaf between two layers of glass, known as *Zwischengoldglas*.

WHEEL CUTTING AND ENGRAVING

A design is engraved or cut into a glass body by holding it against a spinning wheel or disc. A number of factors, including the size, material, and shape of the edge of the wheel affects the result. Fine engraved work is often done with a thin copper disc. Thicker wheels with a V-shaped edge produce mitre and bevel cuts, which can be deep.

Cut glass The decorative effect is created by deep cuts into the glass

Engraved glass A detailed design is made by removing thin sections of glass.

End of day

A term used to describe typically multicolored glass made from the remains of glass left in the pots after the day's production has ended. Made by the glassmakers in their spare time, shapes can be whimsical as well as functional. Colors and designs are usually random and each piece is unique.

Diamond point & stipple engraved

A sharp stylus with a diamond as a point is used to scratch a very fine, shallow line into the surface. Lines are built up and used in combination to form a design. The technique was often used on extremely thin glass that could not be cut. Stippling is a variation where the point is gently tapped onto the surface, leaving a shallow dot.

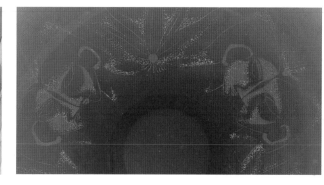

Zanfirico

Twisted strands of white or colored glass are embedded in rods of clear, colorless glass. These rods can then be assembled and fused together to create a form, or fused to the outside of a glass body and fused and melted to form a uniform surface. It is also known as *vetro a retorti,* or *latticino* when white strands are used.

Opaline

A lightly translucent glass typically found in pastel tones of pink and blue, but also in other stronger colors and an off-white. It is made by adding ground calcified bones to the glass mix. Opaline glass is often blown or pressed into molds, and can be further embellished through cutting, gilding, or enameling.

The interrogation
Bohemian glass

GLASS HAS BEEN PRODUCED in the area known as Bohemia (modern-day Czech Republic) since the 16th century. Initially a distinctive dark blue glass was made by adding cobalt oxide to the batch. At the end of the 17th century, Johann Kunckel made a deep pink-red glass by adding gold chloride. Friedrich Egermann was known for his experiments with colored glass. He invented staining, an inexpensive technique for coloring glass in which the initial gather was painted with a stain of color and fired at a low temperature to fix the color. He also invented flashing, where the first gather of glass (often clear) was covered in a different color and fired to fuse the layers.

19th-century Bohemian goblet and cover

This Bohemian ruby-flashed goblet and cover may have been engraved by Karl Pfohl, who is one of the greatest and most sought-after 19th-century Bohemian engravers. Both he and August Böhm were well known for their engravings of Arabs on horseback. The goblet was first entirely covered with the ruby color and then cut to reveal the clear glass beneath. Although the piece is unsigned, its quality and excellence are evident. The depth and power of the cutting and engraving can be felt by running a thumb over the surface. The cover is engraved to the same high standard as the goblet, is in perfect proportion, and fits snugly.

Horse and rider
The engraving is so fine on the figure you can clearly see his beard, eyes, hands, and the folds of his clothes. The horse's muscular body, mane, tail, and reins are sensitively engraved.

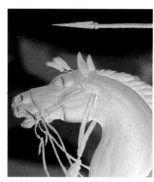

Horse's head
The horse's face has great expression, with its teeth bared, ears pricked, and nostrils flaring. Details such as the wrinkled skin under the neck add to the strong sense of realism.

The back of the goblet
The reducing lens to the rear is also of a high quality, with good engraving on the flash resist.

Attention to detail
The flashing is extremely well executed and the detail on the vines, including the veining, is naturalistic.

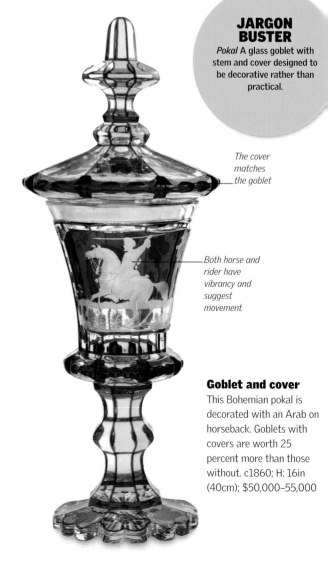

JARGON BUSTER
Pokal A glass goblet with stem and cover designed to be decorative rather than practical.

The cover matches the goblet

Both horse and rider have vibrancy and suggest movement

Goblet and cover
This Bohemian pokal is decorated with an Arab on horseback. Goblets with covers are worth 25 percent more than those without. c1860; H: 16in (40cm); $50,000–55,000

OVERLAY GLASS

Another technique characteristic of Bohemian glassmakers was overlaying glass. As this technique was perfected, it was combined with enameling and gilding. Flashing is often confused with overlay, and in the 19th century the glassworks tended to interchange the terms. With overlay glass the layers are thicker, and between the colors there is often shading, rather than the sharp line that denotes flashing.

Bohemian double overlay beaker
The clear glass has a blue and enamelled overlay and gilding. c1840; H: 4½in (11.5cm); $1,200–1,800

Detail Cut roundels are decorated with enameled flowers, insects, and birds.

20th-century Bohemian goblet

The area of Bohemia has long been known for the excellence of its glassmakers but it also produced glassware for the ever-increasing tourist industry. Although some tourists, Queen Victoria, for example, bought fine-quality examples, many pieces were produced for the general tourist as a small memento of a vacation.

Such pieces shows none of the quality, skill, and craftsmanship of the high-end pieces. Glassware such as this goblet is much closer in appearance to mass-produced examples. The clear gather is cased in red and blown into a mold. The wheel-cut decoration is flat to the touch and the execution is mechanical.

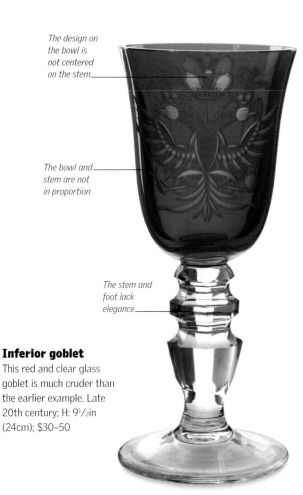

The design on the bowl is not centered on the stem

The bowl and stem are not in proportion

The stem and foot lack elegance

Inferior goblet
This red and clear glass goblet is much cruder than the earlier example. Late 20th century; H: 9½in (24cm); $30–50

The decoration
The wheel-cutting that has been used to produce the engraving has no vibrancy or movement and the design is uninspiring.

Varying quality
There is, however, some definition in the engraving of the eagles' feathers and the crown but it is still simply executed with no life.

Attachment
The bowl has been simply attached to the stem by a small gather of red glass and has been relatively crudely done.

TRADE SECRETS
When examining any piece of cut glass, do the "thumb test" to help check quality. Close your eyes and run your thumb over the surface. Feel how deep and complex the cut surface is. Check how many types of cut and engraving have been used. Feeling the glass will also help you to detect any chips, which are often less obvious on colored glass.

The prime suspects
Colored glass

COLORED EFFECTS CAN BE ACHIEVED by using ingredients that color glass all the way through, by layering clear and colored glass, or by rolling molten glass in powdered glass (enamel). Metallic oxides have been used to color glass since the ancient Egyptians and Romans made dark blue, turquoise, white, and yellow glass. Experiments continued in Venice where, in the mid-15th century, glassmakers used tin oxide to make opaque white *lattimo* glass. Glassmakers in Bohemia used cobalt oxide to make dark blue glass in the 16th century. By the end of the 17th century, they had created a deep pink glass called gold-ruby by adding gold chloride.

Hyalith and lithyalin glass

In the 19th century, Bohemian glassmakers experimented with new chemicals to develop new types of glass. Count Georg Franz August Langueval von Buquoy was the first to make an opaque black or dark red glass known as "hyalith" in 1819. Ten years later, Friedrich Egermann patented "lithyalin," another deep red to black glass. The surface was treated with metal oxides to create the appearance of veins and marbling. Lithyalin was sometimes overlaid on dark green hyalith glass. Such examples command a premium today.

KEY CLUES

- Hyalith was usually decorated with gilding.
- Most lithyalin was cut and polished. It was occasionally decorated with gilding and enameling.
- Hyalith and lithyalin were mostly used for jugs, vases, scent bottles, and bowls, but display cups and saucers were also made.
- Items decorated with gilt *chinoiserie* designs are less common.

Gilded mark
The base of the beaker is marked with a gilt butterfly.

Lithyalin beaker by Friedrich Egermann
The highly polished opaque glass is decorated with oval panels and gilding. c1830; H: 4¼in (11cm); $3,500–5,000

TRADE SECRETS
Red glass is usually more expensive than any other color because it was difficult to make and it contained gold—an expensive ingredient.

Hyalith jug with lid
This black jug by Buquoysche Glashütten is decorated with gilded floral and ornamental motifs. The knob on the lid and the handle are also gilded. c1830; H: 8in (20cm); $2,000–2,500

Overlaid glass

To make overlaid colored glass (also known as cased or *sommerso* in Italian), a piece of clear glass is dipped into one or more differently colored batches of glass to form thick layers. Sometimes the glassmaker cuts through the layers for decorative effect.

KEY CLUES

- There may be shading or thinning between the different layers where the thicker layer of glass has been cut.
- It is heavier, thicker, and shinier than flashed or stained glass.

The red outer layer has been cut to reveal the clear glass beneath

Red overlay goblet
This glass by FP Zach of Munich is engraved with floral motifs and a hunting scene. c1850; H: 8³/₄in (22cm); $5,000–9,000

Flashed glass

Another technique developed by Egermann, clear glass was dipped into colored glass and heated so the layers bonded as they cooled. It was employed for less expensive items using lower-quality materials. However, with higher-quality oxides it was possible to create intricate designs.

KEY CLUES

- It is often decorated with cutting or engraving. There should be a sharp line between the colors.
- Sometimes confused with overlaid glass, layers of flashed glass are usually thinner than overlaid.

Bohemian ruby-flashed goblet
The thistle-shaped bowl has alternate flashed and clear flutes as well as a shaped rectangular raised panel that is engraved with figures in a landscape. c1875; H: 6¹/₂in (16.5cm); $350–400

Stained glass

Staining glass is an inexpensive technique that Friedrich Egermann developed for coloring glass. A clear object was dipped into or painted with a thin layer of metal oxide while cool and then heated at a low temperature to fix the color.

KEY CLUES

- Stained glass has a rich, solid color that was often only applied to specific areas of an item.
- The glass is usually cut or engraved, but this decoration tends to be shallow.
- Beware blue stained glass because it fades easily, lowering value.

The red forms a frame for the clear glass on the stem and foot

Goblet
This goblet was made by Carl Günther, Steinschönau. The red layer is engraved with a mare and foal. c1855; H: 6¹/₂in (16.5cm); $2,000–2,500

URANIUM GLASS

Experiments during the 19th century included adding uranium to the batch (mixture) to make new yellow and green shades that fluoresced under ultraviolet light. In 1830s Bohemia, Josef Riedel created transparent glass called Annagrün (yellow-green) and Annagelb (green-yellow). A similar glass was developed at the Whitefriars glassworks in London. In the 1840s, Baccarat in France made a uranium glass named chrysoprase. Vaseline glass—transparent glass that looks like petroleum jelly—also contains uranium.

In the 19th century, many glassblowers working with uranium glass died relatively young of lung cancer. It was believed that this was caused by contact with molten uranium glass. This is now thought unlikely because uranium tends to affect the thyroid gland rather than the lungs.

Bohemian glass decanter
The yellow-green tinge comes from uranium. 1840; H: 13in (33cm); $500–700

Applied and painted decoration

APPLIED DECORATION consists of prunts (blobs) or trails of molten glass. Enamel colors in the form of metallic oxides are painted onto the glass and heated. Gilding uses gold leaf or paint. Both enamels and gilding were used in ancient Rome but it was Islamic glassmakers who first combined these decorative techniques. Venetian glassmakers in the 15th century were the first in Europe to use the techniques and they inspired German and Bohemian glassmakers. German decorators developed new types of enameling in the 17th and 18th centuries, including *Schwarzlot* (opposite) and *Zwischengoldglas* (see pp110–11).

Applied decoration

In the 15th century, Venetian glassmakers refined a technique known as lampwork to create small, complex shapes from tubes of glass. The tubes were heated then twisted in a small flame to create sophisticated shapes such as mythical beasts and snakes and patterns known as "threading." Lampwork was typically used to form stems for wine glasses and tazzas (stemmed dishes). The technique was copied in the Low Countries where it was called *façon de Venise* (Venetian style, pp126–27) and revived in the 19th century.

KEY CLUES

- Complex shapes, blown or manipulated, used as ornamentation.
- 16th- and 17th-century *façon de Venise* is usually a combination of clear and blue glass.
- It can be hard to differentiate between originals and copies.

The lampwork has been pulled to give a lace-like edge around the base of the bowl

A glass trail has been used to create a ruffle effect

Sweetmeat dish

This Venetian Revival sweetmeat dish by Salviati & Co. is made in the traditional Venetian style. Lampwork decorates the stem. c1890; H: 5³⁄₄in (14.5cm); $500–700

Trailed snake vase

Spiral trail decoration is a quick and easy form of decoration. Here, a green glass vase is decorated with a trailed blue glass snake. c1900; H: 4³⁄₄in (12cm); $80–100

Raspberry prunt

Römer with prunts

This German drinking glass has been decorated with prunts. These have been impressed with a stamp to make "raspberries." 18th century; H: 6in (15cm); $500–1,000

The mouth and ears were pulled from the head with pincers

German Schnapps flask

Molten glass has been applied to the blown glass body of this dog-shaped flask to make legs and a tail. 18th century; L: 5¹⁄₄in (13.5cm); $500–1,000

WATCH OUT!
Any decoration— whether glass, enamel, or gilding— that has been applied to the outside of a piece of glass is vulnerable to damage. Always check carefully.

EASTERN INSPIRATION

The 1878 Paris Exhibition saw a plethora of "Islamic" glassware inspired by the designs of 13th- and 14th-century mosque lamps. Prize-winning glassmakers included Frenchmen Philippe-Joseph Brocard and I. J. Imerton and the Austrian firm of J. & L.

Lobmeyer. They all combined the techniques of enameling, jeweling, and gilding to produce glass decorated with vividly colored designs, which could resemble *cloisonné* work in their intricacy.

Each decorative technique needed to be heated to a different temperature, which meant that cracking was a constant hazard during the decorative process.

Arab Series vase J. & L. Lobmeyr copied motifs such as arabesques, scrolls, and stylized flowers from Islamic lamps. c1875; H: 10¼in (26cm); $8,000–10,000

Enameling and gilding

Enamel is a mixture of metal oxides and ground glass in oil, painted onto the glass then heated to fix it. Different colors require different temperatures so the process has to be repeated several times. To gild a piece of glass, gold is applied using something sticky such as honey, or by mixing it with mercury before heating to fix it. Many 19th-century German drinking glasses were decorated with thin, transparent enamels. Thicker, opaque enamels were used on Bohemian glass from around 1825. Multiple layers of enamel create high-relief enameling.

Light and shade
Dots and hatching have been used to create shadows on the face.

Fine brushwork creates detailing on the clothes

The naïve painting is typical of the period

Swedish beaker
Enamels have been used to create this portrait of King Carolus (Karl) XII of Sweden with a lion at his feet. c1715; H: 9in (23.75cm); $20,000–25,000

KEY CLUES

- Cold enameling and gilding—in which the enamel or gold is not heated to fix it—are vulnerable to wear. They are usually reserved for decorative items.
- Enamel stands slightly proud of the glass surface.
- Mercury gilding appears thinner and brassier than honey gilding.

Black transparent enamel is painted on freehand to create a hunting scene

Gilding was often used to decorate the rim of a drinking glass

Schwarzlot wine glass
Schwarzlot (black lead) decoration began in the late 1700s using black or brown enamels. c1730; H: 8¾in (22.5cm); $1,000–1,500

Portrait beaker
This example is gilded and also features an enamel portrait of Franz I of Austria. c1800; H: 5in (12.5cm); $4,000–5,000

Viennese Cupid beaker
The number of colors and the gilding on this beaker would have required several firings. c1825; H: 4¼in (11cm); $8,000–14,000

JARGON BUSTER
Jeweling Applying drops of colored glass onto a piece of glass so the "jewels" stand proud. It is often combined with gilding.

Handblown and molded glass

GLASS CAN BE FORMED using a variety of techniques. Once techniques for blowing glass had been discovered by the ancient Romans or Phoenicians, the variety of forms that could be produced was dramatically increased. To blow glass, the glassmaker extracts molten glass from a pot using a hollow iron rod. He blows air through the rod to expand the mass into a bubble, and then shapes it using a variety of tools. This technique is still practiced today but, over the past two centuries, other methods have been introduced. These include blowing the glass bubble into a mold by hand or machine, and injecting or pressing molten glass into a mold by machine.

Handblown and formed glass

After the glass has been blown into a bubble, it is manipulated using wooden paddles, hollow molds, pads, and metal tools to form it into the desired shape. Complex forms such as this goblet will be made up of a number of separately made components, which are joined and fused together while the glass is still hot. Smaller masses of glass can be flattened to make a foot, stretched into shapes such as stems, or dripped onto a form and manipulated further.

KEY CLUES

- Often a slightly irregular form, with areas on the same part of the body of different thicknesses.
- The presence of a pontil mark on the base, although this may have been polished away.
- Designs with applied elements that cannot be molded, or that look the same but vary slightly upon closer inspection.

Hand-working
The dolphin-shaped stem is formed by the glassmaker manipulating and shaping the molten glass as it is dripped onto the foot.

Sea creatures are a classic Venetian motif

Murano glass goblet
Although made recently, this handmade piece was produced using centuries-old techniques and styles. 2004; H: 10³⁄₄in (27cm); $400–600

Bonnet was an alcoholic drink

Molten white glass was dripped around the body

English bonnet glass
Although a mold was used to create the pattern, the irregular form shows this was handmade. c1790; H: 3¹⁄₄in (8cm); $400–500

Alpine bottle
The shape was formed using paddles and pads, then decorated with white bands. c1840–c1860; H: 4¹⁄₂in (11.5cm); $500–700

English water glass
A mold with a low-relief diamond pattern inside was used to form this glass. c1770; $150–200

JARGON BUSTER
Pontil The iron rod onto which a hot piece of glass is attached at the base while the top is finished. When the glass is snapped off the rod, a rough mark is left.

GLASSMAKING TECHNIQUES

A piece of handmade glass may be made up of a number of sections, which are assembled at the last stage. The traditional Venetian goblet on p122 requires three components: the bowl, stem, and foot. Multicolored glass canes are melted together to make a striped gather, which is blown to make the separate bowl and foot. The stem is made by dribbling molten glass onto the foot and shaping it into a dolphin with fins and a curled tail. Finally, the bowl is joined to the stem. For a skilled glassmaker the process takes about 45 minutes.

Shaping the bowl
The base has been decorated with a frill of glass and the rim is stretched by hand so that it flares outward.

Molded glass

The 1820s saw the development of mechanized techniques that allowed glass to be pressed into molds, and the late 19th and 20th centuries saw advancements made in the mechanical and manual techniques of blowing glass into molds. All these developments allowed glass to be mass-manufactured at low economic costs. The glass was also consistently regular in form and size. René Lalique mastered press-molded techniques, combining them with Art Deco designs.

KEY CLUES

- An entirely regular form that perhaps cannot be made easily by hand.
- An even, thin distribution of glass across areas of the body.
- Interiors with depressions that match the outside decoration.
- Rounded detailing, which is too smooth to have been modeled by hand. Details may also often be less fine.

The fish appear to swim out of the water, giving a sense of movement and perspective

Lalique molded vase
Although much Lalique glass was pressed into molds, it was also blown into them, as with this Formose vase. c1924; H: 6½in (18cm); $10,000–14,000

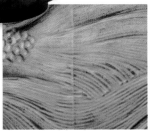

Mold lines
Low relief lines show where the two parts of the mold were joined together.

Riihimäki molded vase
The Finnish company spun molds mechanically at high speed to ensure the glass spread evenly. H: 10in (25.5cm); $50–100

Walter Butterfly vase
This German vase is typical of press-molded glass of the time, with detail on the exterior. 1920–30s; H: 8¾in (22cm); $250–450

Depression glass bowl
Produced to imitate costly cut glass, the rounded edges show the pattern is molded. H: 3in (7.5cm); $20–30

The lineup
Cut glass

THE ANCIENT TECHNIQUE of decorating glass by cutting into its surface was revived in Germany and Bohemia in the late 16th century. Most glass there had thin walls, which limited designs to simple, shallow-cut patterns. In 1676, British glassmaker George Ravenscroft developed a soft, heavy-bodied lead crystal. It was ideal for deep-cutting elaborate designs and prisms. The technique became fashionable for decorating glassware during the late 18th and 19th centuries at Stourbridge in England, across Ireland, and in the United States. Designed to reflect the light, the process of cutting with tools allowed the glass to be decorated with sharp-edged complex patterns in either relief (standing out) or intaglio (incised). These could then be polished to produce a smooth, reflective shine. The repeal of tax on glass in Britain in 1845 led to a surge in the production of cut glass. Forced to compete with British and Irish wares, glassmakers in Bohemia, France, and Belgium copied the technique of cutting glass, while across the Atlantic, American glassworkers developed "Brilliant" glass. European glassmakers continued making traditional cut-glass designs in the 20th century but also introduced Art Deco and modernist styles.

JARGON BUSTER

Intaglio A design that has been cut into the glass and lies beneath the surface.

The high lead content gives the thick glass a brilliant finish

Bowl by Ludwig Kny. 1930s; D: 12in (30cm); $700–1,000

UK, Stuart

Stourbridge-based Stuart & Sons made some of the best British Art Deco glass, by designers such as Ludwig Kny and Eric Ravilious.
- Strong shapes combine with modern designs.
- Most designs were clear glass but from the 1930s amber and green were reintroduced.
- Delicate engraving is 1920s; abstract or geometric, deep-cut patterns are 1930s.

The deep and sharp cutting of the clear, heavy glass exploits its refractive quality

Colored glass with floral decoration is typical of Stevens and Williams

The heavy lead crystal has a distinctive gray tint

Diamond-cut body

Round, radially molded foot

Cased and intaglio bowl and stand. c1920; H: 6¼in (15.75cm); $200–250

UK, Stevens and Williams

Established in 1847 and known for art glass and quality engraved and cut tableware.
- Cutting, engraving, acid etching, cased, and cameo glass were all factory specialities.
- The 1930s bold, abstract cut-glass designs by architect Keith Murray for decanters, vases, and tableware are especially valuable.

Pickle jar. c1815; H: 7in (17.5cm); $700–900

Ireland

To escape the heavy taxes from 1745, British and Irish glassmakers established glasshouses in Belfast, Cork, Dublin, and Waterford.
- 18th-century pieces have simple geometric patterns with shallow, lateral bands.
- Distinctive Irish forms such as canoe-shaped bowls with scalloped edges and heavy, square "lemon squeezer" feet replaced English styles.

Flower holder attrib Libbey. Late 19th century; $700–1,000

US, Brilliant cut

In the late 19th century, American glassworkers developed "Brilliant" glass. It was cut in bold, elaborate patterns and was highly polished.
- The high lead content has a gemlike quality.
- Motifs include stars, diamonds, and scallops.
- When struck gently, the glass of a good-quality piece should ring like a bell.

The hard, brilliant potash glass of Bohemia was ideally suited to deeper, more elaborate cutting

Strawberry diamond cutting

Vertical fluting

Many display pieces have flamboyant cut decoration such as this stylized rooster

Covered beaker. 1836; H: 7¾in (19.5cm); $2,000–3,000

Decanter. 1830–35; H: 10in (25.5cm); $250–350

Display plate. 1950s; D: 14in (36cm); $2,000–2,500

Bohemian

Bohemian glassmakers combined color and virtuoso cutting in their cased and stained glass from mid-19th century into the 20th century.
- Cut glass was often combined with engraved decoration, as well as gilding and color.
- Forms and cutting become more geometric and angular in the 1930s when Art Deco-style Czech cut glass was widely exported.

UK

Despite tax restrictions, by the early 19th century, many British glassmakers were making fine-cut tableware in the typical Regency style.
- After the 1845 tax repeal, decorative tableware such as decanters became heavier in weight with elaborate, deeper cutting.
- Decoration includes relief, strawberry diamond, vertical fluting, and pillar cutting.

Czech

Independent in 1918, Czechoslovakia continued the Bohemian tradition of colorful, heavy-cut glass while also introducing new looks.
- Pre World War II Czech glass displays a complexity and virtuosity of design built up over centuries of experience and tradition.
- After World War II, the same techniques were use to create radically modern designs.

Glass vessels are frequently cut both outside and inside to reveal colors

High-quality lead crystal

The vase is deeply cut with staggered elliptical panels linked by finely engraved meandering lines

Notched neck rim

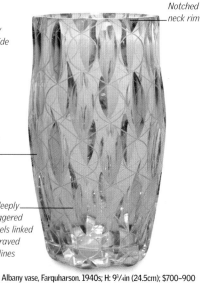

Cased glass vase. 1930s; $12,000–18,000

Belgium, Val St Lambert

From the mid 1920s until World War II, the Belgian glasshouse Val St. Lambert combined traditional designs and modern taste.
- Techniques include "flashing" a colored layer of glass onto a clear body, which was cut in repeating Art Deco motifs or window facets.
- The high-quality lead crystal is deeply cut in bold linear, angular, and geometric patterns.

Albany vase, Farquharson. 1940s; H: 9¾in (24.5cm); $700–900

UK, Walsh Walsh

Established in Birmingham in 1851, the John Walsh Walsh glassworks looked to update its image in the 1930s by employing William Clyne Farquharson to design in the Art Deco style.
- Pieces by Clyne Farquharson are signed in diamond point on the base.
- Popular modern designs Kendal, Leaf, and Albany combine cut and engraved glass.

PRESSED GLASS

Introduced in the US in 1827 at the New England Glass Company near Boston, Massachusetts, pressed glass was mechanically made using a plunger to press molten glass into a mold. Because it was designed as a cheaper alternative to cut glass, many typical cut-glass styles and patterns were copied, including hobnails, fans, and diamonds. Pressed glass is usually lighter than cut glass.

Lidded dish This Canadian dish is decorated with a hobnail pattern that copies cut glass. c1880s; H: 8in (20.5cm); $50–70

18th-century wine glasses

GLASS HAS BEEN USED FOR DRINKING vessels since antiquity. The modern wine glass—with bowl, stem, and foot—evolved from both German vessels embellished with blobs of hot glass (known as prunts) and 16th- and 17th-century sophisticated Venetian goblets. On the whole, European countries produced nationally distinctive styles, sometimes decorated with enameling or engraving. A wide variety of English wine glasses were made from lead glass from the early 18th century and these influenced glassmakers across Europe. The demands of a more sophisticated and affluent clientele saw the creation of high-quality goblets with distinctive decoration. Largely in response to the 1745 Excise Tax on glass, English glassmakers replaced the heavy baluster (thick-stemmed) glass popular in the early part of the century with a smaller, lighter form with complex twist or faceted stems or finely engraved bowls.

Pan top bowl

Single series opaque twist corkscrew cable stem

Pan-top glass. c1765; H: 6in (15cm); $800–850

UK, Opaque twist

White threads were enclosed inside clear glass. Opaque or cotton twist stems flourished in England from 1760 to 1780.

- Most opaque-twist stems are double series (one spiral within another); single series twists are very rare.
- Made in three pieces; joins are visible where the stem meets the foot and bowl.
- Knops are unusual.

FAÇON DE VENISE

Meaning "in the style of Venice," *façon de Venise* describes the ornate, quality glassware that flourished throughout Europe from the mid-16th until the early 18th century. Typical shapes included ornamental serving dishes and distinctive winged or serpent-stemmed drinking glasses. Most goblets were made of a combination of colorless thin soda glass and blue glass. The stems were tooled into ornate shapes such as mythical beasts, loops, snake-like patterns, and complex geometrical designs.

Round funnel bowl

Red corkscrew core entwined by broad, opaque spiral

Conical foot

The ornate snake-like pattern on the stem is a typical feature

Decorated goblet
This piece was made in the style of 15th century Venetian glass. c1690; H: 12¼in (31cm); $2,500–3,500

Color twist stem glass. c1765; $3,500–5,000

Color twist stem glass
From the 1760s, glassmakers started decorating stems with colored spiral threads. Enamels cool at varying rates so the color rods are fragile: color twists tend to be rarer than opaque ones.
- Red and green are the most common colors used for twists; yellow and blue are very rare.
- Continental copies of English color twists are made of soda glass and have no gray tint.

JARGON BUSTER
Knop The decorative bulge on the stem of a drinking glass. It takes a variety of forms, including an egg, tear, cylinder, cone, drop, cushion, ball, or acorn.

Enameling is thin, applied and of high quality

Round funnel bowl

Opaque double series stem

Conical folded foot

Opaque twist glass. c1765; H: 6in (15cm); $2,000–2,500

Beilby glass
From the early 1760s, William and Mary Beilby used the technique of painting opaque white enameled decoration on clear glass.
- Delicate designs of flowers and fruiting vines, landscapes, and hunting and sporting scenes.
- A double series opaque twist stem with a conical foot is most common.
- Armorial and commemorative ornament in colored enamels is rare and highly prized.

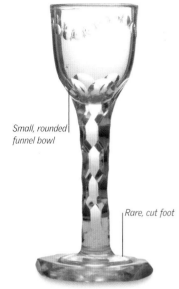

Small, rounded funnel bowl

Rare, cut foot

Facet-stem glass. c1765; H: 5½in (14cm); $500–550

Facet-stem wine glass, UK

In response to taxes imposed on glass from 1745, English glasscutters reduced the weight of glasses by cutting the stems with complex diamond, hexagonal, or plain flat patterns.

- A relatively long stem is typical.
- Toward the end of the 18th century, the flat foot superseded the conical folded foot.
- Often engraved with flowers, birds, insects, and *chinoiserie* patterns.

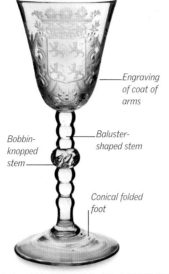

Engraving of coat of arms

Bobbin-knopped stem

Baluster-shaped stem

Conical folded foot

Light baluster goblet. c1750; H: 7½in (19cm); $4,000–5,000

Dutch wine glass

With a long tradition of quality glassmaking, The Low Countries were renowned for engraved glassware. In the 18th century, the Dutch adopted the technique of wheel-engraving. Lead crystal was used, which was well suited to work on the wheel.

- Engraved designs include armorials; scenes celebrating battles, marriages, and politics.

Molded decoration was common in the mid-18th century

Molded bowl wine glass. c1730–40; $500–700

French wine glass

Until the 17th century, most pieces were made in the Venetian style from a local glass called *verre de fougère* (forest glass). From the early 18th century, Normandy glasshouses made small, light wine glasses from quality soda glass.

- Later, the Compagnie des Cristalleries de Baccarat and the Louis Glassworks began to make lead crystal and went on to create distinctive French styles.

Made from potash-lime glass

Engraved wine glass. c1730; H: 9½in (24.5cm); $7,000–10,000

German wine glass

In the 18th century, early German drinking glasses developed into a more sophisticated European goblet known as the "Pokal." Glassmaking centers developed their own style.

- Battle scenes, Classical ruins, hunting scenes, and commemorative armorials are typical.
- Polished highlights often enhance the sculptural effect of the engraving.

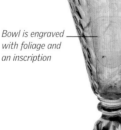

Bowl is engraved with foliage and an inscription

Green and red threads

Bohemian goblet. H: 8½in (21cm); c1700; $1,500–2,000

Bohemian glass

Having pioneered the formula for a colorless, easy-to-cut glass by adding lime to the recipe, the highly accomplished glassmakers of Bohemia perfected the wheel-engraving.

- Typically engraved with portraits, armorial crests, hunting scenes, and landscapes.
- Cutting methods included sculptural high relief or deep engraved intaglio or a rich combination of both.

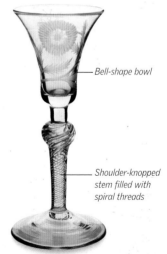

Bell-shape bowl

Shoulder-knopped stem filled with spiral threads

Engraved glass. c1750; 6¼in (16cm); $2,000–2,500

Jacobite glassware, UK

Glassware used to promote the cause of Bonnie Prince Charlie were embellished with sometimes secretive symbolism including portraits, mottoes, oak leaves, and the Scottish rose and thistle.

- Designs include armorials, flowers and foliage, and political slogans—usually diamond-point or wheel-engraved.
- Stem shapes include baluster, air-twist, opaque-twist, and a mixture of the three.

Cameo and faux cameo glass

CAMEO GLASS HAS BEEN MADE since ancient Roman times. It underwent a revival during the 19th century, after the Duke of Portland lent the Roman Portland Vase to the British Museum in 1810, where it was put on public display to great acclaim. It inspired Britain's J&J Northwood to produce an exact copy, a task that took 20 years and saw the introduction of a range of cameo glass. Other companies such as Thomas Webb & Sons followed suit. From the late 19th century, Art Nouveau cameo glass was made by French masters Emile Gallé and Daum Frères, who reached new artistic heights. Soon other companies such as Honesdale in the US joined them.

Cameo glass

Cameo glass is made by coating a gather of glass with one or more layers of differently colored glass. The outer layer, and any underlying layers, are then removed in areas by carving, cutting, or other hand-executed methods, to leave a design marked out in the differently colored glass layers. Running a finger over the surface allows you to feel that the design and details are modeled in low relief.

KEY CLUES

- Two or more different colors of glass.
- Slightly raised feel to the design on the surface.
- Complex design, often incorporating themes from nature, a Classical subject, or the human figure.
- Subtle tones in color, achieved by partially removing a layer.

Signature
As with all Gallé vases, his surname is included on the body, within the design.

The layers have been cut back and removed using a spinning wheel, which requires great skill

The form is complex and time consuming to create

The organic design is typical of the Art Nouveau movement

Gallé cameo vase
There are four layers of color, with the flowering orchid shown in purple.
c1900; H: 8in (20cm); $15,000–20,000

The pine cone motifs on the neck echo the wintry scene below

White has been partially removed to show pink tones

Stylized peony flowers

The best landscapes have a sense of perspective, fine details, and tones suggesting light and shadow

Daum vase
Landscapes are common designs.
c1910; H: 10³/₄in (27.5cm);
$3,000–4,000

De Vez vase
Trees often frame a landscape design. c1915; H: 10¹/₂in (26.5cm);
$2,000–2,500

Thomas Webb vase
White is a common color used for the outer layer. 1889; H: 10¹/₂in (26.5cm); $4,500–5,000

Schneider vase
This *Pivoine* vase has four layers of color. c1926; H: 19³/₄in (50cm);
$3,000–4,000

THE INFLUENCE OF EXHIBITIONS

Companies exhibiting at the international exhibitions popular in the late 19th century displayed their best, often largest, work to showcase their products. In 1878, British glassmaker Joseph Locke also produced a copy of the Portland Vase, which he exhibited at the Paris Exhibition that year. Four years later, he emigrated to the US and introduced his cameo techniques to American glassmakers. Other makers such as the Daum brothers were inspired to create cameo work after seeing Gallé's display at the 1889 Exhibition.

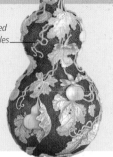

The form and pattern are inspired by Chinese examples

Thomas Webb vase This complex cameo carved and stained gourd-shaped vase is of exhibition quality. Many such wares were so complex and labor intensive they were never made commercially. c1888; H: 9in (22.5cm); $70,000–90,000

Faux cameo glass

True cameo glass is executed by hand, but faux cameo glass uses acid to remove the glass layers and produce the design. The areas that are to remain are coated with an acid-resistant layer. The body is then exposed to acid that eats away at the uncoated glass until it is removed. Layers are thinner to let this happen faster. The technique was introduced to increase production and cut costs, but almost became an art form in its own right.

JARGON BUSTER

Faux From the French word for false, a technique or material that copies or fakes another such as faux cameo or ruby.

KEY CLUES

- Fewer fine details upon closer examination, as the process cannot replicate hand-executed detailing.
- Less subtle toning or gradation to the colors, or no shading at all.
- The design is less complex overall.
- Fewer different layers of glass.

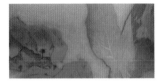

Gilding
The gilding adds visual appeal and a feeling of depth.

There is less detail on the leaves and flowers, as they have not been handworked

The layers are thin, indicated by their transparency, and feel flat to the touch

Only two similarly colored layers have been used

Baccarat faux cameo vase
This footed vase has an acid-etched pattern of a Datura plant. c1900; H: 14¼in (36cm); $1,000–1,500

The foot and rim are gilded

Honesdale vase
Honesdale often applied gilt decoration to their designs. 1915–20; H: 10in (25cm) $2,000–3,000

Webb Cameo Fleur vase
The Cameo Fleur range combined acid-etching and cutting. c1935; H: 10in (25cm); $500–1,000

The range comes in emerald green or amethyst

Stevens & Williams cameo
This decanter is part of the unusual transparent range. c1897; H: 9¾in (24cm); $700–1,000

Iridescent glass

Glassmakers were first inspired to create iridescent glass after the discovery of iridescent Roman glass in the 19th century (see right). Louis Comfort Tiffany in the US and Loetz in Austria perfected the techniques at around the same time: in 1893, Loetz exhibited a range of iridescent glass at the Chicago World's Fair; a year later, Tiffany patented his glass, which he named Favrile.

Loetz vase. c1900; H: 6 ³/₄in (17cm); $2,000–3,000

Both these Art Nouveau ranges were a great success and copied by makers across the US and Europe. Techniques varied: expensive art glass was made by adding metallic salts to the glass batch. Inexpensive items were molded and then sprayed with salts while hot, before being sprayed with hydrofluoric acid and dipped in vinegar. The processes varied depending on the finish: Steuben's Aurene glass relied on salts in the batch, which formed a metal film when heated, and other chemicals sprayed on later that changed color when heated.

Loetz

Loetz glass is difficult to identify because it was often unsigned and was widely copied.

- Pinched forms are highly typical.
- Rich colors, typically blue-green, ocassionally with red, gold, or silver threads or patches (silver patches are known as oil spots).
- Best-known mark is "Loetz Austria," thickly engraved. Acid-etched marks are forged.

Long stem vulnerable to breakage

WATCH OUT!
The Tiffany mark—a cut or etched "L.C. Tiffany"—is easy to copy and so it cannot be relied on as a sign of authenticity. Above all, it is the quality of Tiffany's glass that sets it apart from fakes and copies.

Pulled-feather decoration in gold and green on ivory ground

Gold Favrile vase. Early 20th century; H: 6in (15cm); $2,000–2,800

Tiffany

Highly collectable and valuable, Tiffany's range of iridescent glass dates from 1894. Designs are painted on to the glass using metal oxides.

- Blue and gold are the most common colors.
- Typical shapes are plant inspired (floriform).
- Surface decoration includes peacock pattern, feathering, trailing leaf, and flower shapes.

Steuben Aurene vase; c1915; H: 9in (23cm); $2,000–2,500

Steuben

Steuben Glassworks started producing its Aurene range in 1904, challenging Tiffany.

- Pieces have a soft, even sheen.
- Vases, dishes, and bowls were made in gold or in blue, red, brown, opaline, and green.
- Glass with surface decoration in contrasting colors is the most valuable.
- Pieces are usually marked "Aurene" or "Steuben."

Gold iridescent vase. c1910; H: 9 ¹/₄in (23.5cm); $1,500–2,000

Quezal

Former Tiffany employees set up Quezal in 1902 and produced high-quality glass made to imitate Favrile ware.

- Decoration more regular than on Tiffany pieces; distinctive "pulled-feather" patterns.
- Early pieces were unmarked and many have been given false Tiffany signatures. Later pieces were engraved "Quezal" in block letters.
- Undecorated blue or purple pieces are rare.

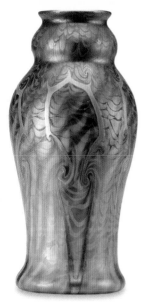

Gourd-shaped vase. c1910; H: 10in (25.5cm); $400–700

Kew Blas

This range of art glass was influenced by Quezal. Characteristically, it has a smooth opalescent (milky) finish.

- Designs tend to be dramatic.
- Symmetrical shapes are decorated with clearly defined feathered decoration in strong, brilliant colors.
- Engraved mark "Kew Blas" on the base. Etched marks have been forged.

ROMAN GLASS

The ancient Roman glass unearthed at sites around the Mediterranean in the 19th and early 20th centuries had become iridescent as a result of a chemical reaction with the damp soil or sand it had been buried in. Roman glass was of a very high quality and so its years underground resulted in corrosion rather than destruction. Glassmakers re-created its iridescent and pitted surface, using various chemical techniques. Some glassmakers also copied Classical glass shapes such as flasks and water sprinklers.

Roman bottle flasks These two *unguentarium* (tear bottle) flasks date from around 1st–3rd century CE.

Strong iridescence is sought after by Carnival glass collectors today

Gold trailing vines decorate the iridescent blue ground

Dugan diamond "Question Marks" compote. 1910–20; W: 6½in (16cm); $80–100

Carnival glass

Mass manufactured in the US and later Europe and known as the poor man's Tiffany.

- Popular colors were marigold, blue, green, and purple; pastels less popular; red is rare.
- Patterns include Oriental motifs, fruits, flowers.
- Deeply molded elaborate patterns are sought after.
- Most early pieces were unmarked.

Solifleur bud vase. c1920; H: 6¾in (17cm); $350–450

Imperial

One of many manufacturers to create iridescent glass in ranges of differing quality and price. Art glass made after 1916 was often worked freehand to create a stretched effect.

- Better pieces mimic Art Nouveau designs with pulled and trailed patterns.
- Pieces may be marked NUART.

Egyptian-inspired "King Tut" swirls

Gold pedestal foot

Durand platinum vase. c1930; H:14in (35.5cm); $2,500–3,000

Durand

Durand started by copying Tiffany designs in 1897. Soon after they made their own simple shapes using an amber glass called Ambergris.

- Decoration included Egyptian-inspired "King Tut" swirls, random trails of glass (spiderwebbing), and peacock feathers.
- Early pieces were usually unsigned. Later pieces were usually marked "Durand," sometimes across the letter V.

Lalique—real, fake, or copy?

FRENCH DESIGNER RENÉ LALIQUE (1860–1945) is the best-known maker of molded, opalescent glass. He began his career by designing jewelry, experimenting with glass in the 1890s when he also created designs for perfume bottles. This proved successful and by 1911 he concentrated only on glass, producing most of his best designs during the 1920s and 30s. His company produced press-molded or mold-blown vases, bowls, perfume bottles, and figurines that have become highly desirable and valuable today. His stylized Art Deco designs tend to be the most sought after. Due to its popularity, his work has been copied and faked ever since it was first made.

Authentic Lalique

Many of Lalique's designs use motifs taken from the natural world such as animals and leaves, as well as exotically posed women. All are stylized, often with pared-down, geometric lines typical of the Art Deco style. He also incorporated abstract geometric patterns. The basic forms he used are simple and unfussy, aiming to display the complex molded pattern to its best advantage. Although his designs were produced using mechanical methods, other techniques such as staining and frosting were done by hand.

KEY CLUES

- Lalique's designs were molded, with the molten glass being pressed or blown into a mold.
- Stylized motifs from the natural world are typical.
- Repeated motifs generally cover the entire piece.
- Clear opalescent glass is typical (though he also used many other transparent colors).

Molded detailing
The molded details are crisp, fine, and realistic, and show a variety of depths.

Staining the surface with another color helps to highlight the molded design

Athletic women in extravagant poses are a recurring Art Deco theme

Molded pair of parakeets (perruches in French) on a flowering branch

Perruches vase
The cased glass has a whitish patina. This vase is extremely rare in red. c1919; H: 10¼in (26cm); $12,000–18,000

Malesherbes vase
The clear opalescent body has a green stain to highlight the Art Deco stylized leaf pattern. c1927; H: 9in (22.5cm); $2,500–3,500

Bacchantes vase
This amethyst glass vase has a sepia patina (brown stain) and is molded with dancing women, each in a different and life-like pose. c1927; H: 10in (25cm); $8,000–12,000

JARGON BUSTER
Opalescent Glass with a soft, milky blue sheen that emulates the opal gemstone. It is created by adding metal oxide chemicals to the glass mix.

LALIQUE SIGNATURES

Virtually all Lalique glass is marked on the base with a variation on the name "R. Lalique," which may be molded, etched, engraved, or sandblasted using a stencil. It can give a clue to the period a piece was produced in, how it was made, and if it is authentic.

A molded name uses simple, blocky capital letters and was usually used on pressed pieces. From the late 1920s, the words "France" or "Made in France" were often included, but not "Paris." His forename "René" was never used and, after his death in 1945, only his surname was used.

Engraved signature
Engraved marks were usually used on mold-blown pieces. The inclusion of the initial "R" dates this to before 1945.

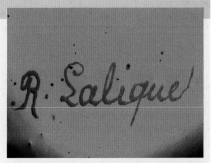

Copies and fakes

Lalique's designs have been copied and faked since the 1930s. While a fake is made to deliberately deceive, a copy is simply in the style of Lalique. Many copies and fakes were produced in Czechoslovakia. French factories also copied his designs, but some such as Etling and Sabino were inspired by them and produced designs of their own that imitate Lalique. Copies and fakes are typically not as well molded, with less pronounced detailing. Colors and shapes may also be different from those used on authentic designs.

Poor definition
The molded details are not as crisp or as finely modeled as on authentic examples.

KEY CLUES

- The molded details are not as fine, with weaker, less precisely defined modeling.
- Colors of glass are not those used by Lalique.
- The shape and size of the body is often different.
- The Lalique mark can be in a style or position not used on authentic pieces.

Lalique did not use this color of glass

Lalique did not use this precise form or design, which is based on his Bacchantes vase (see left)

Bacchantes style
This unsigned Czechoslovakian clear art glass vase is in the style of René Lalique. 1930s; $100–150

Fake Bacchantes
This fake vase has an acid-etched Lalique mark to the base. It is too small to be a real Lalique vase. 1930s; H: 6in (15cm); $50–70

Murano glass

POST WORLD WAR II 20TH-CENTURY glass from the Venetian island of Murano has an unrivaled variety, confidence, and flair. From the late 1940s, innovative glassmaking made a resurgence on Murano after decades of stagnation. Glassmaking families, who had been content to create glass in safe, historical styles, collaborated with international artists who had trained as painters, sculptors, and architects. The result was imaginative designs interpreted by skilled glassmakers, which revolutionized Italian glass design. Named designers produced one-off and limited-production pieces for the major factories, which, in turn, inspired mass-produced pieces from smaller makers.

Murano art glass

Many traditional techniques were revived in innovative ways to create a "new look" in Murano glass. Murrines – small colored *tesserae* used to decorate the surface of a piece of glass—were used in modern color combinations that expressed postwar exuberance. Designs exaggerated the visual effect of techniques such as lampwork, the use of colored canes (*filigrana* glass), and cased and colored glass (*sommerso*). A few designers combined murrines with the techniques of *filigrana* and *zanfirico*—rods containing lace-like twists of colored glass threads.

The diagonal rim brings an asymmetrical quirk to a traditional vase shape

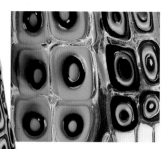

Murrines
The glass canes and murrines are set on clear glass.

KEY CLUES

- Exuberant and stylish designs use a combination of vibrant color and abstract decoration.
- Thickly blown vases of simple, modern form often have elaborate colored decoration.
- Pieces may be signed on the base by the artist or the factory.

Vase by Ansolo Fuga for AVEM
Vertical colored canes in a pattern known as a *canne* are combined with a band of murrines. c1960; H: 9¾in (25cm); $3,500–5,000

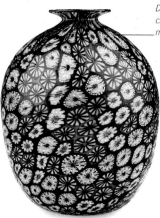

Daisy and chrysanthemum murrines

Margherita and Kiku Vase
In this piece by Ermanno Toso, murrines are arranged into a *millefiori* pattern. 1960; H: 8½in (22cm); $7,000–9000

Intarsio vase by Barovier
Triangular *tesserae* are applied to clear glass and the vase blown to expand it. 1961; H: 12¼in (31cm); $3,500–5,000

Pezzato vase by Fulvio Bianconi for Venini
Playful *pezzato* (patchwork) is created with squares of glass. c1950; H: 8in (20.5cm); $8,000–10,000

WATCH OUT!
An icon of postwar Murano glass, the Venini Fazzoletto (handkerchief) vase has been widely copied and widely faked. Authentic versions are delicate and of high quality and bear the acid-etched Venini (with a lower case "v") Murano mark—which has also been faked—on the base.

QUALITY MURANO GLASS

Good: A *sommerso* triple-cased swan. Although not attributed, this is high-quality tourist ware. 1950s; H: 15¹/₂in (37cm); $200–250

Better: Alessandro Pianon encased this *pulcino* (chick) in textured glass. Its eyes are murrines. 1961–62; H: 8³/₄in (22cm); $3,500–5,000

Best: This blown-glass pigeon from Ercole Barovier's Primavera series is one of four known examples. 1929; H: 12¹/₂in (31cm); $14,000–17,000

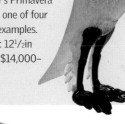

Murano factory glass

Many smaller Murano factories adapted the new techniques and glass styles used by their larger neighbors to create a range of glassware such as ashtrays, figures, and ornaments—many of them aimed at Venice's growing tourist trade. For example, the *sommerso* technique (see pp118-119) perfected by Venini in 1934 was soon being exploited by smaller workshops. Because these pieces had to be manufactured in large numbers and sell for modest prices, the designs were kept relatively simple to make even though they required technical skill.

Layers of pink, purple, and blue are cased in clear glass

The shape echoes the flowing quality of molten glass

KEY CLUES

- Simple shapes and strong, contrasting colors.
- Stylized designs are more conservative than their art-glass counterparts and lack individual flair.
- *Sommerso* pieces may be facet-cut to add visual interest.
- The glass is often unsigned or bears a paper label identifying it only as a piece of Murano glass.

Sommerso vase
For a skilled glassmaker the organic asymmetric shape of this triple-cased *sommerso* vase was easy to produce. c1950; H: 11in (28cm); $250–350

Table lamp base
In this piece, colored glass ribbons were twisted into a spiral and cased in clear glass. c1960; H: 18¹/₂in (47cm); $400–500

Sommerso vase
The strong colors associated with Murano can be seen here. It bears the remains of its original label. 1950s; H: 4¹/₂in (11.5cm); $80–120

Sculptural ashtray
The glassmaker introduced bubbles into the glass before pulling and curling the rim. 1950s; W: 8¹/₂in (21.5cm); $50–90

Handkerchief-style vase
This mass-produced vase lacks the delicate, naturalistic folds of the late 1940s *Fazzoletti* vases. c1960; H: 6in (15cm); $200–300

20th-century glass

THROUGHOUT THE 20TH century, glassmakers combined traditional techniques and inspiring ideas to create innovative designs. The success of cameo and iridescent glass in the early years of the 20th century was followed by that of Lalique with pressed and mold-blown glass. In Scandinavia, trapped air and engraving techniques were taken to new levels of sophistication in the cool, elegant glass produced at Kosta Boda, Orrefors, Holmgaard, and Riihimäki. Scandinavians also made textured glass. Their glass inspired British factories such as Whitefriars in the 1960s. On the Venetian island of Murano, traditional techniques were updated in bold colors and new shapes by Dino Martens, Fulvio Bianconi, and Lino Tagliapietra. The influence of this fresh wave of glass design can be seen in the work of studio artists such as the American Dale Chihuly, whose glass sculptures and chandeliers represent a new art form.

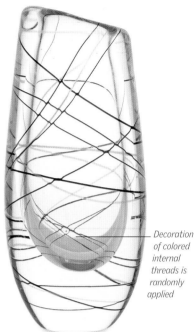

Decoration of colored internal threads is randomly applied

Vase by Vicke Lindstrand, for Kosta. c1960; H: 6³/₄in (17.5cm); $500–600

Kosta, Sweden

The style that came to epitomize 1950s Scandinavian glass was popularized by Vicke Lindstrand at Kosta. Kosta merged with the Boda and Åfors factories in 1964 and with Orrefors in 1990.

- Lindstrand's heavy, blown, clear-cased art and domestic glass usually featured simple, thick-walled, curvilinear, organic shapes.
- Internal decoration included spiral and vertical stripes, trapped-air techniques, and patterns created by trapped air bubbles.

Glass set with filigree decoration is pulled into a spiral

Irregularly shaped bands of colored glass

Large powder inclusions

Large murrine

Dinosaur. 2003; H: 15in (38cm); $35,000–50,000

Lino Tagliapietra, Italy

Designer and glassmaker Lino Tagliapietra was apprenticed to Muranese glassmaker Archimede Seguso at the age of 11.

- Combines classic and contemporary— Venetian filigree on a vase or sculpture pulled or blown into an exaggerated shape.
- The optical effect of expanding the filigree decoration is enhanced by cutting the glass.

Oriente jug made by Aureliano Toso. c1954; H: 13in (32.5cm); $10,000–15,000

Dino Martens, Italy

Artist-designer Dino Martens designed for Aureliano Toso and for Salviati.

- Focus is on color and decoration not form.
- At Salviati, Martens designed vessels with elaborate handles and spouts that made an irreverent reference to traditional Venetian serpent-stemmed drinking vessels.

Folds are designed to look like a falling handkerchief

Fazzoletto vase by Fulvio Bianconi, made by Venini. c1950; H: 5³/₄in (14.5cm); $2,000–3,000

Fulvio Bianconi, Italy

The *Fazzoletto* (handkerchief) vase is an icon of postwar Italian glass. It was developed by Paolo Venini and Fulvio Bianconi in 1948–49.

- It has been made in a variety of types of glass, colors, sizes, and decorations.
- Authentic pieces are superb quality with an acid-etched Venini Murano mark.

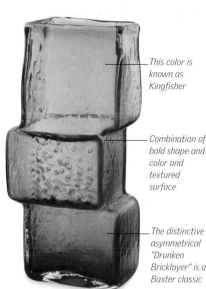

This color is known as Tangerine

This color is known as Kingfisher

Combination of bold shape and color and textured surface

The pattern echoes the curvaceous shape

The distinctive asymmetrical "Drunken Bricklayer" is a Baxter classic

Genie Bottle designed by Wayne Husted for Blenko. c1960; $500–1,000

"Drunken Bricklayer" vase. c1970; H: 13in (33.5cm); $2,000–2,500

Grain Barn vase by Helena Tynell. c1970; H: 8¼in (21cm); $200–250

Blenko, US

William John Blenko began by specializing in stained glass in 1922. When demand fell toward the end of the decade, he developed a range of brightly colored domestic glassware.

- Most glass was made in vivid, single colors.
- In the 1950s, Wayne Husted began a series of large, shaped decanters. The larger and more vibrant pieces in more outrageous shapes command a premium.

Whitefriars, UK

In the 1960s, Geoffrey Baxter established a new look with Scandinavian-inspired designs, many in relatively strong colors.

- Baxter's experiments with texture to create pieces such as Bark and Banjo vases are now seen as quintessential 1960s designs.
- Whitefriars glass was unmarked and unsigned, although it is possible to find pieces bearing the original paper label.

Riihimäki, Finland

In the 1930s, the Riihimäki factory organized design competitions for good, modern pieces.

- In the 1950s and 60s, Helena Tynell, Nanny Still, and Tamara Aladin dominated its design.
- Output includes mold-blown bottle vases, cased vases in undulating shapes, and textured glass.

JARGON BUSTER

Seeds Groups of air bubbles accidentally caught in a piece of glass are referred to as seeds.

Orange-red glass with fine random internal air bubbles

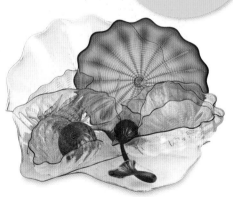

"Dexel-Ei" (egg) Ikora-Kristall vase by Walter Dexel. 1937; H: 5½in (14cm); $200–350

Graal vase with aquarium design. c1950; H: 7¾in (20cm); $1,000–1,500

Carnival Persian Set comprising 12 pieces. 2000; W: 22in (56cm); $35,000–50,000

WMF, Germany

The Württembergische Metallwarenfabrik (WMF) is best known for its Art Nouveau metalware but also produced two successful glass ranges: Myra-Kristall and Ikora-Kristall.

- Ikora was made in many shapes, colors, and decorations, much of it thick, cased glass.
- Decoration was often complex.

Orrefors, Sweden

Innovative designers and a skilled workforce put Orrefors at the forefront of C20th glass design.

- The Graal technique consists of colored decoration held between two clear layers.
- Orrefors also pioneered the Ariel technique where sandblasted channels or holes trap air when the outer layer of glass is applied.

Dale Chihuly, US

Chihuly is known for his complex, sculptural forms, which are made by a team of glassblowers.

- Known for designs featuring intense, vibrant colored glass enhanced with glass threads.
- Work ranges from single vessels to massive chandeliers made up of many components and assembled on a metal frame.

METAL

.WARE

METALWARE

Renaissance metalware, often lavish gold or silver pieces, was prohibitively expensive and usually the preserve of the Church or monarchy. From the early 18th century, however, silverware became steadily more affordable.

Josef Lorenzl figure
Art Deco designers in particular worked with bronze, especially for modelling the elegant female figures that came to epitomize the style.

Helmet-shaped ewer
Silversmiths found silver the perfect material for engraving with armorials (coats of arms). This Louis XIV French ewer features a coat of arms and applied leaves around the base.

The earliest forms of silverware for domestic use were the simple, cylindrical beaker in the 15th century and the solid silver tankard with hinged cover, derived from earlier, wooden examples and made toward the end of the 16th century. Spoons were the earliest form of flatware. Forks were only used for eating sweet foods until the 16th century in Europe and the 17th century in Britain.

Early silverware

During the 1700s, new pastimes of taking tea, coffee, and chocolate created a demand among the wealthy for stylish vessels from which to serve and drink them. Silversmiths responded to this by creating teapots, coffee pots, and chocolate pots, along with numerous accessories such as sugar bowls, cream jugs, and tea caddies. Another popular pastime was wine drinking, which led to the development of the silver wine cooler and the Monteith—a silver bowl with a notched rim used for holding the stems of wine glasses while the bowls were suspended in iced water for chilling.

Early candlesticks tended to be simple affairs raised (hammered) from sheet silver. Toward the end of the 17th century, Huguenot craftsmen

JARGON BUSTER
Raising The process of shaping hollow silverwares by hammering sheet metal rotated on a stake or anvil.

John Emes teapot
London silversmith John Emes was well known for pieces in the Empire style. Typical details here include the Greek key pattern and exaggerated design of the handle.

Art Nouveau cup and cover
This silver and enamel pedestal cup and cover by Eugène Feuillâtre illustrates the trend for enameling silverware that arose during the Art Nouveau era.

Silver-plated box
As manufacturing processes advanced, designers experimented with shapes and combined silver pieces with other innovative materials such as Bakelite.

introduced methods of making solid silver candlesticks by casting the components—base, stem, and sconce—separately and soldering them together. These cast candlesticks were heavier and more durable and could take more elaborate forms of decoration.

Technological advances meant that, by the end of the 18th century, candlesticks could be mass produced—with larger numbers stamped from rolled sheet metal and loaded (weighted with base metal) for stability. Candlesticks and candelabra were usually in matching pairs. Early candelabra—from the mid-17th to late 18th century—were simple, with just one or two branches. Later, more branches were added. The 18th century also saw the introduction of matching sets of cutlery.

Prevailing styles

At the turn of the 17th century, silverware tended to be simple in design, with minimal decoration. As the century progressed, however, designs reflected the Rococo style from France, epitomized by the work of Juste-Aurèle Meissonnier, who produced lavish wares decorated with a mass of scrollwork, cartouches, and shells. Toward the end of the 18th century, with trends moving to the restrained Neoclassical style, designs were simpler and more elegant. Designers favored plain surfaces with the minimum of engraved or applied ornament. Designs of the early 19th century reflected the grandeur of the Empire and Regency styles, while the late 19th century saw silverware in a range of rival styles, predominantly Rococo.

20th-century metalware

Toward the end of the 19th century, resistance to mass production encouraged a return to hand production. This resulted in high-quality pieces made in the Arts and Crafts style, then in the Art Nouveau and Art Deco styles. Working with copper, brass, and bronze as well as silver, designers produced candlesticks, drinking vessels, elegant vases, boxes, salvers, and light fittings.

Dominant names are Josef Hoffman of the Wiener Werkstätte, who produced rectilinear pieces pierced with geometric shapes; Liberty & Co. in England, inspired by Celtic art; and the Roycrofters in the US, with their hand-hammered copper wares. A number of companies, including the German factory Württemburgische Metallenwerk Fabrik (WMF), mass-produced designs.

Possibly the name most associated with 20th-century silverware is Danish company Georg Jensen. Founded in 1904, the name Georg Jensen is synonymous with the Art Nouveau designs he created in the early 20th century. His company continues to produce silver of exceptional quality.

The briefing
Looking at silver

PRECIOUS METALS SUCH AS SILVER are valued for their intrinsic worth although the finished design may be far more valuable than this. Many pieces have been melted down to make coins in times of crisis. Much silver is marked, yet these marks cannot always be relied on as they may have been faked or altered to enhance the value of a piece. So, it is important to know what else to look for, to make sure the marks are telling the truth or to help to identify an unmarked piece.

WATCH OUT!
A hallmark that has been faked will appear soft around the edges when compared to a genuine one.

Finial
Lid
Spout
Handle
Embossed decoration
Base
Gadrooning

George III Samuel Courtauld London coffee pot
The pot has a baluster shape, embossed decoration, an ivory handle, and marks to the base and cover. 1763; H: 11½in (29cm)

Closer inspection
Examine the overall shape of the piece and its detail, including the underside where all sorts of clues may have been left by the maker.

Decoration

Embossing
Also called "repoussé," a relief pattern is created on the front of a thin piece of silver by hammering it from the back, leaving deep indentations.

Bright cut engraving
A pattern is cut into the surface of a piece of silver. The cuts are made at an angle to create facets that reflect the light. Cuts are easily worn through overpolishing, which will reduce value.

Chasing
The opposite technique to embossing: a relief design is created on the front surface using a hammer and punch to push the silver backward. Chasing leaves blurred marks on the back of the silver.

Engine turning
Parallel lines, usually curved, are cut into silver using a machine-driven lathe. Introduced in the late 18th century, it was mostly used to decorate small items such as snuffboxes and vinaigrettes.

Enameling
Colored ground glass bound into a paste is placed on a metal base and heated to set it. It can be painted on using a brush or set into grooves or compartments. The technique was revived in the 19th century.

What to look at

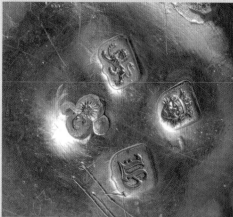

Marks

Look to see whether the piece has any marks. A British piece will typically have four. Each mark serves a different purpose: it tells you where the piece was made, who by, when, and with what standard of silver. Check for, for instance, a rooster, lion, crowned harp, crown, or other symbol—each has its own meaning. *See pp218–219 for more information.*

Lid or cover

If there is more than one part to a piece, such as a lid or cover, check to see whether that too is hallmarked, giving you more clues to identity. *See pp218–219 for more information on silver marks.*

Joints and seams

Check all surfaces for seam lines that tell you the piece has cast components. If the surface is rubbed and you can see a copper glow it is plate rather than solid silver.

Handle

If there is a handle check what it is made from: it may be solid silver or of another material such as wood, bone, or, as here, ivory. The shape of the handle may also give a clue to the age of the piece. This scrolling shape is typical of the Rococo style in the mid-18th century, which started in France and influenced Georgian silver. *See pp220–223 for more on silver and metalware shapes.*

Decorative technique

If the piece is decorated, try to work out what technique has been used. This pot is embossed, giving it a relief pattern. Embossing is often used in conjunction with chasing. *See box opposite.*

Decorative style

Look at the motifs used and their treatment. The asymmetrical shellwork here and foliage pattern above are typical of the lively curves and naturalistic themes that characterize Rococo. The gadrooning on the base and lid, on the other hand, is a Classical motif, often used to edge silver. *See pp206–209 for motifs.*

Neoclassical silver

THE NEOCLASSICAL STYLE first developed in France in the 1750s, with designers and silversmiths adopting Classical urn and lantern shapes for everything from teapots to two-handled vases, Corinthian columns for candlesticks, and tripod forms for candelabra and perfume burners. These were embellished with ornamental motifs copied from Greek and Roman architecture. In Britain, the style was influenced by the latest pattern books as well as imports from abroad and the neat and formal rendering of the "Etruscan" antique championed by Scottish architect Robert Adam. In the US, the Federal style interpreted Neoclassical with a distinctive American flavor.

French

The shapes and decorative vocabulary of Greek and Roman antiquity were adopted by silversmiths in incarnations from the early *goût grec* to more restrained and elegant designs. These featured motifs such as scrolling acanthus leaves, fluting, and mask heads. The Empire taste for strong, heavy forms and opulent sculptural decoration mirroring antique prototypes enjoyed a revival in France in the mid-19th century. Royal as well as highly placed patrons and institutions across Europe ordered magnificent silver for the dining table from celebrated silversmiths, including Jean-Baptiste Claude Odiot and Marc Jacquart.

Handles are in the form of flying bees, symbolic of the sweet contents of the bowl

The lidded bowl takes the form of an antique urn or perfume burner

KEY FACTS

- Cast, chased, and embossed decoration included palm and acanthus leaves, anthemia, swags of flowers and foliage, and masks alongside Egyptian motifs.
- Silver is often combined with silver gilt.
- Many pieces have die-stamped designs prompted by the French adoption of Sheffield plating.

Neoclassical mask
Symmetrical masks (faces) were a common decoration, inspired by recent archaeological discoveries.

Confiturier
Made by Jean-Baptiste Claude Odiot, this confiturier was for serving jams and stewed fruits. The fluted pedestal holds 12 silver-gilt spoons. 1818–39; H: 11in (28cm); $8,000–12,000

Dragonfly

Palmette

Marc Jacquart cruet stand
Palmettes and a column topped with a pharoah's head are typical Egyptian motifs. c1800; H: 12¼in (31cm); $2,000–3,000

Cressand sweetmeat dish
Raised on four claw feet, this boat-shaped dish is adorned with Classical sea nymphs amid seaweed. c1825; L: 10in (25cm); $10,000–15,000

Marc Auguste Lebrun pot
This swan-necked ovoid coffee pot is inspired by the simplicity of English Georgian silver. c1810; H: 13½in (34cm); $3,500–4,500

Circular swags

Delicate openwork gallery

Pierre Bourguignon dish
Rams' heads, a lion finial, and swags combine with an openwork gallery on this sweetmeat dish. c1800; $3,500–4,500

EGYPTIAN REVIVAL

During the first quarter of the 19th century, Egypt became a powerful source of inspiration for artists in Europe and North America. The robust Empire style promoted during Napoleon's reign favored Egyptian ornament. Many motifs featured in the illustrations of antiquities that were made by artists. The most famous was Dominique Vivant-Denon, who accompanied Napoleon on his military campaigns in North Africa. Silversmiths decorated vessels with distinctive Egyptian birds, snakes, lions' masks, sphinxes, lotus leaves, obelisks, and pharaohs. Similar Egyptian motifs were used a century later by designers inspired by the discovery of Tutankhamen's tomb in 1922.

Footed bowl
Made by R&W Wilson of Philadelphia, this bowl was designed as a table centerpiece in the Egyptian revival style. c1825; H: 7in (17.75cm); $2,000–3,000

British

In the elegant designs of Robert Adam, the shapes and ornamental vocabulary of Classical antiquity were cherry-picked and freely interpreted, bearing little resemblance to their antique ancestors. Vessels intended to hold sweetmeats took the shape of ancient sarcophagi, while cups, coffee pots, and teapots echoed the form of antique vases and urns. All were decorated with restrained ornament inspired by Greek and Roman patterns, including garlands and husks, beading, trailing foliage, palmettes, and anthemion flowers.

Urn-shaped finial echoes shape of cup

Engraving
Swags of harebells and other flowers are engraved around the cup.

Beaded handles with acanthus leaf ends

Two-handled cup
A favorite English shape, this silver two-handled George II cup was designed by Charles Wright of London. 1778; H: 12¼in (31cm); $3,500–4,500

KEY CLUES

- The shape of Classical vases and urns was adopted for two-handled cups and dining silver.
- Cast, chased, and engraved decoration of antique motifs.
- Opulent fluting, bold scrolled handles, and robust cast and chased medallions often decorated traditional English shapes.

TRADE SECRET

From the 1770s, mechanization meant candlesticks could be stamped out from thin sheets of silver, then weighted (loaded) internally for support. A loaded candlestick feels as heavy as a cast one, but when turned upside down a cast candlestick is hollow while a loaded one has a metal plate and inset wooden base to contain the filling. Unlike the cast version, the hallmarks of a loaded candlestick are usually in a straight line on the outer edge of the base rather than under it.

Stem shaped as Classical Corinthian column

Gadrooning

Thomas Jeanes coffee jug
The elegant lines and acanthus-wrapped spout of this pear-shaped jug show French influence. 1767; H: 9½in (24cm); $1,800–2,000

James Taitt silver waiter
This Scottish waiter anticipates the Neoclassical with hoofed feet and a molded piecrust border. 1734; D: 7½in (19cm); $700–1,000

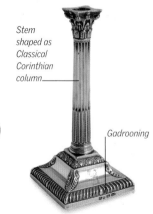

John Carter taperstick
Smaller versions of candlesticks, tapersticks mirrored Neoclassical style in shape and ornament. 1771; H: 7in (18cm); $2,000

The interrogation
Silver-plated candelabra

SILVER WAS HUGELY EXPENSIVE in the 18th century. The demand for silver was such that cheaper alternatives were sought. In 1742, Thomas Boulsover discovered the technique of fusing copper and silver with heat. He rolled out the fused metal into a sheet, which could then be formed into objects. Old Sheffield plate was widely used from the 1750s to the 1840s. As well as in Sheffield, it was made in the city of Birmingham, and in Russia, Austria, and France. Electroplating was introduced by Elkington and Co. in the 1830s. It involved depositing a thin layer of silver onto base metal by electrolysis. Within a decade it had replaced the Old Sheffield plate technique.

Old Sheffield plate candelabra

Candlesticks and candelabra, particularly in silver with its reflective qualities, were in demand in the 18th century. With the newfound Old Sheffield plate process, large numbers could be made more cheaply. Candelabra found a new marketplace with the burgeoning middle classes. 18th-century candelabra often have two lights, with a third dummy light or knop in the center to balance the appearance. After 1805, three lights were much more common. Before 1780, candlesticks were often cast. After this time, hollow metal was held together by a metal spike. One of the best ways to identify Old Sheffield plate is to look for joins. Not all pieces will have a makers's mark.

The urn shapes and overall symmetry are typically Neoclassical

Decoration is kept to a minimum, letting the graceful shapes speak for themselves

The urn-shaped swellings on the column are echoed in the candle sockets

The surface has a warm patina and is not particularly shiny

Candle sockets
The component parts were made in a number of sections, with seams running down the middle.

Seams
If you breathe heavily on the decorative balls (knops) you may be able detect a seam dividing the two halves.

Roll-over edges
Look for roll-over edges—where the sheet of silver has been rolled over to hide the copper edge.

WATCH OUT!
Sheffield (without the word "Old") plate is a term for any item plated in silver. It usually means an item plated in Sheffield rather than anywhere else. It could be a genuine Old Sheffield Plate piece from 1760 (unlikely!) or new electroplate from 2006.

Old Sheffield candelabra
George 11 Old Sheffield plate candelabra. Late 18th century

WEAR AND TEAR

Old Sheffield plate candlesticks are unlikely to have their original 18th-century plate. Servants in the 18th century cleaned energetically and often because candles, open fires, and pollution dulled the plate. Plated ware has usually been replated because it wears

easily, exposing the copper. This can be seen with the late 18th-century candlestick, right, where the stick has worn right down to the copper base. Because it tended to wear, silver was often added to the most vulnerable areas such as joins and sconces, as on this worn copper

candlestick. Pieces that have been recently replated, as well as new pieces, can look extremely shiny and white. This is because 100 percent silver has to be used to attach it to the copper effectively. In the 19th century, plating of about 92 percent silver was more commonly used.

Beneath the plate An Old Sheffield Plate candlestick worn back to copper. c1795; H: 11½in (29cm)

Electroplated candelabra

The demands of the mass market led companies to try to discover an even cheaper way to create silver plate. Electroplating was attributed to cousins Henry and George Elkington in the 1830s, although other inventors may have tried the process earlier. A piece made of a base metal such as brass or nickel was immersed in a tank of silver and an electric current was passed through it to bind the silver to the surface. Electroplated wares such as the 19th-century candelabra below are often less valuable than Old Sheffield plate. However, this will depend on the quality of the design. Generally, electroplated articles are brighter in color, as they are covered in a layer of pure silver.

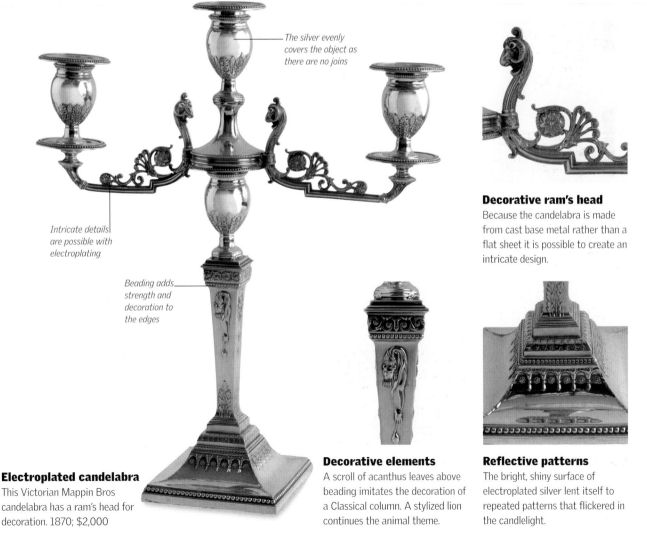

The silver evenly covers the object as there are no joins

Intricate details are possible with electroplating

Beading adds strength and decoration to the edges

Decorative ram's head
Because the candelabra is made from cast base metal rather than a flat sheet it is possible to create an intricate design.

Electroplated candelabra
This Victorian Mappin Bros candelabra has a ram's head for decoration. 1870; $2,000

Decorative elements
A scroll of acanthus leaves above beading imitates the decoration of a Classical column. A stylized lion continues the animal theme.

Reflective patterns
The bright, shiny surface of electroplated silver lent itself to repeated patterns that flickered in the candlelight.

The lineup
Silver boxes

FROM THE 17TH CENTURY, silver boxes were richly embellished with cast, chased, or engraved decoration featuring elaborate coats-of-arms, landscape and hunting scenes, Classical subjects, and inscriptions. Silver and silver-gilt boxes were made to adorn the dressing table of a fashionable lady, with essential articles, including toilet boxes for powders, patches, soaps, and lotions that sometimes featured enameled decoration or exotic materials such as tortoiseshell and mother-of-pearl. Silver boxes were also made in the form of nutmeg graters, snuff holders, and sewing kits. The development of mechanical techniques in the late 18th century guaranteed a plentiful supply of sheet silver from which boxes could be manufactured to meet the growing demand of the rising middle classes.

The box is engraved with emblems that relate directly to the Stuarts

Rare Jacobite snuffbox. c1700; $15,000–20,000

Snuffboxes

Silver boxes to hold ready-grated snuff were made from the beginning of the 18th century. Some were simple; others lavishly decorated.

- Many have engraved initials, coats-of-arms, emblematic inscriptions, or political mottoes.
- Snuffboxes can be distinguished from other small boxes by the lip tucked under the lid on the interior, which helps to keep the snuff dry and prevents spillage.

Tiny sewing accessories include scissors, needles, and thimbles

The case is in the form of Mr Punch's dog Toby

Vignettes of garden scene painted on mother-of-pearl panels

French gilt étui. Early 19th century; $700–1,000

Étuis

An étui contained items deemed necessary for running a household. It was often designed to hang from a *châtelaine*—a clasp worn at the waist with two or more chains or clips.

- Étuis were made in many shapes and often decorated with chasing, enamels, and gilding.
- Tiny sewing accessories such as needles, tweezers, and pencils may be inside the étui.

Birmingham match case. c1890; $1,500–2,000

Match cases

Cases made for friction matches were known from the late 19th century as "vestas," from the Roman goddess of the hearth. In Britain, Birmingham was the main center of production.

- Engraved, chased, or enameled decoration is typical.
- Novelty bird and animal forms, well-loved characters, and erotica were highly popular.

Silver embellished with semi-precious stones

Silver box and cover by Alwyn Carr. 1921; $5,000–9,000

Arts & crafts boxes

With English silversmith Omar Ramsden, Alwyn Carr specialized in designing handmade silver.

- Boxes such as this could be used on dressing tables to hold powder.
- In the tradition of handmade wares fostered by the Arts & Crafts movement, the hammered marks on the surface were not polished smooth, but were left as decoration.

Relief decoration of rams' heads and swags

Lid decorated with portrait of a courtier

Simulated bamboo

Box with hinged lid. Late 18th century; $700–1,000

French toilet boxes

From the 17th century, elaborate toilet services met the fashion for dressing-table silver.

- 18th-century French boxes were often lavishly decorated in the Rococo style with festoons of flowers, fluting, and scrollwork.
- The hinged lids of toilet boxes fitted tightly to prevent the powder from drying out and frequently featured mirrors on the inside.

Tea caddy by Hodd & Linley. 1867; $2,000–2,500

Tea caddies

Tea was imported in large chests and sold loose, to be stored in boxes called caddies.

- Decoration often reflects the European taste for Chinese and Japanese wares and *chinoiserie*.
- Reflecting the high cost of tea, 18th-century examples were fitted with locks to stop theft by servants. By the late 19th century, prices had fallen and locks were no longer needed.

JARGON BUSTER

Pomander Derived from *pomme d'ambre* (French for apple of amber or "ambergris"), a strong-smelling secretion of the sperm whale widely used in perfume.

Russian silver cigarette case. c1870; $1,000–1,500

Cigarette cases

In the late 19th century, boxes for containing cigars and cigarettes reflected the increase in smoking. Lacking filters, cigarettes before 1900 were short and early cases often small.

- Cigarette cases are usually oblong with rounded corners, slim enough for a pocket.
- Embossed, engraved, or enameled hunting and battle scenes, animals, landscapes, or inscriptions were popular decoration.

Foliate scrolls

View of St Paul's cathedral

Castletop card case by Nathaniel Mills. 1842; $1,800–2,000

Victorian card cases

Lavish cases for presenting calling cards were first produced in the 1820s. Birmingham was the center for manufacture in Britain.

- Die-stamped views of monuments, cathedrals, or stately homes, known as "castletops," are most popular, especially by Nathaniel Mills.
- Early examples feature a scene on both sides; later ones a scene on one side only.

VINAIGRETTES

Inspired by pomanders and made from the late 18th until the late 19th century, vinaigrettes are small, hinged boxes with pierced, hinged silver grilles that concealed sponges soaked in perfume, vinegar, or aromatic salts. Tucked away in pockets, vinaigrettes were sniffed to combat unpleasant smells or "fainting fits." Early vinaigrettes were small and simple, but by the 1830s, they were larger, with more elaborate decoration and fanciful grilles. The interiors were always gilded to protect the silver from corrosion caused by the aromatic perfume oil.

Silver grille is embossed with image of HMS Victory

Portrait of Admiral Nelson

A George III vinaigrette The subject, the English naval hero Nelson, adds value. By Matthew Linwood of Birmingham. 1806; $5,000–9,000

The lineup
20th-century silver

DEVELOPMENTS IN MANUFACTURING techniques from the end of the 19th century made it possible to produce silverware on an unprecedented scale. In the first half of the 20th century, domestic silverware in the latest styles included organic Art Nouveau pieces from the Württembergische Metallwarenfabrik (WMF) in Germany and streamlined Art Deco pieces by Christofle in Paris. At the same time, a number of influential silversmiths, including Georg Jensen and Jean Puiforcat, were handcrafting wares of exceptional quality and design.

The second half of the 20th century saw increased mass production, often in materials other than silver, such as stainless steel and aluminum. Leading makers commissioned well-known designers to develop new styles, many finished by hand. These included David Mellor for Elkington in Britain and Henning Koppel for Georg Jensen in Denmark.

The metal resembles stretched fabric

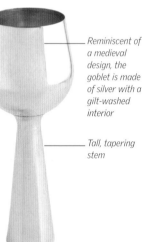

Silver-plated teapot and creamer for Christofle. c1900; H: 11¹/₂in (29cm); $3,500–5,000

Paul Follot

Sculptural designs with sinuous, sweeping lines were a hallmark of Art Nouveau. The designer Paul Follot, also known for his later Art Deco furnishings and interiors, created silverware that was daringly innovative in its day.

- Organic, curvaceous forms.
- Exaggerated spouts and handles.
- Fluted decoration to emphasize shape.

JARGON BUSTER

Biomorphic This term is used to describe a shape that is abstract but nevertheless suggests an organic life form.

Made in Mexico, this coffee service is more European Art Deco in styling

Coffee service. c1960; H (coffee pot): 9¹/₂in (24cm); $3,500–4,500

William Spratling

William Spratling trained as an architect and moved to Taxco, Mexico, in 1929. His work incorporated Mexican symbols and motifs, although he also worked in a Modernist style.

- His Modernist work shows the Art Deco fashion for streamlining.
- Simple geometric shapes.
- Minimal ornament.

Silvershade silver–plated candlesticks by Ettore Sottsass for Swid Powell. 1986; H: 13¹/₂in x (13¹/₂in); $2,000–3,000

Swid Powell

The sleek design of Sottsass's work for Swid Powell contrasts starkly with the boldly colored plastic wares he also made.

- Simple, geometric forms.
- Deliberate lack of ornament.
- Function of the piece is paramount.
- Satisfied trend for architect-designed pieces.

Reminiscent of a medieval design, the goblet is made of silver with a gilt-washed interior

Tall, tapering stem

Postmodern goblet designed by Angelo Mangiarotti for Cieto Murani. 1981; H: 8in (20cm); $1,800–2,500

Cieto Murani

Toward the end of the 1960s, the Modernist dream that it was possible to create a better world using machines and technology came to an end. Designers looked to the past, combining themes and motifs with wit and irony.

- Purity of form.
- Plain, unornamented surfaces.
- Re-interpretation of historical forms.

Geometric ornament emphasizes tall linear forms

Unornamented bowl

Elegant, sculptural stem

Grape motif similar to Jensen's

Art Deco powder boxes. 1934; H: 4–5in (10–12.75cm); $1,300–1,800

Grape tazza. c1918; H: 7½in (19cm); $3,500–5,000

Goblet. Mid-20th century; H: 4½in (11.5cm); $700–1,000

Eliel Saarinen

Finnish-born architect Eliel Saarinen designed pieces for International Silver as well as Art Deco furniture. He was president of the Cranbrook Academy of Art in Michigan.

- Tall, linear forms.
- Geometric ornament to emphasize form.
- Plain, flat surfaces.
- Function of the piece is paramount.

Georg Jensen

Jensen established a studio in 1904 and his company produces silverware to this day. His early designs were in the Art Nouveau style. Jensen was hailed as the greatest silversmith of the last 300 years when he died in 1935.

- Clean, rounded shapes.
- Nature-inspired decoration, including grapes and flowers.

Petersen

Having served as an apprentice under Georg Jensen, Danish-born silversmith Carl Poul Petersen moved to Canada in 1929.

- Handcrafted designs using traditional techniques.
- Simple, geometric shapes.
- Style reminiscent of Jensen's.
- Sparse, naturalistic ornamentation.

SCANDINAVIAN SILVER

In the years immediately after World War II, silver was a luxury item. The arrival of the sculptor Henning Koppel at Georg Jensen in Denmark signaled a change in fortune for the company and silver design. Koppel is best known for his biomorphic forms with strong, fluid lines and sinuous curves. They helped to revolutionize silver design in Scandinavia and as a result the region's silversmiths were the leaders in their field in the middle of the century.

Georg Jensen bowl designed by Koppel
Koppel was a master at balancing purity of form with the function of a piece. 1950s; D: 15in (38cm); $15,000–20,000

Flat, disc-shaped top joined with a conical stem to a square, plinth-like base

Salt shaker. 1994; H: 2½in (6cm); $500–750

Ettore Sottsass

In 1986, Sottsass left the Memphis design group he had founded in 1981. He worked for his own company, Sottsass Associati, and other firms. In the mid-1990s, Ettore Sottsass's postmodern designs included pieces that were simply a collection of geometric forms.

- No ornament.
- Takes reference from historical styles.
- Form more important than function.

Coffeepot and milk jug, part of the Bascule range designed by Lino Sabattini. 1960; H (pot): 4¾in (12cm); $500–900

Christofle

The influential Italian designer Lino Sabattini's Modernist style favored simplicity. As design directory of the French firm Christofle, he created a number of pieces that feature sleek, abstracted, organic shapes.

- Simple geometric shapes.
- Function is paramount.
- Complete absence of ornament.

The lineup
Other metals

PURE METALS—copper, iron, tin, and lead—and various alloys, including brass, bronze and pewter, have been used across the globe for thousands of years. A natural and abundant resource, metals are both malleable and extremely durable, which makes them suitable for all manner of practical purposes. Metals have played a significant role in the development of human civilization: bronze and iron are inextricably linked to the production of early tools and weapons, while copper and lead have been used in plumbing since ancient times. Pewter and spelter proved successful as inexpensive alternatives to more precious metals. Over the centuries, drinking and eating vessels, musical instruments, jewelry, and coins have been fashioned from metal. Metals have long been a mainstay of toy-making and the decorative arts.

Giving tin gifts for a 10th wedding anniversary was a tradition in late 18th- and 19th-century USA

Doll's cradle, Pennsylvania. Mid-19th century; L: 10in (25cm); $2,000–2,500

Tin
Tin-mining dates back to Classical times when trade developed between mines in Britain and southern Europe. The metal was alloyed with copper to produce bronze.
- Tin is easy to mold and hammer into shape.
- It is resistant to oxidization and corrosion.
- It can be polished to give a shiny surface.

A high resistance to corrosion makes lead suitable for garden statuary

Goose neck spout

This is a rare piece since most examples are black

Bird bath. c1900; H: 30¾in (78cm); $700–1,000

Coffee pot, New England. c1820; H: 10¼in (26cm); $14,000–18,000

Kettle, France. 19th century; H: 11in (28cm); $400–500

Lead
In use for at least 7,000 years, the applications of lead are broad—from Roman pipework to toy soldiers.
- Soft, heavy, and malleable, lead is ideal for casting figures.
- A soft, blue-white metal, lead turns dull gray on exposure to air.
- No longer used in toy-making because toxic.

Tole ware
The practice of painting on metal (tole) dates to late 18th-century Europe. Traditions grew in Central Europe and Scandinavia in particular, and were taken to the US by immigrants.
- Metals of choice were tin and pewter.
- Time-consuming technique, so often reserved for giftware.
- Functional, but mainly used for display.

Copper
This soft, dense, red-brown metal has been used prolifically, in its pure state and as an alloy.
- Very malleable and ductile, it is ideal for molding, shaping, and hammering.
- Resistance to corrosion makes it perfect for jewelry and coins.
- High conductivity of heat makes copper useful for cooking vessels.

Pewter oxidizes to a dull gray over time

The bust has been patinated to simulate bronze

Wrought iron is a good medium for intricate work

Tankard, Philadelphia. Late 18th century; H: 7³/₄in (19cm); $35,000–45,000

Pewter

Pewter is an alloy of tin and lead. Used throughout the Middle Ages for domestic wares, pewter enjoyed a revival with the Arts and Crafts movement of the late 19th century.

- Malleable and soft, it is ideal for casting.
- Durable and inexpensive, it is an obvious choice for household wares.
- Many pieces stamped with maker's marks.

Bust of Lloyd George. c1910; H: 10in (25cm); $180–220

Spelter

An alloy composed mostly of zinc (with lead or aluminum), spelter was popular in the late 19th century, when it was used to resemble bronze.

- Very malleable, spelter was used for casting figures and candlesticks.
- Used as cheap substitute for bronze.
- Identifiable by scratching the surface to reveal silver instead of bronze.

Toasting frame. Late 19th century; H: 18¹/₄in (46.5cm); $350–450

Wrought iron

Used since the Middle Ages, wrought iron has a lower carbon content than pig iron, which makes it more malleable. It was popular with late 19th- and early 20th-century designers.

- It is easily forged and welded, so perfect for large-scale items.
- Rusts slowly, so suitable for outdoor use.

Cast and engraved with foliate scrolls and flowers

French candlesticks. 19th century; H: 11¹/₄in (29cm); $400–500

Brass

Brass is an alloy of copper and zinc and is yellowish in color. Since the Middle Ages, it has been a popular choice for household wares.

- Highly durable and resistant to tarnishing, it is ideal for furniture mounts and inlay.
- Small holes are the result of over polishing and this will lower value.

WEATHER VANES

Weather vanes are thought to have derived from the medieval banners that gave archers an instant indication as to which way the wind was blowing. Later fashioned from metal, similar devices were used to help farmers, who needed wind power for grinding wheat. When Europeans first landed in the US, they mounted weather vanes on their churches and meeting halls, and American colonial communities began to make their own for rural and domestic use.

Sheet-iron tail

Cast-iron body

Made from copper, the figure is mounted on an arrow rod with a cast zinc tip

Cockerel This motif is thought to represent the cock that crowed three times at Jesus's betrayal. H: 23in (58.5cm); $8,000–10,000

Native American archer Motifs from America's social history were not uncommon. L: 45in (112.5cm); $300,000–350,000

Art Deco bronze figures

IN THE 1920s AND 30s, the demand for decorative small-scale sculptures that had flourished from the second half of the 19th century in continental Europe continued. They were carved in ivory, or cast in bronze, which was often gilded, silvered, or cold painted, or made from an expensive amalgam of bronze and ivory called chryselephantine that looked back to antique sculpture for inspiration. Self-possessed and stylish young women with elegant, elongated limbs were the favourite subjects of Art Deco sculptors from Paris to Berlin. These stylized figures, produced at well-established metal foundries, are expensive and widely faked. Along with children and characters from Classical mythology or distant lands, sleek animal sculptures were also popular.

Commonly portrayed either as naked or scantily clad erotic fantasies, bold and muscular Amazons, or sensuous young women engaged in Jazz Age pursuits such as dancing, bathing, or athletic activities.

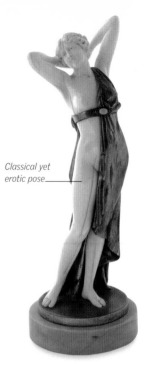

Classical yet erotic pose

Aphrodite. 9in (23cm); $4,000–6,000

Ferdinand Preiss

Having founded the firm Preiss & Kassler with Walter Kassler in Berlin in 1906, German artist Ferdinand Preiss was prolific and successful.

- Naturalistically modeled sculptures are exquisitely carved in ivory, bronze, or chryselephantine.
- Figures are signed with a full signature or "PK" for Preiss and Kassler.

Bronze and ivory dancing figure wears tight, jewel-encrusted costume and headdress

Le Verrier specialized in nude female dancers, erotic motoring mascots, and animals

Exaggerated poses

Flamboyant costumes of exotic dancers have intricate patterns painted in strong bright colors on the bronze

Janie. H: 12½in (32cm); $1,500–2,000

Max Le Verrier

French sculptor and ivory carver Max Le Verrier established his craft company in 1926.

- Lamps, wall brackets, and ashtrays were embellished with sensuous female figures.
- Output of signed bronze sculptures included male athletes such as archers and Classical subjects such as Roman warriors.

The hoop girl. H: 19in (48.5cm); $17,000–25,000

Demêtre Chiparus

Romanian-born Chiparus worked in Paris sculpting theatrical subjects as well as dancers from the stage in elegant poses and costumes.

- Details were cold painted and highlights gilt.
- Inspired by ancient Egypt and the Ballet Russes.
- Signatures are cast in the bronze or engraved on a base of at least two colored marbles.

Dancer. H: 13½in (34.5cm); $10,000–15,000

Gerda Iro Gerdago

Austrian-born Gerda Iro Gerdago created outrageously stylized sculptures.

- Futuristic Folies Bergère-type figures of dancers are modeled in bronze and ivory.
- Black enamel was often applied to the finely carved ivory hair, which is sometimes visible beneath an elaborate headdress.

Figures of dancers are frequently captured as if executing a series of complex dance steps

The surface of the bronze is usually silvered or cold painted

Green onyx bases are often faceted

Fayral was famed for the originality of his poses

The Russian dancer. c1925; H: 16in (40.5cm); $5,000–7,000

Dancing girl. c1920; H: 11in (28cm); $2,500–3,500

Exotic dancer. c1925; H: 15in (38cm); $700–1,000

Paul Philippe

A talented German sculptor working in Paris, Paul Phillippe specialized in female dancers, pierrots, and mannequins in bronze and ivory that echo those of Belgian sculptor Colinet.

- Delicately carved female figures are typically long and lean with fashionably bobbed hair.
- Subtly tinted ivory heads and hand- and cold-painted cast-bronze costumes are typical.

Josef Lorenzl

Austrian-born sculptor Josef Lorenzl had a dramatic and distinctive style. He depicted lively figures in athletic or acrobatic poses.

- Lithe female dancers with elongated limbs and slim boyish bodies are nude or scantily dressed.
- Sculptures are signed with an impressed signature at the base or "Lor" or "Enzl."

Pierre Le Faguays

"Fayral" was the pseudonym used by celebrated French sculptor Pierre Le Faguays.

- Strong, athletic semi-clad or nude female figures are typical of his work.
- Bronze, ivory, wood, and stone used.
- Sculptures bear the signature "P Le Faguays"; those examples reproduced from the 1960s are signed "Fayral" or "Favral."

Some pieces feature intricate detailing on the bronze

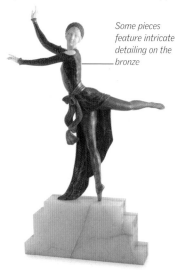

Dancer on points. $17,000–20,000

Joé Descomps

French sculptor Joé Descomps specialized in small-scale female figures in ivory and bronze.

- Although a number of his chryselephantine figures are eclectic or derivative, others such as "Beauty of Paris" are highly original.
- Small female nudes in carved ivory are especially charming and well executed.

STYLIZED ANIMALS

Art Deco sculptors produced a range of animal figures with simplified curvilinear forms and geometric planes. Artists, including Max Le Verrier, Maurice Prost, and Gaston Le Bourgeois, emulated the pioneering sculptor François Pompon by depicting the elegance and dynamism of animals such as deer, doves, and horses. Reflecting the Art Deco allure of the exotic, they also sculpted African and tropical wildlife, including antelopes, monkeys, and angelfish. Panthers were the most popular, as well as other predators such as foxes, eagles, and cobras.

Stag and Hound This rare iron sculpture by Wilhelm Hunt Diederich depicts the animals in a dynamic pose.

JARGON BUSTER

Chryselephantine Originally a term for gold and ivory statues, it also denotes Art Deco objects made of ivory and another material, usually bronze.

COLLEC

TIBLES

COLLECTIBLES

Commercially made dolls from the mid-19th century onwards, teddy bears from the early 20th century, ivory and wood carvings, quilts, samplers, and costume jewelry are all items once regarded as collectibles, but they are now viewed as collectible antiques.

May Frères doll
Fine porcelain dolls were mass produced but years of play and their fragile nature means examples in good condition, like this French Bébé Mascotte in original costume, are scarce. c1885; H: 18in (45.75cm)

Ivory carving of Napoleon
Ivory, bone, and wood have been carved to make decorative and practical items for centuries. Ivory is perfect for detailed carvings such as this French figure of Napoleon Bonaparte in full military dress. 19th century; H: 4³⁄₄in (12cm)

OFTEN, A DOLL, teddy bear, or piece of costume jewelry is marked with the maker's name, taking out a lot of the detective work. Even then, it is important to be able to tell genuine from fake and decide whether something is rare. Understanding and identifying the specialities of different makers and how these affect value and desirability are essential. The four factors to bear in mind when evaluating an item are Condition, Age, Rarity, and Desirability—the easiest way to remember these is CARD. You can add the two Ps: Provenance and Pretty.

Condition is always important. Mint condition, when something is as good as new, is rare and highly prized. Unless something is exceptionally rare, a chip, tear, or repair considerably reduces value. Some wear is accepted on items such as teddy bears that have been played with ("playworn"), and quilts that have been used. While condition is important, the key factor is desirability. Wear can be a sign of genuine age: a Japanese netsuke that has hung on a cord will have been worn when the cord rubbed against the ivory; and a teddy bear may have received many loving cuddles that have smoothed its fur. Connection with an original owner adds desirability.

Age and rarity

When it comes to age, the theory that the older something is the more valuable it must be does not always bear scrutiny. While an 18th-century sampler or treen snuffbox may be more valuable than a late 19th-century one, many 20th-century items are gaining in value and collectibility. For example, costume jewelry only decades old has come

Steiff bear
A Steiff bear—such as this cinnamon plush—always commands a premium, but other bears, even by unknown makers, are hotly collected today. c1908; H: 13in (33cm)

Trifari fur clip
Costume jewelry followed the latest fashions and can rival precious pieces for the quality of its design and manufacture. 1940s; L: 3$^1/_2$in (9cm)

Pennsylvania quilt
Textiles such as this handmade Star of Bethlehem quilt, as well as young girls' samplers, appeal both as colorful objects and pieces of family history. 19th century

to be appreciated for its design and quality of manufacture, even though the materials do not have the intrinsic value of the real thing. Many pieces were made using the same techniques as precious jewelry and can have the same—some might say more—WOW factor. Ten years ago, at valuations, owners were often disappointed to hear that, while beautiful and of great sentimental value, these pieces had no commercial worth. Those days are gone. An auction house in Indianapolis recently sold a Trifari pin of a crane on a lily pond designed by Alfred Philippe for $7,000.

Rarity must always be taken into account. Again, just because something is old does not necessarily mean it is rare. Roman glass was made in vast quantities. The Industrial Revolution brought about mass manufacture on an unprecedented scale, and ceramics have survived in huge numbers. But items made by hand or in genuine limited editions may be rare because few were made. If demand is there, their value will rise and rise.

Objects of desire

It is desirability that has the greatest effect on value, although this is hard to pin down. Fine craftsmanship may increase desirability, especially when combined with exquisite materials. Fashions can dictate what people collect and add both value and desirability. Provenance can help to identify the age of an item and increase its value.

For example, if you can find a photograph of the original owner of an antique doll or teddy with their toy, that will increase its value—especially if the picture shows the owner as a child. However, the most valuable provenance is proof that something once belonged to a famous person.

If beauty is in the eye of the beholder, then prettiness can be just as hard to define because it is a matter of personal taste. However, as a general rule, if you have two 18th-century portraits, both well painted but with no knowledge of the artist, a portrait of a pretty girl will fetch much more than that of an ugly old man.

For many people, the appeal of collectibles is that it is often the item least popular at the time it was new that is the most desirable—and will sell for the most money—today. So in this collecting area a thorough knowledge of the market is essential.

JARGON BUSTER
Provenance Verifiable proof of an item's origins or history. An interesting provenance, or one linking a piece to a famous maker, owner, or event, adds significant value.

The interrogation
Dolls

DOLLS HAVE BEEN MADE from clay, fur, and wood since ancient times. China and parian (made of unglazed untinted porcelain) dolls were first made in Thuringia, southern Germany, and were popular from the end of the 1840s to the 1890s. These dolls are rare and expensive. In the 1850s, German doll-makers introduced bisque heads and exported them all over Europe. From c1860, the high-quality French dolls were coveted, particularly fashion dolls and *bébés*. The most expensive were produced by Rohmer, Maison Huret, Bru Jeune & Cie, and Jumeau. German makers concentrated on producing cheaper dolls, which impacted on the French market by the end of the century.

Jumeau doll

Pierre François Jumeau began manufacturing dolls in Montreuil-sous-Bois in France, around 1842. Jumeau dolls are the zenith of the French doll trade. They were highly regarded for their beautiful faces and couture dresses, many created by Ernestine Jumeau. In 1872, the company began to produce its own porcelain heads. In 1878, Jumeau won the Gold Medal at the Paris Exhibition. This was advertised on the dolls' bodies, boxes, shoes, and even dress labels. Jumeau's Golden Age lasted from the late 1870s to the late 1890s.

The head
The head is cut away on the diagonal revealing the cork pate (material). The pate (hidden by the wig) is made of cork. The bisque head was made from a mold.

The eyes
Blown glass "paperweight" eyes are fixed and spherical. They extend bulbously from the socket. The thick, heavy eyebrows are almost knitted together giving the doll an intense, inquisitive look.

Face is beautifully formed

The fingers and hands are realistically molded with separate fingers and dimples in the skin

Mouth is closed

The wrists are fixed

Marks
The head is marked DÉPOSÉ with a size number and a red mark. The lower back has a stamped blue mark.

Limbs
The body has eight ball joints. The chunky legs are solid and stable so that the doll can stand up.

Large early Jumeau doll
Visual appeal is highly important when assessing the value of a doll. The original couture fashion outfit and rare marked shoes of this doll add to the desirability. c1860–70; H: 32in (81cm); $8,000–10,000

ASSESSING VALUE

Various factors can influence the value of a doll. The one shown here once belonged to the Queen of Romania and has authentic documentation and letters relating to the provenance. She also has her original crown in gold metal and lapis lazuli, and the original traditional Romanian dress. These factors make her more desirable and valuable.

However, the doll has a crack on her forehead. Any hairline crack or damage to the face of a doll can reduce the value by at least 70 per cent. Always check a bisque head for hairlines. Carefully remove the wig and the pate. Place a black light or flashlight in the head. Any cracks will show though as black lines. A Bru in perfect condition will sell for around $25,000. Thanks to the provenance and the fact that the crack is not within the mask of the face (the eyes, nose, and mouth) the decrease in value is held at just over 50 per cent.

Bru Jeune doll
She has a crack above the eyebrow. c1860; H: 21in (53cm); $12,000

Armand Marseille doll

Armand Marseille founded his doll company in 1885 in Thuringia in southern Germany. German dolls in the 1890s were cheaper than the French. But they were still well made and popular with little girls, even if they were by no means as elegant or graceful as the best Jumeau dolls. From 1890, Armand, with his son also called Armand, were prolific producers of bisque dolls' heads. From 1900 to 1930, they were the largest suppliers of dolls' heads to other manufacturers, producing up to 1,000 per day. The most common Armand Marseille doll is the 390 series made from c1900. The most popular of the Armand Marseille range are the Dream Babies made in the 1920s.

The wig is good quality

Open mouth with teeth

Armand Marseille 390 doll
The doll wears a beige dress with a lace fabric shawl and hat. c1910; H: 23¹/₂in (59.5cm); $80–100

The face
The molding of the features is not particularly fine. The doll has brown glass fixed eyes that are flatter to the head. The eyebrows are lighter. There is no character to the face.

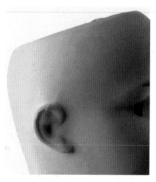

The head
Marseille dolls' heads have a smaller opening positioned at the top. The pate is usually cardboard. The ears are not pierced.

The body
The doll has a simple jointed composition (a mixture of glue and sawdust or wood pulp) body, with slender legs. The torso is out of proportion—too large for the legs.

Marks
The doll is fully marked on the back of the head with the name of the maker and numbers.

German dolls

BY ABOUT 1900, the demand for German dolls took over from the French. German firms dominated the doll market up to the 1930s. While French dolls were superb to look at, children all over Europe and the US could actually play with German dolls, which were well made and cheaper. At the same time, the quality of the French dolls was decreasing. Some of the most successful types were realistic character *bébés*, Googly dolls, and fashion dolls, with distinctive thin waists. Much of the current value is based on "cuteness," condition, sensitivity of painted expression, and possession of original clothes. Heubach and Simon & Halbig are two important German makers.

Gebrüder Heubach dolls

The Heubach brothers concentrated their porcelain factory production on figurines and dolls' heads from about 1840. In about 1910, the factory began to produce whole dolls. They used artists and sculptors from a local art school to work on the dolls' heads and create their high-quality realistic and amusing character dolls. The skill, attention to detail, and personality of the dolls all contributed to the price they commanded at the time and now. Some of the dolls were large, which also increases the value.

Heavily molded hair

Original clothes are in excellent condition

KEY CLUES

- The character dolls are highly sought after for their visual appeal.
- Much effort was devoted to the heads, with well-painted molded hair, rosy cheeks, and faces full of personality.
- Their eyes were realistic with an indented pupil and an iris highlighted with a white dot. Many were lever-moving.
- Original bodies can be a little crude. Bisque (unglazed, matte porcelain) is better than over-shiny reproductions.

Character child

This rare doll has a typical bisque socket head, painted intaglio (hollowed-out) eyes, fully jointed composition body, and original clothing. c1890–1910; H: 19in (48.5cm); $28,000–30,000

The Scottish uniform and the googly lever-moving eyes make this doll desirable

Girl doll

Wearing highly desirable original clothing, this doll has a shoulder plate (allowing the head to swivel) attached to a cloth body. c1900; H: 20in (51cm); $400–600

Doll in Scottish uniform

This doll was made for the English firm Eisenmann & Co. who traded under the name Einco, and later became Chiltern Toys. c1915; H: 12in (30cm); $4,800–5,000

German schoolboy

The slightly chubby body and highly detailed face with open mouth and teeth are extremely realistic. c1900; H: 16in (40.5cm); $1,500–1,600

TRADE SECRETS

Many factors, in addition to the state of the bisque head, influence the value of a doll. A body in very poor condition can reduce the value by 40 percent. A replaced body can reduce the value by 50 percent. However, a doll in mint condition, with original clothes and original trunk containing additional dresses and accessories can add 200–250 percent.

GOOGLIES

Googly dolls were inspired by the drawings of an American illustrator called Grace Debbie Drayton. They were an immediate success, particularly in the US, thanks to their cute bisque faces, large sideways glancing eyes, tiny snub noses, and closed smiling watermelon mouths. Bodies tended to be of jointed composition. They are still especially popular in the US.

Googlies were produced from c1912 to c1938 by many German makers, including Armand Marseille, Kämmer & Reinhardt, Gebrüder Heubach, and Hertel, Schwab & Co.

Hertel, Schwab & Co googly boy
This toddler boy doll 173–6 is in later clothes. c1915; H: 15in (38cm); $4,000–6,000

Hertel, Schwab & Co She has sideways-looking eyes, melon mouth, and original shirt. c1915; H: 15in (38cm); $5,000–6,000

Simon & Halbig dolls

Simon & Halbig began making dolls in the 1870s and production soon became prolific. They made many china and bisque dolls themselves and also supplied dolls' heads, often with fine wigs, to the French Jumeau factory and Kämmer & Reinhardt. Kämmer & Reinhardt bought Simon & Halbig in 1920. Simon & Halbig dolls are fully marked. The ampersand was added to the mark in 1905 and it is generally accepted that dolls marked without the ampersand were made before that date.

KEY CLUES

- Kid-bodied shoulder heads (dolls with head, neck, and shoulders molded in one piece) from the 1880s closely followed the French.
- Sleep (open and close), paperweight (blown glass), flirty (move from side to side), or intaglio (hollowed-out) blue-painted eyes.
- Very rosy-cheeked baby or toddler dolls.

The black cap with "1908 Baseball Fan" pin is a real collector's item

Closed pouty mouth

Fully jointed limbs

Character boy
This male doll has all the desirable qualities: a poured bisque socket head, intaglio blue-painted eyes, fully jointed composition body, and blonde mohair wig. It is marked "S&H 150/2". 1908; H: 21in (53.5cm); $27,000–30,000

Fashion doll
This doll is for the French market and is dressed in elegant French clothes, including a fashionable red jacket with bustle. c1890; H: 13in (34cm); $2,000–2,500

Lady doll No. 1159
This character doll has a good wig and glass eyes. Original clothes in good condition add to the value. c1910; H: 12in (30cm); $1,200–1,500

Always check to see if the body marks match the head—this doll is by two makers

Simon & Halbig/Adolf Wislizenus toddler doll
Wislizenus bought the head from Simon & Halbig and used a jointed composition body made in his own factory. Early 1900s; $1,500–2,000

"Flirty" glass eyes

Simon & Halbig/Kämmer & Reinhardt 126 doll
The rosy-cheeked look of this doll reflects the improvement in health in babies from 1900. c1920; H: 17in (43cm); $600–800

The lineup
Dolls

FROM THE LATE 19th century, doll-makers created a range of styles to appeal to different tastes. Many dolls are marked but marks are not always a guide to quality, as a proportion of the desirability of an early doll lies in its decoration, eyes, and hair, which can vary on the same model. Plastic dolls from the 1930s onward should be boxed and in mint condition.

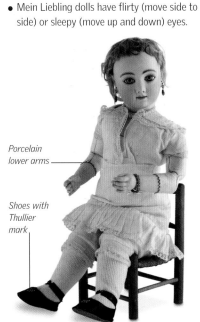

Period outfit adds to the value

Jointed bodies were popular, as they enabled dolls to stand and pose

117n Mein Liebling (My Darling) with flirty eyes. c1890; H: 25in (63.5cm); $4,000–5,000

Kämmer & Reinhardt, Germany
Founded in 1886 and the first company to produce character dolls, it made girl or boy dolls with bent-limb or jointed bodies.
- Most have painted eyes, painted closed mouths, and mohair wigs.
- Mein Liebling dolls have flirty (move side to side) or sleepy (move up and down) eyes.

Pierced ears still have the gold and opal drop earrings

Fixed blue glass eyes with painted brows and eyelashes

Le Petit Parisien. c1890; H: 19in (42.5cm); $6,000–7,000

Jules Steiner, France
The factory made good-quality dolls from 1855 to 1908. Many have eyes that can be opened and shut using a lever at the side of the head.
- Fingers are stubby and the mouth is always close to the nose.
- Bodies are usually papier mâché (referred to as "composition") and jointed.

Blonde mohair wig

Kid-leather body dressed with original outfit

"G" fashion doll. c1880; H: 22in (55.8cm); $2,000–3,000

Kestner, Germany
J. D. Kestner began making dolls in 1820, and started producing porcelain child dolls in 1860. Character dolls were introduced in 1909. Kestner was one of the few companies to make its own heads and bodies. The company closed in 1938.
- Heads are high quality and in many styles.
- Bodies are leather, composition, or wood.

Porcelain lower arms

Shoes with Thullier mark

Bébé. H: 21in (53.5cm); $70,000–90,000

Thullier, France
Thullier made top-quality dolls from 1875 to 1893. They are highly sought after today.
- Dolls have enchanting porcelain faces with paperweight eyes made from blown glass with realistic depth of color.
- The bodies are wood, kid leather, or composition, wigs are mohair, and the quality clothing is accessorized with jewelry.

Porcelain head with set or sleepy eyes

Bébé, mold 301. c1900; H: 30in (76cm); $2,500–3,000

SFBJ, France
The Société Française de Fabrication des Bébés et Jouets was a group of French doll-makers who joined forces to challenge the German industry. They were active from 1899 to c1950.
- Initial quality was high but tailed off.
- Dolls tend to be slim, with high-cut legs and composition or wooden bodies.
- Character dolls, made from 1911, were best.

— Applied ears

— Although not in original clothes, she is in good condition, which adds value

— Painted shoes and stockings

"Indestructible" baby. H: 18½in (47cm); $3,500–4,000

Alabama, US

Alabama dolls were made by Ella Smith Doll Co, of Roanoke, Alabama, from 1899 to 1925.

- Made from cloth with molded faces, the hair and features are applied with oil paint.
- A little wear will not affect the value but repainting and repairs will reduce it.
- Early versions have applied, not molded ears. Later dolls have a bobbed hairstyle.

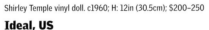

Original pearl necklace, hair slide, and hat

Shirley Temple vinyl doll. c1960; H: 12in (30.5cm); $200–250

Ideal, US

Ideal Novelty & Toy Co. made dolls modeled on child star Shirley Temple from 1934 to 1963.

- Initially dolls were made from papier mâché but in 1957 the first vinyl dolls appeared.
- Made in five sizes.
- Most wore 1950s fashions, but some had outfits from Shirley Temple's films. Additional outfits were available.

TWO-FACED DOLLS

Introduced by Jumeau, two-faced dolls feature a knob, concealed in the hair, which turns the head around. One face is smiling, the second crying. Bru Jeune & Cie produced a number of high-quality and unusual bébé dolls, now highly sought after. The best examples have a porcelain head, shoulders, and hands on a kid-leather body.

Bru, Jeune & Cie On this rare two-faced doll, marked No. 4, the bonnet flips to reveal a second face of a crying red-faced child. H: 15in (38cm); $20,000–22,000

— Painted hazel eyes

No. 7534 cloth child. c1930; H: 20in (51cm); $2,000–2,500

Käthe Kruse, Germany

Käthe Kruse made cloth-bodied dolls 1911–1956 and plastic dolls from the late 1940s.

- The heads are made from molded muslin with hand-painted features.
- Early dolls have three hand-stitched seams on their heads and fetch a premium.
- The bodies are jointed at shoulders and hips.
- Clean fabric and intact paint increase value.

Dolls are fully — posable

Dolls were sold — dressed or patterns were available to make your own clothes

"At The Beach" doll. 1950s; H: 13in (33cm); $500–700

Mary Hoyer, US

In 1938, dolls were made by Ideal Novelty & Toy Co. to showcase Mary Hoyer's dolls' clothes. A year later, composition dolls were first made, most stamped on the back of the neck. Production ended in the late 1960s but since 1990 new dolls have been made.

- Hard plastic dolls made from 1946 have mohair wigs, sleepy eyes, and closed mouth.

Original outfit in perfect condition

"Morocco" bent knee doll. c1970; H: 8in (20cm); $250–350

Madame Alexander, US

The company made dolls from fabric in 1923; composition in the 1930s; plastic from 1948; vinyl from the late 1950s. It continues today.

- Dolls are collected for their highly detailed and well-made costumes (rather than for the doll itself), made in over 6,500 variations.
- Dolls were made to be displayed on a shelf rather than played with.

Steiff teddy bears

AMERICAN PRESIDENT THEODORE "Teddy" Roosevelt's refusal to shoot a bear on a hunting trip in 1902 started a craze that continues to this day. A newspaper cartoon commenting on the incident inspired entrepreneur Morris Michtom to produce a toy bear, named "Teddy Bear," to commemorate the event. The toy was sold from his store in Brooklyn, New York. Others copied his idea and the teddy bear was born. Although the first boom in bears was in the US, Germany produced the most, and arguably the best. The German firm Steiff (founded in 1886) is considered the finest maker and is the best known. Its bears command high sums and have been faked.

Genuine Steiff teddy bears

Steiff marks its teddy bears and other soft toys with a metal button in the ear. Early buttons had an elephant logo or were left blank; later ones bear the word Steiff. Even if the button has not survived it is often possible to see the hole it made. Early bears were stuffed with wood shavings and the fur was commonly beige or gold mohair plush. Like many early 20th century bears, early teddies should have a pronounced snout and a thinner, more elongated face than a modern bear. Good condition is important, but most bears will have received a lot of hugs. Look for wear that is consistent with cuddles.

KEY CLUES

- Long, curved limbs with large, out-turned paws covered with felt pads and narrow wrists and ankles. Replaced pads lower value.
- Seam across the top of the head from ear to ear.
- Button in one of the ears or a hole left behind.
- A pronounced, humped back.
- Ears are original and in correct position: if they have been moved or replaced there will be repaired holes in the head seams.

The pale brown stitched nose is original and intact

Colored fur (in this case white) is rare and in good condition—adding to desirability

Steiff white mohair bear
This early bear has a rare blank button in its ear, boot-button eyes, and a stitched nose and mouth. c1904; H: 20in (51cm); $7,000–10,000

Steiff center seam bear
The seam down the center of the nose appeared on one in seven bears. c1907; H: 20in (51cm); $7,000–10,000

Dark brown Steiff bear
The shape of the bear and its glass eyes are clues that it dates from the 1920s. c1920; H: 18in (45.5cm); $5,000–7,000

Bear with kapok stuffing
This early Steiff bear has a button in its ear and is stuffed with a lot of kapok, dating it to 1905–1906. H: 17in (43cm); $6,000–8,000

Button in ear
The style of button helps to date the bear. This one is from around 1920 to the 1950s.

HUMPED-BACK BEARS

Like real grizzly bear cubs, early German bears, and some American ones too, had a pronounced humped back. A grizzly's hump is a mass of muscle needed to help it dig holes or pack a punch. Its toy counterpart's hump was made of the soft mixture of long, thin wood shavings used as stuffing and known as excelsior or wood wool. This feels crunchy when the bear is squeezed. British bears were stuffed with a mixture of kapok and excelsior, making them lighter in weight. Although Steiff bears became chunkier during the 1910s and 20s, the humped back remained. It was not until the launch of the Original Teddy in 1951 that the hump all but disappeared.

Early Steiff bear The pronounced hump on this Steiff blonde bear is typical of a bear made in about 1905.

Fake Steiff teddy bears

Early Steiff bears are so valuable that many fakes have been made. Beware examples that appear to be made in the old shape, are worn and well stuffed. Although the stuffing in old bears was hard, years of love and attention should have softened and redistributed it. Wear is often faked using a drill with a sanding attachment, so look out for worn patches where the pile of the fur has been smoothed into circles. Wear should be all over and consistent with the bear being played with—especially notable on the top of the head, back, arms, and chest. Fake bears are often made in rare and unusual colors, which should arouse suspicion, especially if the bear has no labels, or remnants of them.

Top of head should show more wear

Stuffing strong and hard despite wear to fur

KEY CLUES

- Most fakes are of bears made from 1902 to c1930.
- Be cautious of old-style shaped bears made in modern fabrics.
- Wear that does not fit with being given years of loving hugs should immediately arouse suspicion.
- Use your nose: old bears have their own smell from years of play and house dust. A modern bear does not.

Foot pads are intact despite so much wear to the fur

TRADE SECRETS

Rarity and condition are all-important when valuing a bear. Original tags, labels, and buttons increase value – however, safety-conscious parents often removed buttons. Conversely, being nibbled at by moths and faded by the sun will decrease desirability and value.

Dark cinnamon teddy bear
This color of fur is highly unusual and is the first clue that the bear may not be what it seems. Late 20th century; H: 17in (43cm); $50–70

Worn in patches
The missing fur on the top of the shoulders is not consistent with being hugged every night.

Condition of the face
It would be hard to wear the fur around the eyes this much through play.

The lineup
Teddy bears

BY 1906, THE TEDDY BEAR craze was in full swing and new companies sprang up across North America and Europe. The market for bears was so strong that Steiff took on 2,000 more workers to satisfy orders, which increased 80-fold in five years. In Britain, J. K. Farnell & Co, Chiltern, Merrythought, and Chad Valley were among the new teddy bear makers. Their bears tended to have straighter limbs and flatter faces than their German cousins. Few American makers survived long in the Depression, with the exception of the Ideal Novelty and Toy Company and Gund. Germany, with its history of toy-making, fared better with Gebrüder Bing, Schuco, and, of course, Steiff. French bears can be distinguished by their simple joints, colorful ear linings, and short bristle mohair. It is not always easy to identify the maker, although M. Pintel Fils and Fadap (both closed in the 1970s) are among the best known.

Body is made from luxurious mohair

The Chad Valley label was stitched under the foot

Brown mohair bear. c1930; H: 11in (28cm); $350–450
Chad Valley, England
Chad Valley began making bears in 1915. Early examples were made of mohair, usually gold, and the limbs were stuffed with soft kapok.
- Early bears had vertically stitched, triangular noses. Later, the muzzle was shaved.
- Later bears have large, flat, wide-apart ears and oval paw pads with cardboard inserts.

Stitched woollen nose

Mechanism allows the body to be lifted over the arms

During the 1930s, the shaved muzzle became gradually longer

Fabric label

Tumbler bear. c1910; H: 11½in (29cm); $2,000–2,500
Bing, Germany
Gebrüder Bing began to make high-quality, mechanical toys in the 1890s. It produced its first bears in 1907 and soon introduced mechanical elements.
- Tumbling bears have long, metal-framed arms and a clockwork mechanism that lifts the body over the arms.
- Bears were made from golden mohair plush with a stitched woollen nose and claws.

Golden mohair bear. 1930s–40s; H: 23in (58.5cm); $500–700
Merrythought, England
Merrythought was founded in 1930 and is still making bears today.
- Bears made in the 1930s have a celluloid button in the ear as well as a fabric label.
- Until the 1950s noses were stitched vertically. The outermost stitches on each side were elongated and stretched down.
- Paw pads sometimes have webbed stitching.
- Before the 1960s, snouts were shaved.

Hugmee teddy bear. c1930; H: 15in (38cm); $120–180
Chiltern, England
The Chiltern Toy Co. first made bears in 1915. Chad Valley took over Chiltern in the 1960s.
- The first bear was googly-eyed Master Teddy who wore a shirt, pants, and bow tie.
- In the 1920s, Chiltern introduced Hugmee, a mohair bear with soft kapok stuffing, cotton or velveteen paw pads, and a shaved snout.
- In the 1930s, bears that contained squeakers and musical boxes were made.

Triangular head

Feet have original felt pads with cardboard inserts

Shaved snout

Long, plump arms

Solid form

White Steiff bear. 1920s; H: 18in (45.5cm); $7,000–9,000

Gold mohair bear. c1905; H: 24¹/₂in (62cm); $2,500–3,500

White mohair bear. 1920s; H: 19in (48.5cm); $2,500–3,500

Colored bears

Many companies made colored bears, including Steiff, Merrythought, Chiltern, and Farnell. White, pink, and blue are very desirable.

- Colored bears tend to be more valuable than bears in the less common darker and lighter shades of brown.
- Steiff and Farnell made a limited number of black bears to commemorate the *Titanic*.

American bears

Many American companies started up to meet the demand for teddy bears, only to close as a result of the Depression.

- The majority of bears were not marked and so it is impossible to say who made them.
- Many are based on the Steiff shape.
- Often have round ears set low in the head.
- Long, pointed feet are typical.

Farnell, England

J. K. Farnell & Co was founded in 1908 and is known as the "English Steiff" for its high quality bears. The factory closed in the 1960s.

- Ears tend to be angled.
- Like most makers, they used black boot button eyes before World War I. In the 1920s, Farnell was one of the first companies to use glass eyes.

The original tag adds to the value

Steiff gold plush bear. 1950s; H: 6in (15cm); $500–600

Post World War II bears

Post-war bears are becoming more desirable as pre-war bears diminish in number.

- Rounder faces with a less pronounced muzzle and ears closer together.
- Bodies are plumper and arms shorter and straighter than pre-war bears.
- Limited-edition bears, made since the 1970s, should grow in value, especially if they are in mint condition with their box and paperwork.

NOVELTY BEARS

The German firm of Schuco is renowned for its range of miniature toys, including bears, monkeys, and rabbits, which were produced between the 1920s and 1970s. Gold is the most common color, with unusual colors such as red and green rare and highly sought after. Bears were made from mohair. They had swivel heads and were jointed at the shoulder and hip. Many of its miniature bears had a novelty use and may conceal a perfume bottle or manicure set, for example. The company also made mechanical toys and produced miniature tumbling bears and a "yes/no" bear that nodded or shook its head depending on how its tail was moved. The company was sold in 1976.

Schuco A Schuco scent bottle teddy bear. The head lifts off to reveal a glass bottle concealed in the body. c1950; 5¹/₂in (14cm); $200–300

The lineup
Ivory and bone

HARD, FINE-GRAINED CREAMY-WHITE IVORY has been used for centuries for useful wares and novelties, especially in miniature. Valued for its tactile surface and adaptability to carving, ivory lends itself to a high degree of detail. Chinese craftsmen first made ivory carvings c1500BCE. In Japan, craftsmen did not start to carve ivory until the 17th century, but they soon became renowned for their netsuke (see pp172–73). In the West, ivory was used as a furniture inlay from the 17th century and later carved into figures, chess pieces, and card cases. Elephant tusks were the primary source, but walrus, sperm whale, narwhal, ram, and wild boar tusks have all been used.

All ivory objects must legally conform with the Convention on International Trade in Endangered Species (CITES). However, the illicit trade continues so check the origin of items offered as "antique ivory" before buying and obtain a written statement from the seller (see opposite).

Indian ivory workbox. c1780; W: 12½in (32cm); $4,500–6,000

Indian boxes

Indian decorative objects were imported into Europe from the 17th century. By the late 18th century, many designs reflected prevailing European styles such as the Neoclassical.

● Ivory was often combined with ebony.
● In the 18th and 19th centuries, craftsmen in the Indian town of Vizagapatum produced boxes and furniture inlaid or covered with panels of ivory, mainly for the British market.

American pair of miniatures on ivory. c1845; H: 3¼in (8.5cm); $800–1,200

Ivory miniatures

In the late 17th century, ivory joined the favored materials of vellum and enamel as the ideal base for painted miniature portraits.

● The ivory shines through the pigments making the paint look luminous.
● In the 19th century, ivory miniatures in larger formats were turned into small imitations of oil paintings for display on a desk or wall.

Complex carving includes two wheels and two figures

Prisoner-of-war bone spinning jenny. c1800; H: 6in (15cm); $750–850

Prisoner-of-war carvings

During the Revolutionary and Napoleonic Wars against France (1793–1815), some French prisoners of war were kept in floating prisons. To pass the time—and earn money—many prisoners made bone carvings.

● Ships were a popular subject, but working models of machines such as the spinning jenny and the guillotine were also made.

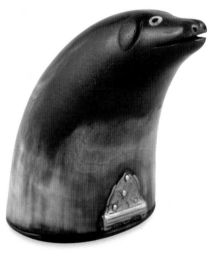

Horn snuff mull, in the shape of a seal. 18th century; H: 3in (7.5cm); $1,000–1,200

Horn snuff mulls

Scottish for a snuffbox, a mull originally incorporated a mill for grinding the snuff.

● Snuff mulls were frequently fashioned from the horns of rams and decorated with silver mounts, which are usually unmarked.
● Made in a variety of imaginative shapes, mulls often had a decorative lid and were meant to stand on a table.

Crowned with a coat of arms and shell

Female figure representing summer with sickle and cornucopia

French ivory snuff rasp. 18th century; L: 7³/₄in (19.5cm); $3,500–5,000

French ivory snuff rasps

By the early 18th century, the fashion in Europe for taking snuff had spread to the nobility and then the middle classes. Snuff rasps were used for grinding the tightly twisted rope tobacco.

- Made in lavish materials including ivory.
- Ivory is often carved in the round and follows the shape of the original tusk.
- Easily carved, ivory allowed for delicate decorative motifs and complex armorials.

SCRIMSHAW

From the 19th century, decorative objects from the teeth and tusks of whales and walruses were fashioned by craftsmen and sailors on both sides of the Atlantic, as well as in Australia and New Zealand. Using simple tools, the surface of a tooth or piece of bone was scraped smooth. Pictorial designs were pricked out with a needle through a paper image, then scratched, engraved, or lightly carved. Soot, tar, or black India ink and sealing wax were used to join up the pricked-out dots to reveal decorative pictures such as whaling scenes or ships. There are many replicas on the market— they are often heavier, milkier, and have a whiter finish and a highly polished base.

Scrimshaw This whale's tooth is engraved on both sides with a ship. Early to mid-19th century; L: 8¹/₄in (20.5cm); $70,000–90,000

WATCH OUT! According to CITES, all ivory taken from the wild and significantly altered to make a piece of jewelry, art, tool, or musical instrument before June 1, 1947, is an antique. Any piece made after this date is illegal. Any piece of ivory sold in its natural state is also illegal.

Silver-mounted beaker recording an incident when a lioness attacked a mail coach. c1816; H: 3¹/₄in (8.5cm); $1,500–1,600

Horn drinking vessels

Derived from the horns of animals such as rams and goats, horn was used for drinking vessels and later knife handles and spoons. In the 18th century, London was a center for shaping horn.

- Beakers frequently mounted with silver.
- Horn was also used to fashion snuffboxes, medallions, brooches, combs, and in thin sheets for lanterns as an alternative to glass.

Modeled in full military dress and mounted on square plinth base

French carved ivory Napoleon Bonaparte figure. 19th century; H: 4³/₄in (12cm); $500–700

Ivory figures

Easily carved, ivory has always been a popular material for making figures.

- Figures made from the hard, fine-grained and creamy-white material derived from the teeth or tusks of various animals resemble biscuit or *blanc de chine* porcelain.
- Popular subjects include politicians, actors and actresses, street sellers, and animals.

Shibayama scene of storks in a garden

Shibayama (Japanese inlay technique) visiting card case c1880; L: 4in (10cm); $5,000–7,000

Visiting card cases

Presenting calling cards was widespread in polite society in the 18th century, but it was not until the 1820s that cases were made for them.

- In the late 19th century, many card cases were made in the Far East to satisfy the European fashion for Oriental wares.
- Shibayama cases had carved tortoiseshell and ivory set into a gold lacquer or ivory ground.

The prime suspects
Netsuke

NETSUKE WERE MINIATURE sculptures for use as toggles in traditional Japanese dress. They were attached to the *obi* (sash) around a kimono, from which hung a pouch, pipe case, or series of boxes on a cord. Produced from the 16th century, netsuke were carved from ivory, bone, or wood in many shapes, including peasants, gods, and mythical or real beasts, sometimes humorous. Netsuke had no sharp or projecting areas that would catch on the cloth, and the best examples were finely carved with details. Many artists signed their netsuke using Japanese symbols, and the work of some of the best known is highly sought after.

Authentic netsuke

Look closely at a netsuke to find irregularly placed fine veins, which occur naturally in ivory. If it is ivory, consider the size and subject matter, because they can affect desirability. Important factors also include how well the form has been conceived, and how finely the details have been carved and highlighted with staining. If the piece is charming, or perhaps whimsical, this can also increase desirability, as can the presence of an artist's signature. Netsuke were functional objects, so look for wear on pronounced or protruding areas and around the holes, and consider where dirt and grime would have built up through use.

Genuine netsuke
This netsuke was carved and signed by Rio (Kawara). The ivory has a good patina and the details are consistently finely carved. c1850; $8,000–12,000

Staining has been skilfully applied to highlight details

Himotoshi

The carver's signature is visible

Netsuke holes
The cord was threaded through small holes, or spaces between a leg or tail, which are known as *himotoshi.*

KEY FACTS

- The veins in the ivory will be visible upon close inspection.
- Ivory is usually cold to the touch and feels heavy.
- The details should be finely carved.
- Sepia staining is apparent.
- Wear and dirt will be visible in the places where it is expected.

Kwangu on horse
The carver has cleverly adapted the shape of a stag antler to create this netsuke. $20,000–25,000

Monkey and baby
The carver of this whimsical netsuke, Kaigyokusai Masatsugu, is very well known. c1870; $30,000–35,000

Monkey trainer
All parts of Japanese life and culture were captured by netsuke artists. 18th century; L:5cm (2in); $2,000–3,000

Shishi dog
Used to ward off evil spirits, shishi dogs are typical of the mythical animals portrayed. 18th century; L:4.5cm (1³⁄₄in); $2,500–3,500

OKIMONO

Netsuke became sought after as souvenirs, and then as works of art, after Japan was opened to the West during the mid- to late 19th century. This demand led many netsuke carvers to produce similar, larger wood and ivory sculptures, known as *okimono*. These were also displayed in the *tokonoma*, the display alcove in a traditional Japanese home. Themes used were the same as for netsuke, with many illustrating traditional Japanese myths, characters, or activities. Values are based on the artist, age, and size of the sculpture, and on the complexity of the carving. Chisel marks have the same appeal to the collector as brushstrokes in a painting, although *okimono* made for export are usually smooth.

Japanese *okimono*
This ivory fisherman is well carved with plenty of detail. c1900; H: 14in (35cm); $3,500–5,000

Fake netsuke

As values and demand from tourists grew toward the end of the 19th century, netsuke began to be faked. Well-carved ivory or wood modern examples have a value of their own, but most fakes are made of molded resin. These typically have poorly defined details, with a rounded, not crisp, feel. Staining or dirt may have been applied, but this may be in the wrong places and not consistent with the details or wear and tear. Most do not have holes, and where holes do appear, they are drilled in a uniform size and show no signs of wear through use.

KEY CLUES

- Uniform pale creamy color with no signs of a patina.
- Lack of the fine lines seen on ivory.
- Where lines are seen, they are uniformly parallel, indicating an early plastic.
- Warm to the touch, and often a light weight.

Molded resin netsuke
This fake netsuke bears many hallmarks of resin examples, most obviously a uniform pale creamy color. c1995; H: 3in (7cm); $4–6

Staining
The staining is a dirty brown color and has been applied haphazardly. The turtle's feet are crudely rendered.

The detailing is poor and inconsistent, and is not suggestive of proper wear

Resin owl
Although the stain is applied better than on the turtle (right), the color shows this to be a resin fake. H: 1¼in (3.5cm); $4–6

Resin turtle
The poor stain application indicates that this is a later fake. L: 3in (7.5cm); $4–6

Flat base
Lines on the base are parallel, a sign of an early plastic.

Samplers

UNTIL THE INVENTION OF the sewing machine in the mid-19th century, all cloth was sewn by hand. Needlework skills were important, and wealthy women put examples of their favorite stitches and motifs together on a single cloth known as a sampler. Women helped girls create these useful needlework guides and, to make the lessons more interesting, they arranged the stitches and motifs in attractive compositions. Letters and numbers were added to sampler designs in the 17th and 18th centuries, charting the rise in education. Girls made their first sampler with the alphabet and numbers at the age of six. In their early teens they produced a more complex sampler.

Outstanding samplers

Ideally, samplers should include the name and age of the embroiderer and the date she completed the project. They should be embroidered with the letters of the alphabet, numbers 1 to 10, and a verse from a religious text or a short rhyme. There should be a main focal image—in the mid-18th century, this was usually Adam and Eve; in the early 19th, the girl's home. This should be surrounded by visually exciting motifs and a decorative border that ties the composition together.

The composition is well balanced

The borders are formed by flowers growing from ornamental urns

The verse reads: When youth's soft season shall be over/ And scenes of childhood charm no more/ My riper year with joy shall see/ This proof of infant industry

KEY CLUES

- Sentimental verses are more desirable than religious.
- The different elements of the design should be balanced and create an attractive whole.
- The name of a school or a teacher adds collectability.
- Embroidered text that touches on current affairs such as the abolition of slavery enhances value.

Scottish sampler
Imaginative and unusual details, like the ship *Neptain* here, which reflect their maker's life stories are in demand. c1800; $2,500–3,500

George I sampler
This English sampler features heraldic imagery and the biblical story of Elijah and the ravens. 1720; $7,000–10,000

Sophisticated sampler
A shepherdess and her flock grace the margins. Fine stitching and fresh colors enhance desirability. 1789; $35,000–50,000

Early 19th-century sampler
From its enchanting verse to the charming house, this sampler contains the classic components. Signed Lucy Parham 1822; $20,000–25,000

WATCH OUT!
Gold and silver thread were sometimes used, especially for raised stitches. Only the very wealthy would have been able to afford these threads and so the value of the sampler will be higher.

BAND SAMPLERS

The oldest surviving samplers from the 16th and 17th century are called band samplers (spot samplers in the US). Motifs and stitches were arranged across the surface—some upside down. There are no letters or numbers but sometimes a name and date. Band samplers were not a pretty show of needlework and literacy. Professional needlewomen or rich ladies used them as a record of stitches and designs. Many motifs were adapted from illustrations of plants and animals. Band samplers are long and narrow because they were embroidered on linen woven on narrow looms. Stitches were usually in worked silk—sometimes embellished with gold and silver thread.

English band sampler Samplers this old are scarce. Initialled and dated ML 1611; $15,000–20,000

Dull samplers

There were established conventions that sampler-makers had to adhere to, such as embroidering the letters of the alphabet. The difference between a dull sampler and a great sampler was the spontaneity and creativity with which the maker handled these conventions. No amount of fine needlework will improve the desirability of a routine composition. Assess the quality of a sampler by judging it using the same criteria as a painting. Look for harmonious color combinations, delightful details, and eye-catching images put together in an imaginative and carefully thought-out way.

KEY CLUES

- Pristine samplers are rare but avoid overtly discolored or damaged examples.
- Unless the design is exceptional, it should follow the formula of an alphabet, numerals, verse, and pictorial elements and border.
- Simple samplers with a later date tend to be less desirable than early ones.

The letters are not aligned

The stitches have faded

Mid-19th-century sampler
The later date, weak composition, religious verse, and poor condition detract from this sampler's value. Signed and dated Elizabeth Reamer, 1838; $1,000–1,500

Religious verses are not as highly prized by collectors

Pennsylvanian sampler
This lively and colorful sampler is attractive but would fetch a higher price if it included a verse. 1807; $5,000–7,000

New Jersey sampler
The striking naïve house motif lifts what is otherwise an ordinary needlework exercise. 1827; $1,500–2,000

English sampler
Designs dominated by lengthy devotional text are less desirable to collectors, reflected in the value. 1821; $350–450

New England sampler
Exposure to sunlight has bleached the once vivid embroidery to pastel shades, which lowers its value. c1810; $2,000–2,500

The lineup
Quilts

FROM THE FAR EAST to Europe, quilts have been admired for their craftsmanship and designs as well as their warmth. Most quilts combine three main techniques. In the first, quilting, tiny stitches in elaborate patterns hold layers of fabric together. Wholecloth quilts, with their solid colored or single patterned tops and bottoms, are put together with this technique. The second, appliqué, is where fabric motifs and patches are sewn to the top of quilts. The third is piecing, where pieces of fabric are sewn together to form a quilt. Patchwork patterns like log cabin—strips of fabric stitched together to form squares— are a good example of piecing. Quilters refer to units of design on quilt tops, like log cabin pattern squares, as blocks.

JARGON BUSTER
Cheater's cloth Printed to look like patchwork, cheater's cloth was used by some as a backing or border in the mid- to late 19th century.

Appliqué rosettes give a sense of movement

Wreath quilt made in Ephrata, Lancaster County, Pennsylvania. c1900; $5,000–7,000

Mennonite wreath quilts, US

Mennonites are a Christian sect who live simply and piously. Their principles regarding dress, home decoration, and modern technology are similar to those of the Amish. Like the Amish they are renowned for their quilts.

- Collectors prize Mennonite quilts for their brilliant colors.
- Their fine, detailed quilting is also desirable.

Missing border reduces value

Floral chintz printed in Jouy or Beautiran

Floral chintz probably printed in Jouy

Madras cotton

Tree of Life quilt. 18th century; ££7,000–10,000

Tree of Life quilts, India

In the 17th and 18th century Indian chintz panels decorated with a tree of life, also known as palampores, were all the rage for bedcovers.

- The tree of life might be painted or hand-printed.
- These luxurious imports were so popular they inspired appliqué copies made from scraps of precious chintz, called *broderie perse* quilts.

Boutis quilt, probably Provençal. c1798; $700–1,000

Boutis quilts, France

Boutis quilts are a type of wholecloth quilt made of two layers of fabric with cord inserted in between the backing and the top to raise select areas of quilted design. Trapunto is another name for this quilting technique.

- Boutis quilts were a Provençal speciality.
- A special boxwood needle used to insert the cord is called a *boutis* in Provence.

Provençal quilt. Late 18th century; $1,700–2,000

Provençal quilts, France

Provence has been a quilting center since the mid-17th century, exporting around Europe.

- Typical Provençal quilts, like the one above, have padding between the top and bottom.
- They were made in solid colors or chintz—a printed cotton.
- 18th-century European chintz was inspired by Indian originals.

Border of swags and sawtooth *Compass pattern*

This pattern is also known as Trip Around the World

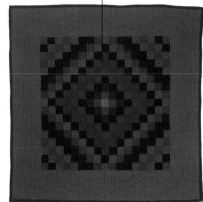

Quaker album quilt, Patterson/Regester family of Delaware, Chester county, Pennsylvania. c1850; $15,000–20,000

Album quilts, US

Album quilts are pieced together from individually decorated blocks. They were made to commemorate events like a marriage or as a farewell present for friends moving out West.

- Appliquéd with flowers, sometimes figures, animals, buildings, and fraternal symbols.
- Many were worked on by several quilters and embroidered with their signatures.
- Album quilts often feature green and red motifs on a white ground.

Mariner's Compass quilt probably Pennsylvania German or from New Jersey. c1845; $10,000–15,000

Mariner's Compass quilts, US

A pinnacle of the quilter's art, the Mariner's Compass pattern is in demand. It is also called Sunburst or Chips and Whetstones pattern.

- Great skill is required to piece or appliqué the main circular motifs from triangular fabric scraps and keep them pointy.
- The compasses should appear to pulsate—the hallmark of a desirable quilt.
- As this pattern is difficult to make, it is also hard to find.

Amish crib quilt in Sunshine and Shadows pattern. Mid-20th century; $2,000–2,500

Amish crib quilts, US

Amish women used sewing machines to stitch the fabric together and bind the edges of a quilt. However, they always hand-stitched the layers of quilting together.

- Crib and other miniature quilts are rare and command a premium.
- To tell a true crib or miniature quilt from one cut from a larger example, check that the design is to the correct scale and that any border is in proportion.

This quilt is pieced with Oxford shirting scraps and dyed with Turkey red

Wool Crazy quilts usually have more restrained designs and embroidery than silk and velvet Crazy quilts

North country strip quilt. c1900; $100–150

Strip quilts, UK

Strip quilts were assembled from long shapes, and were popular in the North of England.

- Strip quilts were often thriftily produced from recycled material.
- They were intended as everyday quilts rather than artistic heirlooms.
- Turkey red (a widely available dye) was used for home dyeing in the 19th century.

Pennsylvania wool quilt. c1880; $7,000–10,000

Crazy quilts, US

Fashionable in the late 19th century, Crazy quilts were pieced from irregular patches of fabrics like satin and velvet and embroidered.

- Pennsylvanian quilters are known for their wool-patched versions of Crazy quilts.
- In comparison with examples made of other materials, patches on Wool Crazy quilts are less haphazardly combined.

Quilt, Barrien County, Michigan. c1864; $60,000–75,000

Civil War quilts, US

Margaret Hazzard decorated this Album quilt with local buildings and gave it to her husband as a reminder of home when he joined the Union army in 1864. Within months he was dead and the quilt was returned to Margaret.

- The poignant history is supported by evidence from the local historical society.
- The detailed provenance enhances value.

Treen

SINCE MEDIEVAL TIMES, wood has been used to make domestic objects. Today, these small items are called treen. Although most were functional, they were also decorative but their beauty also lies in their simplicity and the form, feel, and figuring of the wood. Carved and turned decoration is sought after. Look for well-proportioned forms and figured wood. Condition and patination are important, as are original carved decoration, dates, initials, and mottoes. Many early pieces were hollowed by hand, and gouge marks can be seen. The most popular woods in the early 17th century were beech, elm, and chestnut; in the late 17th century, yew, sycamore, alder, and fruitwoods were also used. In the early 18th century, pine, boxwood, and maple became popular. And, by the second quarter of the 18th century, lignum vitae, ebony, teak, and mahogany were also prevalent.

The wood is inlaid with pewter

Shoe snuffbox. c1760; L: 3³/₄in (9.5cm); $800–1,000

Dutch snuffbox

By the mid-18th century, snuff taking was a growing habit among wealthy Europeans.

- The shoe is a symbol within Freemasonry and Judaic customs. Shoe-shaped boxes are often decorated with Masonic symbols.
- In the Bible, the shoe symbolizes the earthly in contrast with the holy—a shoe-shaped snuffbox was a reminder that snuff taking was a vice.

Glass eyes and intricate carving are a sign of quality

The man's exposed bottom adds humor

Glass eyes and ivory buttons indicate high quality

Fruitwood snuffbox. Mid-18th century; W: 3¹/₂in (8.5cm); $3,500–5,000

English snuffboxes

Early boxes were made of precious materials. As snuff taking became more widespread, so the fashion for wooden boxes grew.

- Treen boxes were often designed as a clever joke: a box shaped as a double-headed man, depicting good and evil, was proof that the owner knew snuff could be addictive.

Carved coquilla nut snuffbox. c1790; H: 4in (10cm); $1,000–1,500

French snuffboxes

The coquilla is a feather-leaved plant from Brazil. The nut has a thick, hard shell, which is ideal for carving. Once carved, the shell resembles boxwood.

- French craftsmen were renowned for coquilla nut carvings, which included snuffboxes, thimble holders, and perfume flasks.

THE SHAKERS

A religious sect renowned for their craftsmanship, Shakers based their designs on function, economy, and proportion. Their work was executed to the best of their ability and any decoration was in the construction: for example, the joinery was left visible. Shakers made furniture, wooden boxes, sewing accessories, and household items such as brooms. Most pieces were made from local timber such as maple or oak.

Oval maple and pine four-finger box

The chrome-yellow finish is original, with a later blue cloth fitted interior with sewing items. 19th century; $20,000–25,000

Lid and thumbrest carved with a lion

JARGON BUSTER

Treen Broadly, *"treen"* means "from the tree." The word was created by the author Edward Pinto for his 1969 book *Treen and other Wooden Bygones.*

Turned fruitwood goblet. Late 18th century; H: 7in (18cm); $500–900

Peg tankard. Late 18th century; H: 7½in (19cm); $2,000–2,500

Snuffbox carved with image of three Jewish peddlers, made in Alsace. c1800; L: 4in (10cm); $1,200–1,800

English goblets

Many pieces of treen were carved by journeymen—craftsmen who had completed their apprenticeship but were not ready or able to start their own business. Instead, they often traveled from town to town working for different employers to gain experience.

- One of the skills craftsmen learned was to carve wood by turning it on a lathe to create a symmetrical shape.

Scandinavian tankards

Tankards could be made from wood, horn, ceramic, or silver. In Scandinavia, wood had a similar status to precious metals.

- Wooden tankards were usually made in traditional shapes with carved decoration.
- Peg tankards are communal drinking vessels with a series of pegs inside marking off equal measures. Each drinker would down a "peg" and pass the tankard to the next person.

French snuffboxes

Judaica—items made for Jewish ceremonies or decorated with symbols or images related to Judaism—are highly collectable.

- As well as ritual objects, Judaica include snuff and other boxes decorated with Hebrew inscriptions, scenes from the Old Testament, or naturalistic fruit, birds, and flowers.

Signed by John Conger, an accomplished carver who designed the New York State coat of arms

Walnut cake mold, carved with a Hessian soldier with rifle and flower. c1835; L: 6in (15cm); $1,500–2,000

South German baking mold. 19th century; H: 13½in (33.5cm); $200–300

Black Forest nutcracker in the form of a dog c1870; H: 4in (10cm); $1,200–1,800

American cake molds

Cakes such as shortbread were made using a firm mixture, which was pressed into a mold and turned out before being baked.

- The wooden molds were carved with motifs, including religious figures, animals, and birds.
- Most cake molds were unsigned. A mold signed by a well-known maker is rare.

European cake molds

Central European cake molds were often decorated with traditional folk art motifs.

- Hearts, tulips, and flowers were love symbols.
- Love tokens were made by young men for a sweetheart. If she liked him she would show off and use the token; if not she returned it. Once married, the couple kept the token.

Nutcrackers

Nuts were a popular snack and many people carried a supply and a nutcracker with them.

- Carved wooden nutcrackers were made from hardwoods such as box and yew and featured a screw or lever action.
- They were often carved in novelty shapes and might also be marked with initials and a date.

The interrogation
Costume jewelry settings

JEWELRY HAS BEEN an adornment since the earliest times. In the 20th century, examples made from non-precious materials became known as costume jewelry, probably because they were often designed to go with the clothes of one fashion season and then be replaced. The settings used are often the same as on precious pieces of the time because, following the Wall Street Crash of 1929, many people were unable to afford "real" jewelry. Jewelry-makers who could not find work with traditional jewelers started to make affordable pieces. Many setting styles were favored by particular makers, which may help to identify the source of an individual piece.

Invisible

The sophisticated invisible setting technique was developed by fine jeweler Van Cleef and Arpels. It was introduced to costume jeweler Trifari by Alfred Philippe, who joined the company as chief designer in 1930. The stones are set so tightly together that sections appear to be made from one large, carved stone instead of many smaller, faceted ones.

Calibre-cut faux rubies and emeralds

Trifari carnation earrings
Invisible setting creates a superb imitation of precious jewelry with faux rubies, diamonds, and emeralds. 1940s; $200–250

Poured glass

Until the early 20th century, the poured glass technique was mainly used to make buttons. Then Maison Gripoix and other manufacturers started to use it to make jewelry for clients such as Chanel. Crushed glass and metal oxides were mixed together before being molded and heated.

The glass sits in a metal wire frame designed as part of the setting

Chanel peacock pin
Poured glass has been used for the peacock feathers, and *pavé*-set (close-set) clear crystal rhinestones decorate the head and body. 1930s; $3,500–5,000

Prong set

One of the most commonly used settings, claw-like metal prongs hold each stone in place. This setting allows as much of the stone as possible to be shown. It was used to good effect by costume jewelers such as Henry Schreiner, who was known for his unconventional combinations of colors and stones.

Inverted stones and unusual colors such as amber and smoky gray are typical of Schreiner

Schreiner flower pin
Prong-set faux moonstones encircle a cluster of prong-set inverted amber rhinestones. The claws do not detract from the beauty of the artificial stones. 1950s; $200–250

DOUBLE CLIP MECHANISM

The clip (a pin worn to accentuate a collar or neckline) was popular in the 1920s. In 1927, the French fine jeweler Louis Cartier developed the double clip mechanism, in which two clips were fastened together and worn as a pin. The US manufacturer Coro created its own version, the Duette, in 1931. Early examples were Art Deco in design and its later figural pieces were a great success.

The bouquets can be worn separately

The frame has a pin fastener

Coro Duette The two enameled silver, red glass, and clear crystal rhinestone bouquets of flowers can be fastened to the frame and worn as a pin. 1930s; $300–500

Each bouquet has a clip fastener that attaches it to clothes and the frame

Hand-wired

Beads are strung onto fine metal wire, which is wound around a metal frame to create the design. Stanley Hagler used hand-wired glass beads and faux pearls to create leaves and petals for his extravagant, three-dimensional jewelry made on shaped, gold-plated filigree backings. The intricacy of the hand-wired sections balanced the boldness of the overall design.

The bracelet is designed to wind around the wrist

Peridot beads

Enameled

First used in ancient Egypt, enamel is a glassy powder placed onto a metal backing and fused by heat. The enamel on costume jewelry is often referred to as "cold" because it was fused at a relatively low temperature. The result tends to be fragile—any damage detracts from the value.

Chipped enamel is virtually impossible to repair

Glued

Flat-backed stones are glued onto a flat surface so that the resulting design is not interrupted by the setting. The technique is often used on affordable ranges, as it is quick and easy to do. However, manufacturers such as Art used it to enhance designs of unusual multicolored stones.

The flowers appear to grow from the stems without a setting

Stanley Hagler bracelet

Five strands of peridot glass beads link two hand-wired flower and leaf motifs, which are made up of beads, peridot glass, and emerald crystal rhinestones. 1960s; $200–250

Trifari plant motif pin

Green and brown enamel are fused onto sterling silver for the leaves. The brooch is decorated with *pavé*-set clear rhinestones. c1940; $2,000–2,500

Art bouquet-of-flowers pin

Colored and Lucite (acrylic plastic) petals are glued onto gilt castings to make flowers, highlighted with glued clear rhinestones. Mid-1950s; $100–150

Costume jewelry

THE COSTUME JEWELRY manufacturers working in the 20th century designed pins that reflected the fashions and materials available as well as their individual style. Many pieces are as beautiful and as well made as precious jewelry. Since they were made in large numbers and to reflect the latest fashions, there are plenty to choose from.

Some designers such as Coco Chanel, Christian Dior, Miriam Haskell, and Elsa Schiaparelli set trends for the rest of the fashion world. Others, including Kenneth Jay Lane and Albert Weiss, made a range of affordable pieces that enabled more people to indulge in high fashion.

With vintage costume jewelry, look out for damage such as missing stones and chipped enamel.

Blue, pink, and clear rhinestones set in gilt metal

Heart-shaped pin. 1950s; L: 1½in (4cm); $200–250

Hobé
The company was founded in New York by the son of a Parisian goldsmith. He used the high standards and techniques of precious jewelry.
- Materials include *vermeil* (gold-plated silver), platinum, pastes, and semi-precious stones.
- Exotic designs and reproductions of historic pieces owned by European royalty.

The rhinestone eyes tremble as the wearer moves

Sun god pin. 1940s; W: 3in (7.5cm); $400–500

Joseff of Hollywood
Eugène Joseff designed jewelry for Hollywood film studios and sold copies to star-struck fans.
- Majority of pieces feature "Russian gold"—a semi-matte copper-gold finish that minimized flare under the studio lights.
- Most pieces are signed but beware bright examples—value plummets if polished.

Rhodium-plated metal with prong and bezel settings

Eisenberg Original fur clip. 1940s; L: 3in (7.5cm); $350–450

Eisenberg
Eisenberg started as a clothing company that made pins to accessorize its dresses. As the pins proved popular they were sold separately.
- Fine materials include Swarovski rhinestones.
- Large pieces are made to bold designs. Early 1940s figural pins are particularly collectable.
- 1930–45 pieces are marked "Eisenberg Original" and after 1945 "Eisenberg Ice."

The colours of the enamels are expertly shaded

Enamel and diamanté pin. c1930; L: 4¼in (10.5cm); $250–400

Boucher
Marcel Boucher learned fine jewelry skills working for Cartier, and his pieces are so well made they are often mistaken for the real thing.
- Innovative designs use exquisite metalwork, rhinestones in cuts and colors that resemble precious stones, and colorful enameling.
- May be marked "MB", "Marboux", "Marcel Boucher", or just "Boucher."

Quality of stones and setting is always striking

Stylized fruit pin. 1962; L: 2½in (6.25cm); $400–500

Dior
Christian Dior's "New Look" transformed fashion after World War II. Jewelry was an integral part of his collections.
- Early pieces were made in small numbers for particular outfits or clients.
- Later pieces made under license in greater numbers, with unusual pastes and stones.
- Most pieces are signed and dated.

Classic 1950s design set with simulated pearls and diamanté

Pearls are attached to a gilt metal chain

Gold-plated brass forms a frame for the petals and leaves

Flower pin. 1990s; L: 3¼in (8.25cm); $350–450

Maison Gripoix

The Gripoix family has made poured glass jewelry under its own name and for fashion houses Chanel and Dior since the mid-1920s.

- The company's skill with the poured glass technique means it can create both subtle and vibrant colors with varying degrees of translucency and opacity.
- Pieces from the early 1990s onward are marked *Histoire de Verre*.

Feather pin. 1950s; L: 3in (7.5cm); $200–250

Schiaparelli

Elsa Schiaparelli founded a fashion house in Paris in the early 1920s. Her range included costume jewelry, which was quirky or highly stylized. From the 1950s, she was based in New York and made abstract or floral jewelry designs using colorful stones and glass.

- Early pieces are usually unsigned; later pieces are signed.
- Fakes have been produced.

Pearl and rhinestone pin. c1950; L: 3in (7.5cm); $350–450

Haskell

Miriam Haskell helped to make costume jewelry as prestigious as and more fashionable than fine jewelry.

- Components include fake pearls and *roses montées*—flat-backed rhinestones in clusters.
- Innovative and complex hand-wired pieces created by a team of designers.
- Missing rhinestones and damaged pearls substantially detract from the value.

Amethyst glass cabochons set in sterling silver

French jet cabochons

Antiqued gold tone setting

Aurora borealis rhinestones

Dragon pin. Late 1960s; W: 2½in (6.5cm); $200–250

Kenneth Jay Lane

Bright, bold, elegant, and affordable designs. Lane began making jewelry in 1963. Pieces made up to the late 1970s are most collectable.

- Distinctive combinations of materials and re-interpretations of traditional styles.
- Stones show exceptional depth of color.
- Signature before 1970 is "K.J.L."; after 1970 "Kenneth Jay Lane" or "Kenneth Lane."

Topaz & amber rhinestone pin. 1950s; L: 2½in (6.25cm); $100–150

Weiss

This highly successful company is renowned for its exquisite floral, foliate, fruit, or figural designs using Austrian crystal rhinestones.

- Convincing reproductions of German smoky quartz crystals known as "black diamonds."
- Stones set in gold and silver alloys may be enameled, or in 1960s japanned (dull black).
- Undervalued for years, prices are going up.

Crown pin. 1940s; L: 2¼in (5.75cm); $350–450

Mazer

From late 1927, Joseph and Louis Mazer made affordable, convincing simulations of precious jewelry. In 1946, Joseph set up his own company, marking most of its work "Jomaz."

- Floral, foliate, or ribbon designs are set with faux pearls and Austrian crystal rhinestones.
- Stones are in sophisticated cuts and settings.
- Pieces remain relatively affordable.

Manufactur·
de S. M. Impératric·
P.L. DAGOTY
A PARIS

COMPOSIT

TE PHOTOS

Composite photos
Wood types

MANY DIFFERENT WOODS WERE USED to make furniture, often in combination. Oak, walnut, and mahogany, in chronological order are most common. Different woods are used for different parts, depending on their hardness, the size of the original plank, and even the original cost. For example, box is a slow-growing tree and yields smaller, narrower sections of wood. Bear in mind that the color or appearance of a wood may differ depending on how it has been cut and finished. The patina of years of use will also often change the color.

Amboyna   Beech

Coromandel   Ebony   Ebony   Elm   Elm

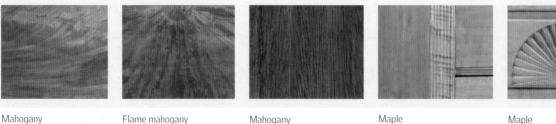

Mahogany   Flame mahogany   Mahogany   Maple   Maple

Oak   Olive   Pearwood   Pine   Pine

Sycamore   Walnut   Walnut   Walnut   Walnut

Birch	Birch	Calamander	Cherry	Chestnut
Burr elm	Harewood (marquetry)	Harewood (parquetry)	Harewood	Kingwood
Bird's eye maple	Burr maple	Tiger maple	Tiger maple	Oak
Rosewood	Rosewood	Rosewood	Satinwood	Satinwood
Walnut	Burr walnut	Virginia walnut	Yew	Burr yew

Composite photos
Pediments

PEDIMENTS ARE USED TO DECORATE the tops of storage furniture such as highboys, wardrobes, and bookcases. Regional and national styles were influenced by fashion and materials. Shaped pediments often feature carved decorations, including finials. Flat-topped pediments, with plainer, molded decoration, were often used to display ceramics and other ornaments. A pediment with a break at the top of the triangle of the arch is called an "open" pediment; one with a break in the base of the triangle is known as a "broken" pediment.

Architectural
Russia
Late 17th century

Architectural
Sweden
Late 17th century

Molded overhanging
England
c1720

Open-arched with finial
England
c1725

Bow-shaped molded
England
c1725

Open-arched with carved
bust and cresting
Germany
c1725

Scrolled with carved crest
and cresting
Denmark
Mid-18th century

Cyma reversa arch with
carved crest
Germany
c1760–70

Bow-shaped
Denmark
c1760

Pierced cresting with scrolled swan-neck
and pinnacles
England
c1765

Open segment with finials
England
Late 18th century

Bow-shaped with carved
crests
South Africa
1780–90

Swan-neck bonnet-top with
fretwork, carved crest, and
finials, Philadelphia
Late 18th century

Swan-neck bonnet-top with
finial
US
Late 18th century

Open-arched with bust
Boston
Mid-19th century

Carved cresting with finials
North Germany
Mid-19th century

Carved domed cresting with
mythological beast finials
France
Late 19th century

Medallion with stepped
scrolls and urn finials
Britain
c1890

Stepped molded arch with
tower finials
Italy
Late 19th century

Renaissance Revival open-
arch with figural carvings
France
Late 19th century

Domed
Germany
Early 18th century

Architectural
Germany
Early 18th century

Queen Anne double-domed
England
c1715

Ogee arched with carved
shell
England
c1720

Center-domed with flanking
scrolls
Austria
18th century

Bow-shaped carved
France
c1730

Rhineland overhanging
molded with floral, foliate,
and cherub carvings in relief
Germany, 18th century

Double-arched with finials
Venice
c1735

Arched and scrolled with
carved crest and finials
Rome
c1740

Double-domed
The Netherlands
Mid-18th century

Swan-neck bonnet-top with
finials
Massachusetts
c1775

Swan-neck
Germany
Late 18th century

Swan-neck bonnet-top with
carved crest
Philadelphia
c1770

Open-arched with finials
Philadelphia
c1775

Swan-neck bonnet-top with
finials
US
Late 18th century

Closed and carved scrolled
Britain
1830–37

Closed-scrolled with carving
The Netherlands
19th century

Swan-neck crested with
finials
Britain
Mid-19th century

Molded and stepped flat-top
Britain
c1880

Renaissance Revival carved cresting with
mythological beasts
Germany
Late 19th century

Renaissance Revival carved,
pierced cartouche with finials
Italy
c1880

Renaissance Revival arched and open-arched with
finials
Italy
c1880

Composite photos
Handles

HANDLES SHOULD FIT stylistically with the piece they are on, and so it is important to compare the style to make sure they match. They were often replaced to follow fashion: check to see whether they are original. A handle that has been in place for decades will be covered with a layer of dirt and grease, which will appear as darker patches in crevices and around the edges. Any moving rings or pulls may have marked the wood. There may be marks from old handles on the front of a piece and plugged holes where they were removed on the back.

Brass baluster drop, round backplate
England, early 18th century

Brass baluster drop, round backplate
England, early 18th century

Régence Rococo
South-west France
Early 18th century

Régence Rococo
Paris
Early 18th century

Louis XIV Rococo
France
Early 18th century

Régence Rococo
Paris
Early 18th century

Régence Rococo
France
Early 18th century

Rococo swan-neck
France
Mid-18th century

Swan-neck
France
Mid-18th century

Swan-neck
France
Mid-18th century

Rococo
France
Mid-18th century

Swan-neck
France
Mid-18th century

Solid backplate
England
Early 18th century

Pierced backplate
England
Mid-18th century

Shaped brass batwing
Pennsylvania
Mid-18th century

Large batwing brass
backplate, Philadelphia
Late 18th century

Brass backplate
England
Late 18th century

Stirrup
England
Late 17th century

Squared
Germany
Mid-18th century

Louis XVI plain squared
France
Late 18th century

Brass swan-neck
England
Late 18th century

Silvered swag
England
Late 18th century

William & Mary brass drop, shaped backplate
US, c1710

Arts & Crafts brass drop, shaped backplate
Britain, c1895

Art Deco split-tail silvered metal drop
France, c1925

Art Deco silvered metal drop
France
c1930s

Louis XIV Rococo swan-neck
Paris
c1710

Louis XV Rococo foliate double handles
Paris, mid-18th century

Louis XV ormolu foliate
France
Mid-18th century

Brass swan-neck
England
Mid-18th century

Colonial Rococo silver
Portugal
Mid-18th century

Foliate and pierced ruffled C-scroll
France, mid-18th century

Foliate curved
Philadelphia
Late 18th century

Rococo
Sweden
Late 18th century

Rococo swan-neck
Britain
Early 20th century

Engraved backplate
England
Early 18th century

Brass batwing backplate
US
Early 18th century

Brass stamped backplate
Britain
Early 20th century

Brass stamped backplate
Britain
Early 20th century

Arts & Crafts
Gustav Stickley, US
Early 20th century

Arts & Crafts
Gustav Stickley, US
Early 20th century

Arts & Crafts
L. & J. G. Stickley, US
Early 20th century

Federal brass swan-neck
US
Late 18th century

Neoclassical squared drop
Italian states
Early 19th century

Brass sunk campaign
Britain
Early 19th century

Squared, flush fitted campaign, Britain
Early 19th century

Squared
France
19th century

Composite photos
Handles

Arts & Crafts squared
Anglo-Japanese engraved
Britain, late 19th century

Sheraton Revival squared,
brass swan-neck
Britain, late 19th century

Arts & Crafts squared, iron
Scotland
Early 20th century

Chippendale embossed oval
Pennsylvania, US
Late 18th century

Federal oval embossed with
fox brass, Pennsylvania, US
Late 18th century

Transitional Louis XV/XVI
ring
France, c1774

Louis XVI ring
France
Late 18th century

Neoclassical ring
France
Late 18th century

Circular lion's head and ring
England
Late 18th century

Sheraton floral embossed
and ring, Scotland
Late 18th century

George III circular lion's
head and ring
Britain, c1800

Regency leopard's head and
ring
Britain, c1810

George III pull
Britain
c1810

Turned mahogany
Scotland
Early 19th century

Federal turned tiger maple
US
c1820

Art Deco chrome button
US
c1940

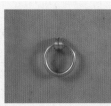

Mid-century Modern
bronze ring, France
c1948

Mid-century Modern
brushed chrome and black
enameled wood, US, c1950

Mid-century Modern
Domed circular brass
US, c1950

Mid-century Modern
Circular brass
US, mid-20th century

Art Nouveau, gilt-bronze
water lily
France, c1900

Art Nouveau gilt-bronze leaf
France
c1900

Art Nouveau bronze tendrils
Belgium
c1894

Art Nouveau gilt-bronze
floral
France, c1905

Art Deco brass scroll,
France
1930s

Sheraton stepped oval
England
Late 18th century

Federal oval embossed with
bust of George Washington
US, late 18th century

Federal oval embossed rope
twist motif
US, late 18th century

George III Neoclassical oval
England
Late 18th century

George II gilt ring
England
c1730

Neoclassical ring, embossed
Empress Maria Theresa bust
Germany, late 18th century

Neoclassical ring, embossed
Prince of Wales feathers
England, late 18th century

Neoclassical lion's head and
ring, England
Late 18th century

Neoclassical rosette and
ring, England
Late 18th century

Neoclassical escutcheon and
ring
France, 18th century

Neoclassical Revival ring
Britain
c1840

Lobed carved mahogany
Scotland
c1840

Arts & Crafts stamped brass
with ring
Britain, late 19th century

Louis XVI-style circular, gilt-
bronze floral
US, early 20th century

Art Deco pyramidal gilt
bronze
US, c1930s

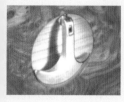

Contemporary cast bronze
inset into wood
Britain, c2000

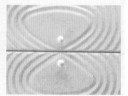

Contemporary carved wood
US
c2000

Regency twisted textured
metal
Britain, c1810

Art Nouveau gilt-bronze leaf
and berry
France, c1905

Art Nouveau gilt-bronze
water lily
France, c1900

Art Deco chromium plated
France
c1930

Art Deco wooden band
France
1930s

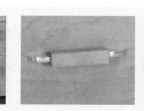

Art Deco wood and metal
US
c1939

Mid-century Modern steel
US
c1946

Postmodern carved wood
Italy
c1960

Composite photos
Chair backs

CHAIR STYLES have evolved through the centuries with shapes from previous eras often revived or inspiring later fashions. Chair backs such as those of the French 18th-century Louis XV style were copied internationally while, in the early 19th century, the French Empire style inspired similar designs in the US, Germany, Russia, and Sweden. As a result, it is important to be able to distinguish national characteristics. The style revivals of the late 19th century exaggerated earlier shapes so look at proportions, wear, and construction to help date a chair.

Barley twist stiles with scroll work and acorn finials
England, 17th century

Yorkshire pattern with lobed and carved rails
England, 17th century

Louis XV-style ladder with salamander slats
Canada, mid-18th century

Lancashire ladder
England
Late 18th century

Windsor spindle with ram's horn cresting
England, c1750

Windsor spindle with ring-and-vase stiles, Pennsylvania
Early 19th century

Windsor spindle bow-back
Mid-Atlantic States
Early 19th century

Embossed and painted leather
Portugal, c1720

George I curved with vase-shaped splat and scrolled top rail, England, c1720

Vase-shaped splat with hooped and scrolled stiles
Chinese Export, c1730

George II pierced and carved giltwood shell splat with scrolled stiles, England, c1740

George II pierced splat with carved shell motifs
England, c1740

Queen Anne vase-shaped splat, Northern Coastal States, c1750

Queen Anne vase-shaped splat with shell cresting
Maryland, c1765

Chippendale vase-shaped splat with shell cresting
Philadelphia, c1770

Chippendale pierced and carved splat
England, c1760

Chippendale pierced vase-shaped strapwork splat
England, c1760

Chippendale Cockpen
England
c1765

Chippendale Gothic
England
c1775

Chippendale ladder
England
c1780

Hepplewhite shield-back
England
c1780

Hepplewhite shield-back with reeded splats
England, c1780

194

William and Mary caned with
S-scroll and shell crestings
England, 17th century

Colonial split-banister and
crown crest with inverted
heart, North America, c1730

Colonial banister with pierced
and shaped crest, North
America, mid-18th century

Late Colonial spindle
North America
Mid-18th century

Late Colonial ladder
North America
Mid-18th century

Windsor rod with raised
comb, Canada
Early 19th century

Windsor hoop spindle with
pierced splat
Britain, mid-19th century

Queen Anne with vase-
shaped splat
England, c1710

Queen Anne with solid splat
and shell-carved cresting
Philadelphia, US, c1760

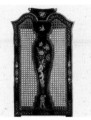

Late Italian Baroque vase-
shaped splat, caned panels
Italy, early 18th century

George II baluster splat with
acanthus carving
England, c1740

Solid vase-shaped marquetry
splat, The Netherlands
Mid-18th century

Chinese export solid vase-
shaped splat with armorial
inlay, China, mid-18th century

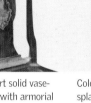

Colonial solid vase-shaped
splat, Cape of Good Hope
Mid-18th century

Rococo-style pierced vase-
shaped splat
Peru, mid-18th century

Chippendale with volute-
carved strapwork splat
Philadelphia, c1760

Chippendale pierced splat
with leaf-scroll carving
England, late 18th century

Chippendale pierced splat
with serpentine top rail
Philadelphia, c1765

Chippendale pierced vase-
shaped splat
England, c1770

HEPPLEWHITE HORNS

These protrusions were
a misunderstanding of
Hepplewhite's drawings.
The inlay should wrap
around the rail but
some makers thought it
was meant to protrude.

Federal shield-back with
pierced urn-shaped splat
Philadelphia, US, c1790

Federal Hepplewhite with
Hepplewhite horns (see box)
Philadelphia, US, c1800

Solid carved shield-back
with pierced centre
Germany, late 18th century

Baroque Revival tooled
leather, carved armorial crest
Germany, late 18th century

Composite photos
Chair backs

Late Baroque upholstered
cartouche
Italy, mid-18th century

Late Baroque upholstered
cartouche, South Germany
Mid-18th century

Louis XV upholstered
giltwood cartouche
France, mid-18th century

Rococo upholstered giltwood
cartouche
Germany, mid-18th century

Louis XV upholstered
giltwood cartouche
France, mid-18th century

George III upholstered
giltwood oval
England, c1775

Louis XVI upholstered
giltwood oval
France, c1775

Louis XVI upholstered
giltwood oval
France, c1775

Louis XVI upholstered
rectangular giltwood
France, c1780

Louis XVI upholstered
giltwood oval
France, c1780

Gustavian painted
rectangular with archtop
Sweden, late 18th century

Gustavian painted with
pierced cipher (GS) splat
Sweden, late 18th century

Gustavian painted oval with
pierced vase-shaped splat
Sweden, late 18th century

French Hepplewhite-style
umbrella with floral
medallion, England, c1785

George III molded oval with
carved splats
England, c1785

TRAFALGAR CHAIRS

One of the most idiosyncratic chairs of the Regency
period is the Trafalgar chair. It is characterized by a
back rail with cable- or rope-molding and appeared
about the time of Nelson's victory over Napoleon. It
was popular from 1805 until well into the 1820s.

Regency Gothic arched with
lancet and pierced frieze
Britain, c1810

Regency painted spoon with
incised gilt decoration
Britain, c1815

Late Federal cornucopia and
fruit basket carved rail with
scrolled stiles, US, c1815

Rope top rail above
inlaid panel

Bar back and rope twist
lower rail

Regency painted with
pierced diaper-pattern splat
Britain, c1820

George IV carved and painted
crescent above curved stiles
and splat, Britain, c1830

George IV cartouche with
reeded swags and scrolled
cresting, Britain, c1830

Rococo upholstered giltwood
cartouche
Germany, mid-18th century

Rococo caned cartouche
Italy
Mid-18th century

Louis XV upholstered
giltwood
France, c1760

George III upholstered
giltwood oval
England, c1770

George III upholstered,
painted, gilded cartouche
England, late 18th century

Gustavian upholstered and
painted oval
Sweden, c1790

Gustavian upholstered and
painted rectangular
Sweden, late 18th century

Louis XVI upholstered
rectangular giltwood
France, c1785

Louis XVI upholstered oval
giltwood with cresting
France, c1785

Neoclassical upholstered,
carved, and painted oval
Italy, late 18th century

George III pierced wheel
Britain
c1800

Neoclassical rectangular
with interlaced oval splats
Italy, early 19th century

George III S- and C-scroll
framed cartouche with
garter star, Britain, c1800

Regency crescent with
carved festoon and C-scrolls
Britain, c1810

Regency lyre splat with
tablet top rail
Britain, c1810

Regency scrolling yoke back,
lobed fan cresting, palmette
pendant, Scotland, c1815

Regency tablet top rail with
ball-mounted C-scroll mid-
rails, Britain, c1820

Empire-style with *demi-lune*
splats
New York, early 19th century

Federal with urn-shaped
splat
US, early 19th century

Regency curved top rail with
carved and pierced mid-rail
Britain, c1820

Sheraton-style bar back with
rosette-centered demi-lune
splat, Boston, c1830

George IV rail back with
twin turned spheres
Britain, c1830

William IV curved and
carved rail back with scrolls
and foliage, Britain, 1830s

Dutch Colonial foliage-
carved curved
The Netherlands, 1830s

Black Forest-style scrolled,
waisted, and pierced
Germany, mid-19th century

Chair backs

Empire trellis splat with
concave crest rail
France, c1800

Empire trophy-of-arms X-
frame with selective gilding
Russia, mid-19th century

Empire shaped top rail with
ormolu mounts
Russia, mid-19th century

Empire spool-turned X-frame
splats with padded backrest
Sweden, mid-19th century

Biedermeier with carved
feather splats and foliage
brackets, Germany, c1825

Openwork crest rail and
back splat
Germany, c1840

Victorian lobed, waisted, and
pierced papier mâché with
gilding, Britain, c1870

Victorian waisted splat with
bow-shaped crest rail
Britain, mid-19th century

Chinese yoke
China
Mid-19th century

Chinese carved asymmetrical
figural and foliate splat
China, mid-19th century

Late Victorian upholstered
shield and columnar stiles
Britain, c1890

Late Victorian upholstered
rectangular with scrolled
crest, Britain, c1890

Victorian carved, waisted
and open with upholstered
splat, Britain, c1870

Victorian upholstered shield,
arched crest, and columnar
stiles, Britain, c1870

Art Nouveau-style pierced
and scrolled with marquetry
medallion, Britain, c1905

Gothic Revival arch with
blind arches and carved
rosette, Britain, c1890

Renaissance Revival figural
and grotesque carvings
Italy, late 19th century

Renaissance Revival carved
and pierced grotesque mask
Britain, c1870

Baroque Revival with leaf-
carved and pierced splat and
crest rail, Britain, c1870

Rococo Revival upholstered
shield, Germany
mid-to late 19th century

Classical Revival carved
shield, Britain
c1860

Chippendale Revival
strapwork with foliate crest
Britain, c1900

Classical Revival lyre
Britain
Late 19th century

Empire Style upholstered
rectangular
Germany, c1880

Mooresque with stylized urn
and flowers
Italy, late 19th century

Biedermeier H-frame with
yoke crest rail
Germany, c1825

Biedermeier stylized and
painted feather splats
Germany, c1835

Biedermeier with central
lozenge splat
Germany, c1835

Biedermeier with palmette
splat
Germany, c1835

Classical Revival scrolling
foliage X-frame with caned
crest rail, Germany, c1840

Rococo Revival pierced,
carved, and upholstered
cartouche, New York, c1855

Victorian spoon with pierced
and scrolled splat
Britain, c1870

Victorian shaped balloon
Britain
c1870

Victorian upholstered oval
with cartouche and husk
cresting, Scotland, c1870

Victorian upholstered
medallion within leaf-carved
oval, Britain, c1870

Late Victorian oval with
pierced and carved vase and
wings splat, Britain, c1890

Gothic Revival Gothic arches
with pierced quatrefoil
New York, c1870

Gothic Revival upholstered
splat and ogee-arch crest
rail, Britain, 1870

Gothic Revival carved with
crockets, cross, and spire
finials, Britain, c1880

Gothic Revival pointed arch,
fleur de lys above, chamfered
columns, Britain, c1890

Rococo Revival upholstered,
carved and pierced giltwood
France, late 19th century

The Aesthetic movement The credo of the Aesthetic
movement, which flourished in the 1870s and 80s, was
"Art for Art's sake": that art and beauty should be
pursued for their own sake. The designers who were
inspired by it had grown tired of the over-cluttered
Victorian interiors. A huge influence on the movement
was the re-emergence of Japan from years of self-
imposed exile. One of the best-known designers in the
style was E. W. Godwin, who adapted Japanese

decorative and architectural elements into his Anglo-
Japanese furniture, which was often ebonized to
resemble Oriental lacquer furniture.

Designs were mainly symmetrical arrangements of
horizontal and vertical lines, and decoration was
restrained. Cheaper furniture was produced by applying
decorative Japanese fretwork to standard shapes.
Higher quality examples featured embossed-leather
panels or sections of carved boxwood or marquetry.

Grotto style
Italy
Late 19th century

*Japonaiserie lattice splats
Britain, late 19th century*

*Beaded top rail, upholstered
Britain, late 19th century*

*Diaper ebonized back
Britain, late 19th century*

*Ladderback with panel
Italy, c1890*

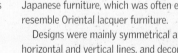

Composite photos
Chair backs

Arts & Crafts vertical back
slats, C. F. A. Voysey
England, c1895

Arts & Crafts fixed back
Gustav Stickley
US, c1900

Arts & Crafts with "V" rail
Gustav Stickley
US, c1901

Arts & Crafts inlaid discs over
elongated fretwork, George
Walton, Scotland, c1900s

Arts & Crafts spindle
L. & J. G. Stickley
US, c1900

Arts & Crafts ladder
Britain
Late 19th century

Jugendstil padded with birch
frame
Sweden, c1900

Art Nouveau padded with
vertical splats
Scotland, c1900

Art Nouveau curved top rail
with tall spindle filled back,
Harry Napper, England, 1890s

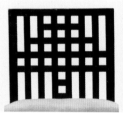

Art Nouveau tree-form back
slats, Charles Rennie
Mackintosh, Scotland, 1904

Art Nouveau bentwood
J. Hoffmann for J. & J. Kohn,
Austria, early 20th century

Art Nouveau bentwood
Austria
c1910

Art Nouveau padded, arched
mahogany frame, Bruno Paul
Germany, 1901

Art Nouveau padded, wooden
"handle," R. Riemerschmid,
Germany, c1905

Art Nouveau oak solid, cutout
heart, R. Riemerschmid
Germany, c1905

Art Deco latticed
Paul Frankl
US, 1920s

Mid-century Modern
fiberglass shell "RAR"
C. & R. Eames, US, 1948–50

Mid-century Modern "Jason"
Carl Jacobs
England, 1950

Mid-century Modern
Charles & Ray Eames
US, early 1950s

Mid-century Modern "Ant"
Arne Jacobsen
Denmark, 1951–52

Mid-century Modern "Heart"
Verner Panton
Denmark, 1959

Postmodern "First"
Michele de Lucchi for
Memphis, Italy, 1983

Postmodern molded plywood
"Sheraton"
Robert Venturi, US, 1984

Postmodern "Garriri"
Javier Mariscal
Spain, 1988

Contemporary laminated wood
"Powerplay," Frank O. Gehry,
US, 1990–1992

Arts & Crafts pierced
lozenge panel, Hans Ofner
Austria, c1910

Arts & Crafts tall, carved,
and panelled
Britain, c1900

Arts & Crafts shaped top rail,
vertical splats, J. M. Olbrich
Germany, late 19th century

Arts & Crafts inlaid top rail
and back splats
Britain, late 19th century

Arts & Crafts curved top rail
and inlaid back splats
Britain, late 19th century

Art Nouveau tapered high
inlaid panel
Britain, c1905

Art Nouveau organic shaped
Georges de Feure
France, c1900

Art Nouveau stylized floral
carved, Léon Jallot
France, c1908

Art Nouveau padded, pierced
floral carving, Lucien Gaillard
France, c1900

Art Nouveau marquetry,
turned spindles, Louis
Majorelle, France, c1900

Art Nouveau entwined
whiplash
Germany, c1900

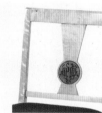
Art Deco central vertical
splat with inlaid medallion
Sweden, 1920s

Art Deco central splat with
burled elm and satinwood
details, Sweden, 1920s

Art Deco oval upholstered
Emile-Jacques Ruhlmann
France, c1920

Art Deco stylized acorn
within "theater drape
curtain," France, 1920s

Mid-century Modern "Grand
Prix," Arne Jacobsen
Denmark, 1955

Mid-century Modern "Swan"
Arne Jacobsen
Denmark, 1957–58

Mid-century Modern "Cone"
Verner Panton
Denmark, 1958

Philippe Starck The designs of Frenchman Philippe
Starck (born 1949) are renowned for blending
primitive imagery with references to highbrow culture
and mischievous details. The WW stool features a
streamlined horn motif, while the Aleph chair has only
three legs—one less for the waiters to trip over.

Contemporary "Pylon"
Tom Dixon
England, 1991

Contemporary reinforced
fiberglass "Felt", Marc
Newson, Australia/Italy, 1994

Contemporary "Museum
Chair," Alessandro Mendini
Italy, 1996

Aleph chair   WW stool

Composite photos
Legs

LEGS ARE A USEFUL INDICATOR of period or date, although earlier styles were copied extensively in the 19th century. The shape and carving should fit with the style of the foot and the rest of the piece. Some carved sections—such as the ear piece at the top of a cabriole leg—were carved separately as a matter of economy and as a result are vulnerable to being broken. Check for replacements by making sure the carving fits with that on the rest of the chair and comparing the patination. A broken leg or legs on a chair will seriously affect its value.

Barley twist
England
17th century

Bobbin-turned, tapering
Indo-Portuguese
Late 17th century

Cabriole, with carved drapery on knee
England, mid-18th century

Cabriole, with leaf carved knees, Philadelphia, US
c1765

Cabriole leg, with leaf carved knees, Colonial India
c1770

Louis XV-style restrained cabriole leg
France, late 19th century

Square cabriole, with ormolu mounts and sabots
France, late 19th century

Empire-style scrolled with caryatid
Russia, early 19th century

Outward-scrolling
France
Early 20th century

Louis XVI carved, with scroll knees
Paris, France, c1775

Louis XVI-style tapering, with leaf carving
Turin, c1780

Tapered, with spade feet
England
Late 18th century

Regency turned, cluster column, Britain
Early 19th century

Late Georgian Gothic turned and reeded, Britain
Early 19th century

Victorian turned, tapered, and fluted
Britain, late 19th century

Molded
England
Late 18th century

Georgian square tapering, molded
England, late 18th century

Arts & Crafts square tapering, Morris & Co
England, late 19th century

Art Nouveau spiral tapering, with root carved block feet
Louis Majorelle, Paris, c1900

Arts & Craft plain, with Mackmurdo feet, Roycroft
US, c1900

Art Deco slender tapering, Emile-Jacques Ruhlmann
Paris, France, c1920

Art Deco molded outswept
Laszlo Hoenig
London, England, c1930

William and Mary tapered, twisting
England, late 17th century

William and Mary cup and vase, Massachusetts, US
Early 18th century

Louis XIV cabriole, with scrolling acanthus toes
France, early 18th century

Cabriole, carved with shell and husk ornament, England
Early 18th century

Cabriole leg carved with shell and husk ornament, Chinese Export, early 18th century

C-scrolled, splaying at front with scrolled toes
England, late 17th century

Louis XIV counter-scrolled France
Early 18th century

Scrolled, with gilt leaf decoration on the knee
Italy, early 18th century

Scrolled, capped with boys' heads, drapery to knees
England, mid-18th century

Egyptianesque scrolled leg with hoof foot
Sweden, late 18th century

Art Nouveau carved and tapered, Auguste Endell
Germany, c1910

Art Nouveau naturalistically carved, Léon Jallot
France, c1910

Sheraton-style turned and reeded, England
Late 18th/early 19th century

Louis XVI square tapered and stop-fluted
France, late 18th century

Louis XVI turned, tapered, and fluted
France, late 18th century

Empire ring-turned, with scalloped collars
Jacob Frères, France, c1800

Half-engaged vase and ring-turned tapered
US, early 19th century

Vase and ring-turned reeded with turned feet
US, early 19th century

Vase and ring-turned US
Early 19th century

Sheraton slender, tapering Scotland
Late 18th century

Art Deco straight, tapered, metal sabot feet, Jacques Quinet, France, c1930

Classical splayed, with brass paw feet and casters
US, early 19th century

Regency splayed, reeded, leaf cast brass caps and casters
Britain, early 19th century

Art Nouveau splayed carved France
c1900

Art Nouveau delicate splayed
France, c1910

Composite photos
Feet

FEET ARE A USEFUL GUIDE to dating furniture, but always bear in mind that they may have been replaced. Centuries of wear and tear: being dragged across floors, dampened with water when the floor was cleaned and attacked by woodworm, can all take their toll. Feet were also replaced as fashions changed—look out for new wood or marks that do not otherwise fit with the construction of the piece. Replacement feet are considered acceptable if they were sensitively done—in keeping with the originals and the work skillfully carried out.

Turned, tapering and faceted bun foot, The Netherlands, Late 17th century

Bun foot
England
Early 18th century

Trifid foot
US
c1755

Intaglio carved slipper foot
US
c1760

Blunt arrow foot
US
c1775

Knife-edge foot
US
c1780

Inverted scroll
France
c1680

Regency scrolled sabot brass
Britain, c1810

Regency brass ram's head capping and caster
Britain, c1820

Regency honeysuckle brass capping and caster
Britain, c1820

Art Nouveau scrolled sabot
France
c1900

Georgian claw-and-ball
England
c1735

Empire lion's paw
US
1830

Empire lion's paw
France
c1830

Empire-style lion's claw
Italy
c1890

Carved paw
Italy
17th century

Classical claw
US
c1815

Chippendale ogival bracket foot with pad below
Philadelphia, c1770

Spurred ogee bracket foot
Pennsylvania
c1775

Georgian block bracket foot
England
c1780

Chippendale ogee bracket foot
US, c1780

Ogee bracket foot
England
Late 18th century

Flattened bun foot
France
c1730

Moorish turned bun foot
Mid 19th century

Pad foot
England
Early 18th century

Pad foot
Ireland
c1740

Pad foot
US
Mid-18th century

Cabriole leg with scrolling
acanthus toes
France, c1710

Counter-scrolled foot with
carving
France, c1710

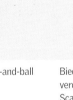

Scrolled foot with brass
casters
England, c1760

Régence scrolled sabot
France
c1720

Louis XV splayed bracket
with ormolu cloven hoof
France, c1760

Georgian claw-and-ball
England
c1745

Chippendale claw-and-ball
US
c1765

Biedermeier gilt and
verdigris claw-and-ball
Scandinavia, c1860

Claw-and-ball
Chinese Export
c1900

Lion's paw
England
c1830

Regency style paw
Britain
c1840

Carved and gilded paw
Italy
c1850

Georgian hoof
England
Mid 18th century

Hoof
Italy
c1880

Classical Revival profusely
carved hoof
Britain, c1890

Bracket foot with stepped
ogee
Britain, c1800

Splayed slender bracket foot
France
c1860

Louis XV square splayed
bracket foot
France, c1780

Splayed bracket foot
The Netherlands
c1850

Curved played bracket foot
Denmark
c1890

205

Composite photos
Motifs

DESIGNERS AND CRAFTSMEN wishing to embellish artifacts have drawn on a huge catalog of imagery. Constantly accumulating and evolving from antiquity to modern times, motifs substantially comprise human, animal, bird, insect, and plant forms. Diverse objects and phenomena are also represented, from fountains and fireworks to geometric and planetary forms. As well as decorative qualities, many have symbolic meaning. The manner in which they are represented—naturalistic or stylized—is an indicator of both period and style.

Napoleonic bee
France
Early 19th century

Empire eagle
Europe
Early 19th century

Art Deco bird and branch
France
1930s

Art Deco gazelle
Britain
1930s

Art Deco hound
Germany
1930s

Neoclassical dolphin
Europe
Late 18th century

Mythological dragon
China
Mid-18th century

Regency Revival panther's head
Britain, late 20th century

Art Deco fox
France
1930s

Neoclassical phoenix
US
Mid-18th century

Neoclassical ram's head
England
Late 18th century

Regency ram's head
Britain
Early 19th century

Régence female mask
France
Early 18th century

Louis XV female bust
France
Mid-18th century

Belle Époque winged female
France
Late 19th century

Empire female bust
Russia
Early 19th century

Provincial female
Germany
Mid-19th century

Egyptian Revival pharaoh
England
Late 18th century

Egyptian Revival pharaoh
US
Early 19th century

Empire pharaoh
France
Early 19th century

Egyptian native bearers
Egypt
Mid-19th century

Provincial human busts
France
Late 19th century

Federal eagle and snake
US
Early 19th century

Biedermeier swan
Germany
Early 19th century

Empire swan
France
Early 19th century

Art Nouveau peacock
France
c1900

Art Deco bird and feather
France
1930s

Palladian lion mask
England
Early 18th century

Neoclassical lion mask
Sicily
Late 18th century

Arts & Crafts mouse
England
1920s

Neoclassical wyvern
England
Late 18th century

Empire wyvern
Sweden
Early 19th century

Egyptian Revival ram
France
Mid-1920s

Arts & Crafts scarab
US
c1900

Egyptian Revival scarab
Europe
1920s

Greek Revival sphinx
Germany
Early 19th century

Empire sphinx
France
Early 19th century

Renaissance Revival
females, France
Mid-to-late 19th century

Art Nouveau reclining
female, Germany
c1900

Art Nouveau female bust
US
c1900

Glasgow Arts & Crafts
female mask
Scotland, c1905

Art Deco huntress and
hound
France, 1930s

Second Empire courting
couple, France
Mid-19th century

Empire woman and centaur
Germany
Early 19th century

Belle Époque putto
France
Late 19th century

Glasgow Arts & Crafts
cherub, Scotland
Early 20th century

Renaissance Revival cherubs
US
c1900

Composite photos
Motifs

Spanish Colonial rosette
New Mexico
Early 18th century

Louis XIV flowers and
scrolling foliage, France
Early 18th century

Pastoral floral basket
France
Mid-18th century

Neoclassical rosette
England
Late 18th century

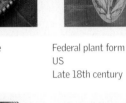

Federal plant form
US
Late 18th century

Early Art Deco floral
France
c1920

Early Art Deco floral
France
c1920

Arts & Crafts fruit
US
Early 20th century

Art Deco acorn
France
Mid-1920s

Regency patera and foliage
Britain
Early 19th century

Art Nouveau oak leaves
France
Early 20th century

Art Nouveau palm-like
leaves, France
Early 20th century

Art Deco stylized foliage
Sweden
Late 1920s

Early Georgian shell
England
Early 18th century

Mid-Georgian leaf form
England
Mid-18th century

Neoclassical shell
England
Late 18th century

Neoclassical shell
England
Late 18th century

Modern Classical shell
US
1940s

Louis XV Rococo feathers
France
Mid-18th century

Neoclassical feathers
Scotland
Late 18th century

Neoclassical festoons
Italy
Late 18th century

Louis XV Rococo foliate
swag, France
Mid-18th century

Directoire cornucopia
France
Late 18th century

American Colonial tulip,
heart, and wave scrolls, US
Early-to-mid-18th century

Neoclassical shield and
ribbon, Britain
Late 19th century

Art Nouveau water lilies
Scotland
Late 19th century

Glasgow Arts & Crafts rose
Scotland
Early 20th century

Art Nouveau floral
France
c1900

Glasgow Arts & Crafts roses
Scotland
c1900

Arts & Crafts floral
US
Early 20th century

Empire acanthus leaves
Germany
Early 19th century

Classical Revival scrolling
acanthus, Britain
Mid-19th century

Empire leaf forms
France
Early 19th century

Arts & Crafts oak leaf
US
Early 20th century

Art Nouveau leaf forms
France
c1900

American Queen Anne shell
US
Mid-18th century

Rococo shells
Italy
Mid-18th century

Rococo shell
Italy
Mid-18th century

American Chippendale shell
US
Mid-18th century

American Chippendale shell
US
Mid-18th century

Late Art Nouveau feathers
France
Early 20th century

Neoclassical feathers
France
Mid-to-late 18th century

Empire lyre
France
Early 19th century

Neoclassical musical trophy
France
Late 19th century

Greek Revival lyre
Britain
Late 19th century

Baroque sunburst
Europe
Late 17th century

Empire star
Russia
Early 19th century

Art Deco fireworks
France
1930s

Art Deco fountain
US
1930s

Classical Revival urn
Britain
Late 19th century

Composite photos
Ceramic marks

MANY CERAMICS are marked on the base. Some marks are easy to decipher as they contain the name of the factory or potter and even a title of the piece and date it was made. Some are so famous – such as the crossed swords of Meissen—that they are easy to identify once you know what to look for. Others take time to decipher as they contain symbols alone. Many marks—such as those of Meissen and Sèvres—have been widely copied and should always arouse suspicion. The following pages contain a selection of marks as a starting point.

Bristol
England
c1773–81

Bristol
England
c1773–81

Frankenthal
Germany
1762–94

Frankenthal
Germany
1770–89

Höchst
Germany
c1763–71

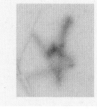

Kloster (Closter) Veilsdorf
Germany
c1760–90

Ludwigsburg
Germany
1758–93

Potschappel
Germany
End 19th century

Rookwood
US
1880–1960

Sèvres
France
1745–53

Sèvres
France
1745–53

Sèvres
France
c1745–53

Vienna
Austria
1762–82

Vienna
Austria
Late 19th–early 20th century

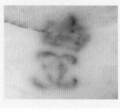

Wallendorf
Germany
Early 20th century

Worcester
England
1751–1800

Worcester
England
1760–70

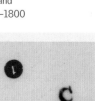

Berlin
Germany
20th century

Bing & Grøndahl
Denmark
20th century

Caughley
England
1755–99

Caughley
England
1775–99

Derby
England
Late 1770s–80s

Chantilly
France
c1725–92

Chelsea
England
Red Anchor period 1752–56

Dresden
Germany
1800–1900

Dresden
Germany
1800–1900

Frankenthal
Germany
1759–76

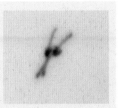

Meissen
Germany
1739

Meissen
Germany
1763–73

Meissen
Germany
c1900

Meissen
Germany
Marcolini period 1774–1814

Paris, Locré factory
France
1771–97

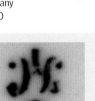

Sèvres
France
Late 18th century

Sèvres
France
c1845–48

St. Petersburg
Russia
1825–55

St. Petersburg
Russia
1855–81

Tournai
Belgium
1763–96

Worcester
England
1770–83

Berlin
Germany
1763–1837

Berlin
Germany
1823–32

Berlin
Germany
1849–70

Berlin
Germany
20th century

Derby
England
Late 1770s–early 1790s

Derby
England
c1891–1921

Helena Wolfson, Dresden
Germany
1843–79

Fürstenberg
Germany
Late 18th century

Gotha
Germany
1802–34

Ceramic marks

Hummel
Germany
1938–50

Hutschenreuther
Germany
c1880–1902

McCoy Pottery
US
20th century

Newcomb Pottery
US
1897–1940s

Niderviller
France
Late 18th century

Roseville Pottery
US
1920s

Worcester Barr, Flight &
Barr, England
1807–13

Amphora, Bohemia (now
Czech Republic), late 19th–
early 20th century

Batchelder
US
1920–32

Boch Frères, Belgium
1920s–30s with signature of
Charles Catteau

Doulton
England
1923–27

Doulton
England
1928 onwards

Fulper, Ink race track mark
US
1909–1917

Grueby Pottery
US
1897–1907

Grueby Pottery
US
1897–1907

Minton
England
c1863–72

Minton
England
c1873–1912

Nymphenburg
Germany
Modern mark

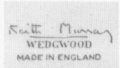

George Ohr
US
1895–1903

P. L. Dagoty, Paris
France
1804–1814

Spode
England
Early 19th century

Copeland Spode
England
c1891 into 20th century

Van Briggle Pottery
US
1902–12

Wedgwood, England
Designed by Keith Murray
1933–67

Weller Pottery
US
Early 20th century

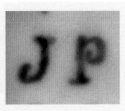

Jacob Petit, Paris
France
c1830–60

Pilkington
England
1892–1920

Rorstrand
Sweden
20th century

Rosenthal
Germany
1897–1945

Rosenthal
Germany
1891–1904

Boch Frères
Belgium
1920s–30s

Coalport
England
1900–20

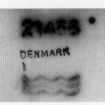

Royal Copenhagen
Denmark
1894–c1920

Royal Copenhagen
Denmark
1897–1920

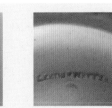

Davenport
England
1850–70

Herend
Hungary
1935–38

Herend
Hungary
1940s–50s

Herend
Hungary
1940s

Leeds
England
Late 18th century

Martin Brothers
England
1873–1915

Edward & George Phillips
Staffordshire, England
1827–34

Poole
England
1978 onwards

Roseville Pottery
US
1900–07

Roseville Pottery
US
1920s on

Spode
England
c1780–c1830

Wemyss Pottery
England
1932–57

Worcester Barr, Flight &
Barr, England
1807–13

Flight, Barr and Barr
Worcester, England
1813–40

Royal Worcester
England
1885 into 20th century

Royal Worcester
England
1889–1902

Composite photos
Glass marks

MUCH GLASS IS NOT MARKED, and is identified from its form, color, method of production, and style. Glass marks, where they exist can be engraved, inscribed, cut, etched with acid, or molded as part of the design. Marks can change in format and method of execution, but may have been used for a specific period of time and can give an indication of age. Some marks, such as most of Lalique's, are impossible to date precisely, as records were not kept or no longer exist. Original labels can help, but many have been removed or have degraded or fallen off.

Amalric Walter
France
Early 20th century

Blenko
US
1958–1961

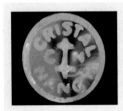

Cristallerie de Nancy
France
1922–1934

Cristalleries de St. Louis
(D'Argental), France
c1890s–c1910s

Daum with Lorraine Cross
France
c1905–1920s

Daum with Lorraine Cross
France
c1905–1920s

Daum, with integral
Lorraine Cross
c1905–c1910

Gallé with star
France
1904–07

Jiri Harcuba
Czechoslovakia
1965

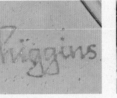

Higgins
US
1957–c1965

Holmegaard, Denmark
(Designer Per Lutken's
monogram), 1962 onward

Honesdale Glassworks
US
c1915–c1920

R. Lalique,
France
c1919

Lalique
France
1920s–30s

Lalique
France
post 1945

Legras & Cie
France
c1900–c1920s

J. & L. Lobmeyr
Austria
1870s onward

Muller Frères
France
c1910–c1920

Archimede Seguso
Murano
1960s

Orrefors
Sweden
1950s–70s

Riihimaki Lasi Oy
Finland
1960s–70s

Joseph-Gabriel Argy
Rousseau, France
c1915–c1930s

Blenko, US, 1930s–1982

Burgun, Schverer & Cie,
France, c1900

Caithness Glass
Scotland
Late 1960s–early 1970s

Amédée de Caranza
France
1903–06

Cenedese
Murano
c1960s

André Delatte
France
c1926

Gallé,
France,
Early 1900s

Gallé
France
1890

Gallé
France
1900

Gallé
France
1898

Humppila
Finland
1950s–60s

Ittala (Tapio Wirkkala
designer)
Finland, 1950s

Schott, Jenaer Glaswerk
Germany
1920s onwards

Kosta, (Gunnar
Wennersburg designer)
Sweden, c1901

Kosta Boda (Ulrica
Heydman-Vallien designer)
Sweden, c1980s

Loetz
Austria
Early 20th century

Loetz
Austria
Early 20th century

Paolo Martinuzzi
Murano
1980s

Ludwig Moser & Sohne
Czechoslovakia
c1925–c1945

Ludwig Moser & Sohne
Czechoslovakia
20th century

Verreries Schneider (La
Verre Français), France
1921–1930s

Tiffany
US
1902–1920

Tiffany
US
1890s–1902

Cesare Toso
Murano
1950s–60s

James Powell & Sons
(Whitefriars), England
1950s–62

Oriental ceramic marks

Chinese Reign Periods and Marks Imperial reign marks were adopted during the Ming dynasty, and some of the most common are reproduced here. Most pieces with these marks were made in kilns at carefully controlled Imperial workshops. These workshops made ceramics for the Emperor's household and as tribute for foreign dignitaries. During periods when Imperial control was relatively lax, ceramics made outside the confines of these exalted workshops would sometimes be painted with reign marks. Many Chinese ceramics have reign marks that actually predate the object. A piece of Kangxi porcelain made in the late 17th century, for example, might bear the mark of the Emperor Chenghua who reigned between 1465–87. This was designed not to deceive, but to show reverence for a golden age of production.

Marks were made using two types of script: the regular *kaishu* script, introduced in the Sui and Tang dynasties; and the *zhuanshu* Seal script, first used on ancient bronze vessels.

Jiajing 1522–66
Ming Dynasty

Longqing 1567–72
Ming Dynasty

Wanli 1573–1619
Ming Dynasty

Shunzhi 1644–61
Qing Dynasty

Kangxi 1662–1722
Qing Dynasty

Kangxi 1662–1722
Qing Dynasty

Qianlong 1736–95
Qing Dynasty

Qianlong 1736–95
Qing Dynasty

Jiaqing 1796–1820
Qing Dynasty

Daoguang 1821–50
Qing Dynasty

Xianfeng 1851–61
Qing Dynasty

Xianfeng 1851–61
Qing Dynasty

Guangxu 1875–1908
Qing Dynasty

Guangxu 1875–1908
Qing Dynasty

Xuantong 1909–11
Qing Dynasty

© "The Handbook of Marks on Chinese Ceramics" by Gerald Davison

Early Periods and Dates

Xia Dynasty	c2000–1500BCE
Shang Dynasty	1500–1028BCE
Zhou Dynasty	1028–221BCE
Qin Dynasty	221–206BCE
Han Dynasty	206BCE–220CE
Three Kingdoms	221–280
Jin Dynasty	265–420
Northern and Southern Dynasties	420–581
Sui Dynasty	581–618
Tang Dynasty	618–906
The Five Dynasties	907–960
Song Dynasty	960–1279
Jin Dynasty	1115–1234
Yuan Dynasty	1260–1368

Ming Dynasty Reigns

Hongwu	1368–1398
Jianwen	1399–1402
Yongle	1403–1424
Hongxi	1425
Xuande	1426–1435
Zhengtong	1436–1449
Jingtai	1450–1457
Tianshun	1457–1464
Chenghua	1465–1487
Hongzhi	1488–1505
Zhengde	1506–1521

The Japanese ceramic industry was on a much smaller scale than the Chinese—with master potters who specialized in one area and small workshops more common than factories that mass-produced wares. There were no reign marks, as used by the Chinese. Master potters often changed their signature as time went by and also added details such as the factory, decorator, customer, exporter, or importer. Ceramics may also be marked "Made in Japan," "Happiness," or "Good Luck." From the 20th century, many factories used several marks at the same time—Noritake is said to have used over 400 marks in the past century.

Registration marks

Tianqi 1621–27
Ming Dynasty

Chongzhen 1628–44
Ming Dynasty

Yongzheng 1723–35
Qing Dynasty

Yongzheng 1723–35
Qing Dynasty

Jiaqing 1796–1820
Qing Dynasty

Daoguang 1821–50
Qing Dynasty

Tongzhi 1862–74
Qing Dynasty

Tongzhi 1862–74
Qing Dynasty

Hongxian (Yuan Shikai)
Republic Period

Hongxian (Yuan Shikai)
Republic Period

Design registration marks In Britain, designs began to be registered following the 1839 Copyright of Design Act and from 1842 the Design Registration Mark was used to denote the date a design was registered. The diamond-shaped mark also showed what material the item was made from (its class) and how many items were included (bundle or package). The Rd in the center of the diamond stands for registered design.

1842–67
a = class
b = year
c = month
d = day
e = bundle

1868–83
a = class
b = day
c = bundle
d = year
e = month

The letters were not used in sequence but as follows: 1842–67 (features a number in the right hand corner of the diamond)

A 1845	H 1843	O 1862	V 1850
B 1858	I 1846	P 1851	W 1865
C 1844	J 1854	Q 1866	X 1842
D 1852	K 1857	R 1861	Y 1853
E 1855	L 1856	S 1849	Z 1860
F 1847	M 1859	T 1867	
G 1863	N 1864	U 1848	

1868–83 (letter in the right hand corner of the diamond)

A 1871	F 1873	K 1883	U 1874
C 1870	H 1869	L 1882	V 1876
D 1878	I 1872	P 1877	X 1868
E 1881	J 1880	S 1875	Y 1879

The months from both periods are shown as follows:

A December	D September	H April	M June
B October	E May	I July	R August
C/O January	G February	K November	W March

Classes Sometimes the clerks mis-classified items so it is possible to find a bookbinding misfiled as a carpet.

Class 1 - Metal	Class 7 - Printed Shawls	Class 12 (i) - Other Fabrics
Class 2 - Wood	Class 8 - Other Shawls	Class 12 (ii) - Other Fabrics
Class 3 - Glass	Class 9 - Yarn	(Damasks)
Class 4 - Earthenware	Class 10 - Printed Fabrics	Class 13 - Lace
Class 5 - Paper Hangings	Class 11 - Furnitures (printed	
Class 6 - Carpets	fabrics)	

A series of consecutive numbers were used from 1884, nearly always prefixed by Rd or Rd No (Registered or Registered Number). This guide is an estimate only:

1: 1884	163767: 1891	311658: 1898	447000: 1905*
19754: 1885	185713: 1892	331707: 1899	471000: 1906*
40480: 1886	205240: 1893	351202: 1900	494000: 1907*
64520: 1887	224720: 1894	368154: 1901	519000: 1908*
90483: 1888	246975: 1895	385500: 1902*	550000: 1909*
116648: 1889	268393: 1896	402500: 1903*	*approximately
141273: 1890	291241: 1897	420000: 1904*	

By 1980 the system had reached around one million. It is still in use today.

Japanese Periods

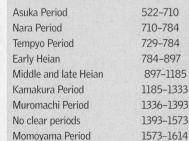

Asuka Period	522–710
Nara Period	710–784
Tempyo Period	729–784
Early Heian	784–897
Middle and late Heian	897–1185
Kamakura Period	1185–1333
Muromachi Period	1336–1393
No clear periods	1393–1573
Momoyama Period	1573–1614
Edo Period	1615–1867
Meiji Restoration	1867–1911

Composite photos
Silver marks

THE STAMPED MARKS found on most silver are the best way to find precise information about it. They indicate or guarantee that the silver content of the metal is of a certain level, often 92.5 per cent. Not all silver is marked, and the type and quantity of marks differ from country to country, and even from city to city.

English silver marks Known as hallmarks, these typically comprise four individual marks, each with its own meaning. The order of the marks may differ from piece to piece. On the London mark for Robert Makepiece and Richard Carter (right), the first mark is the silversmith's, and usually comprises the initials of the craftsman or company who made the piece. The second is the date letter, which indicates the year the piece was stamped, and (most probably) made. It is unique in style to that year and assay office (where the piece was officially tested and stamped), and follows an alphabetical sequence. The third is known as the "lion passant" and indicates that the metal contains 92.5 per cent silver. Before 1544, a stylized leopard's head was used. The final mark is the town mark, where the assay office was based. The most frequently seen marks are for offices in London, Birmingham, and Chester, but there are others. It is best to refer to a specialist guide to fully interpret the many English hallmarks.

Newcastle hallmark Francis Batty, 1705

London hallmark Richard Rugg, 1773

London, Makepiece and Carter, 1777

London hallmark Paul Storr, 1820

Birmingham hallmark Edward Smith, 1850

Chester hallmark Charles Horner, 1887

Scottish and Irish hallmarks Scottish assay offices were based at Edinburgh and Glasgow, but larger burghs or guilds, for instance at Aberdeen, Banff, Elgin, and Montrose, also had identifying marks. Some Scottish silver marks include an additional mark of the assay office master. In Edinburgh, this was replaced with a thistle from 1759 until 1975. In Dublin, the mark of a "harp crowned" was used as well as a maker's mark and date letter. In 1731, the figure of Hibernia was added. However, around 40 per cent of Irish silver does not bear a date letter.

Edinburgh, Edward Lothian, c1750

Dundee, probably John Steven, c1760

Dublin, Richard Williams, c1770

Montrose, Benjamin Lumsden, c1795

Perth hallmark William Ritchie c1795

Elgin, Thomas Stewart c1800

Aberdeen/Montrose for Peter Lambert

Banff, William Simpson, c1810

Castle Douglas, Adam Burgess, c1820

Dumfries, Joseph Pearson, c1820

Arbroath, Andrew Davidson, c1825

Wick J. Sellar, c1825

French silver marks Before the Revolution, French silver typically had four stamped marks. These comprised the stamp of the silversmith or company that made the piece, a town or city mark related to the *ferme générale*, a uniquely styled date mark guaranteeing the silver content, and a duty mark. After 1797, the marks were reduced to three: a mark showing a rooster, old man's head, or the head of Minerva guaranteeing the silver content; a duty mark; and the maker's mark. More modern French marks are limited to two: the Minerva's head mark and the maker's mark.

PF Grandguillaume Besançon, 1743

Joseph Virgile Vilhet, Avignon, c1775

G. CARRE & Cⁱᵉ PARIS
TRAVAIL au marteau de G. Lecomte

Denis Frankson Paris, 1789

François Corbie Paris, 1787

G. Lecomte Minerva mark, c1925

American silver marks The presence of the word "STERLING" in capital letters usually indicates a piece of silver made in the US. The maker's name often appears in full as well, or may be indicated by a stamped symbol. Date letters were generally not used, making it hard to date many pieces precisely, and there is usually no consistent mark for each town or city.

Simeon Soumaine
New York, 1685–c1750

Jacob Hurd
Boston, c1728

J. Lownes
Philadelphia, c1800

Simon Wedge, Sr.
Baltimore assay mark, 1815

E. Lownes
Philadelphia, c1817

R. & W. Wilson
Philadelphia, c1825

Joseph Seymour of New York, c1900

Carence Crafters
Chicago, c1907

Robert Jarvie
Chicago, c1925

Kalo Shop mark
c1925

Tiffany mark
c1925

Other silver marks Silver from other countries may often only be indicated by the word "Sterling" or a number, which is typically ".925." Countries had specific stamped marks, sometimes representing the town or city where the piece was made.

In Germany and Poland before 1886, the silver content was divided into 16 parts. Known as the Loth system, a "16" stamp indicated pure silver and "12" indicated 75 per cent silver content. This was accompanied by a town or city mark. After 1886, the number for the standard minimum silver content was "800," and town and city marks were replaced by a single national mark of a crescent and crown.

Turin, 18th century

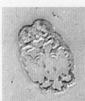

Jamaica, c1800s

Schott, Frankfurt
1786–1811

Hossauer, Berlin
1854–60

H. J. Wilm, Berlin
c1890s

Sy & Wagner, Berlin
c1900

Fahrner, Pforzheim
c1915

19th-century Russian mark

Fabergé
St. Petersburg, Russia

Fabergé, workmaster Henrik Wigstrom, with London import marks for 1910

Georg Jensen
Copenhagen, c1905

C. F. Heise, Copenhagen, 1930

Composite photos
Metal shapes: candlesticks

From the earliest times, candlesticks have reflected the prevailing decorative fashion. By the end of the 17th century, silver candlesticks were cast. This method of production was used until the 1770s when sheet silver was used and the sticks were loaded. Most candlesticks were functional and simple. During the 18th century, candlesticks grew progressively taller—from around 6in (15cm) at the beginning of the century to around 10in (25cm) in mid-century and 12in (30cm) by the early 1900s. The sticks that follow are ordered by style and then date.

Gothic brass candle holder with three-knopped shaft
England, 15th century

Trumpet brass with sausage turned shaft
England, c1650

Rococo silver by Sébastien Igonet
Paris, France, 1730

Rococo silver candlesticks by Simon Jouet
London, England, 1750

Elaborate Rococo silver by William Café
London, England, 1758

Rococo silver candlesticks by William Café, London, England, mid-18th century

Rococo silver candlesticks b
John Carter
London, England, 1769

Rococo Revival silver by Paul Reczka, Bordeaux, France, Late 19th century

Louis XV1-style ormolu and marble, Gervais Maximillian Eugène Durand, Paris, c1880

Classical silver candlesticks by Jonathon Paisley
Dublin, Ireland, c1759

Classical silver candlesticks by Jean Baptiste Dréo
Rennes, France 1756–62

Classical silver candlestick by John Carter
London, England, 1771

Classical Revival silver
Germany
Late 19th century

Classical Revival silver
Germany
c1870

Classical Revival silver
Regency style
England, c1882

Adam-style silver
Martin & Hall
London, c1894

Classical Revival silver
Birmingham
1905

Arts & Crafts bronze candlesticks by Jarvie Shop
Chicago, US c1910

Arts & Crafts hammered copper by Roycroft
New York, US, c1910

Art Nouveau silvered bronze by E. Colin & Cie, Paris, France, Late 19th century

Art Nouveau silver plate by WMF
Germany, c1900

Art Nouveau pewter by Hugo Leven for Kayserzinn
Dusseldorf, Germany, c1900

Trumpet brass with sausage
turned shaft
England, mid-17th century

Trumpet brass candle
holders, England
Late 17th century

Wrought-iron rush light
England
Early 18th century

Hand-forged iron rush light
and candle holder, tri-legged,
penny feet, England, c1740

Rococo silver candle holder
by Antoine Fillassier
Paris, France, 1723

Rococo silver
Edmé-François Balzac
Paris, France, 1772

Rococo Revival silver plate
Sheffield, England
c1820

Rococo Revival silver plate
Sheffield, England
c1825

Rococo Revival silvered
bronze candelabra
France, late 19th century

Russian Rococo Revival silver
candlestick by A. Riedel
Minsk, 1878

Empire silver candlesticks by
Pierre Paraud
Paris, France, 1798–1809

Egyptianesque silver
Berlin, Germany
Early 19th century

Empire-style silver-gilt
Puiforcat, Paris, France
Late 19th century

Classical Revival silver by
John Green & Co.
Sheffield, England, c1834

Classical Revival silver by
Henry Wilkinson & Co.
Sheffield, England, c1835

Secessionist pewter by Albin
Muller
Germany, c1900

Arts & Crafts electroplate
WMF
Germany, c1900

Arts & Crafts silver by
AE Jones
Birmingham, England, 1904

Arts & Crafts silver plate
Britain
c1905

Arts & Crafts silver by Orivit
Germany
c1905

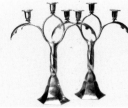

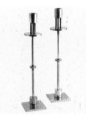

Art Deco silver by Harald
Nielsen for Georg Jensen,
Copenhagen, Denmark, 1920s

Art Deco silver by Kalo
Shop
Chicago, US, c1925

Art Deco silver
Heinrich Eggs
Zurich, c1928

Art Deco Gallia metal (silver
plate), Gio Ponti for
Christofle & Cie, Paris, 1920s

Modernist silver plate
Ettore Sottsass for Swid
Powell, US, c1986

Composite photos

Metal shapes: tea & coffee pots

TEA, COFFEE, AND CHOCOLATE POTS from the 18th century on have survived well, although they are rarer in the US than in Europe. Early 18th-century teapots were small due to the high cost of tea. The Queen Anne pear shape was replaced by the bullet shape, which was fashionable c1730–45. Coffee pots follow the same trends as teapots. Chocolate pots are rare after 1730, except in France. These pots have been ordered by style, maker, assay office, and then date – so Revival styles follow the originals.

Bullet teapot
Francis Batty
Newcastle, 1705

Bullet teapot
Abraham Buteux
London, 1721

Rococo teapot
James McEwan
Glasgow, c1783

Rococo Revival coffee pot
Rebecca Emes & Edward
Barnard, London, 1825

Rococo Revival teapot
Marshall & Sons
Edinburgh, 1836

Rococo Revival teapot
William Marshall
Edinburgh, 1846–47

Rococo Revival coffee pot
Dominick & Haff
New York, mid-19th century

Classical coffee pot
Gaspard Bougarel
Paris, France, 1787

Classical teapot
James Aldridge & Charles
Green, London, 1791

Classical teapot
P. & W. Bateman
London, 1792

Classical teapot
Solomon Hougham
London, c1797

Classical teapot
William Fountain
London, 1798

Biedermeier coffee pot
Maker A. L.
Stockholm, 1833

Classical Revival teapot
W. W. Williams
London, 1867

Classical Revival teapot
E. K. Reid
London, 1868

Classical Revival coffee pot
France
Late 19th century

Art Deco coffee pot
Tétard Silversmiths
Paris, France, 1920s

Oval teapot
Maker's mark worn
London, 1801

Round teapot
Edward and John Bernard
London, 1865

Arts & Crafts teapot
C. Dresser for Hukin &
Middleton, London, c1879

Arts & Crafts silver-plate
teapot, C. Dresser for J.
Dixon & Sons, Sheffield, 1879

Arts & Crafts silver-plate
teapot, C. Dresser for J. Dixon
& Sons, Sheffield, c1879

Bullet teapot, Wm. Aytoun: assay master Edward Penman, Edinburgh, 1729

Rococo teapot by Henri Louis Le Gaigneur Saint Omer, c1740

Rococo chocolate pot Charles-Louis Gérard Douai, France, 1752–55

Rococo coffee pot Lothian and Robertson Edinburgh, 1760

Rococo coffee pot Samuel Courtauld London, 1763

Biedermeier teapot Johannes Bade Hamburg, 19th century

Rococo Revival teapot Russia Late 19th century

Rococo chocolate pot L. Lapar Paris, c1880

Classical coffee pot Maker indistinct London, 1780

Bright-cut Classical teapot Thomas Pratt & Arthur Humphreys, London, c1781

Classical teapot Old Sheffield Plate England, early 19th century

Classical teapot with Greek key pattern John Emes, London, 1805

Classical vase-shaped teapot Argyle Peter & William Bateman, London, 1806

Classical baluster coffee pot Jean-Louis Galliot Lyon, 1809–19

Empire style coffee pot by Amable Brasier Philadelphia, 1810–30

Panelled oval teapot Unidentified mark London, 1798–99

Spherical teapot with flared rim, John Robins London, 1798

Spherical teapot with flared rim, John Edwards London, 1799

Oval teapot Christian Wiltberger Philadelphia, 1793–1817

Oval squat teapot William Birwash and Richard Sibley, London, 1806

Art Nouveau silver-plate teapot, Paul Follot for Christofle, Paris, c1900

Art Deco coffee pot International Silver Co. Connecticut, c1925

Art Deco teapot Georg Jensen Copenhagen, 1928

Modernist stainless steel teapot, Robert Welch for Old Hall, Sheffield, 1960s

Modernist pewter teapot Henning Koppel for Georg Jensen, Copenhagen, 1979

Timeline

	1600	**1625**	**1650**	**1675**

BAROQUE 1600–1720   AGE OF OAK (UP TO c1670)

BRITAIN

Jacobean
1603–25 James I

Carolean
1625–49 Charles I

Cromwellian
1649–60 Commonwealth

● 1642 English Civil War

Restoration
1660–85 Charles II

1685–88 Jam

FRANCE

Louis XIII
1610–43 Louis XIII

Louis XIV
1643–1715 Louis XIV

US

Early Colonial
1600–1690
● 1607 First English settlement in North America established in Jamestown, Virginia
● 1608 Samuel de Champlain founds a French settlement in Quebec
● 1620 Pilgrim Fathers land at Plymouth, Massachusetts

1683 First German ●
settlements in
North America

SCANDINAVIA

1588–1648 Denmark's Golden Age under Christian IV

● 1632–45 Sweden at war with Denmark

ITALY

● 1669 Venice loses
Crete to the Turks

GERMANY

● 1620 Imperial armies and the Catholic League defeat the Protestant
Bohemians at the Battle of White Mountain, Prague

● 1648 The Treaty of Westphalia ends
the Thirty Years' War

LANDMARKS

1602 Dutch East India Company, the first modern public company, founded in Java
1609 Tea first shipped to Europe from China
1682 Palace of Versailles completed and becomes the royal residence of France
1667 Gobelins factory founded
1685 Revocation of Edict of Nantes triggers spread of Huguenot craftsmen

1709 Böttger discovers secret of hard-paste porcelain
1720 France prohibits the export of walnut
1738 Excavation starts at Herculaneum
1748 Excavation starts at Pompeii
1754 Chippendale's *Gentleman & Cabinet Maker's Director* published
1756 Sèvres founded

1700	1725	1750	1775

E OF WALNUT (c1670–1735)   ROCOCO 1720–1760   AGE OF MAHOGANY (c1735–1810)   NEOCLASSICAL 1760–1840

Chippendale
c 1750–1780

iam and
y
3–1694

Queen Anne
1702–14 Anne

Early Georgian
1714–60

Late Georgian
1760–1811 George III

1694–1702 William III

1714–27 George I   1727–60 George II

1788 First settlement founded ●
in Botany Bay, Australia

● 1707 England and Scotland unite as Great Britain

Régence
1715–23

Louis XV
1723–74 Louis XV

Louis XVI
1774–93 Louis XVI

1789 French Revolution begins ●
with the fall of the Bastille

Queen Anne
1720–50

Early Federal
c1775–c1805

Villiam and Mary
690–1720

● 1776 Declaration of
Independence

● 1732 Georgia, the last of the 13 colonies, founded

1775–83
Revolutionary War

Gustavian
1755–1810

1700–21 Great Northern War: Sweden versus Denmark, Poland, and Russia

1789 Gustav III reintroduces ●
absolutism in Sweden

1719–72 Era of liberty in Sweden with parliamentary government

● 1713 Austria rules Milan, Naples, and Sardinia

● 1718 Venetian maritime empire
begins to decline

● 1735 The Kingdom of Two Sicilies
become an independent monarchy

● 1737 Medici line ends in Florence

689 Louis XIV of France invades the Rhineland

1700–21 The Great Northern War. Prussia acquires Pomerania after defeating Sweden

● 1701 Brandenburg, once a small state in Northern Germany, becomes known as Prussia

● 1740 Accession of Frederick II of Prussia

1759 Wedgwood founded
1773 Robert and James Adam publish *Works in Architecture*
1788 George Hepplewhite's *The Cabinet Maker and Upholsterer's Guide* is published
1789 George Washington becomes the first President of the US
1793 Louis XVI goes to the guillotine
1801 Percier & Fontaine publish *Recueil des Décorations Intérieures*

1804 Thomas Sheraton publishes first volume of *The Cabinet Maker, Upholsterer and General Artist's Encyclopedia*
1807 Thomas Hope publishes *Household Furniture and Decoration*
1808 George Smith publishes *A Collection of Designs for Household Furniture and Interior Decoration*

Timeline continued

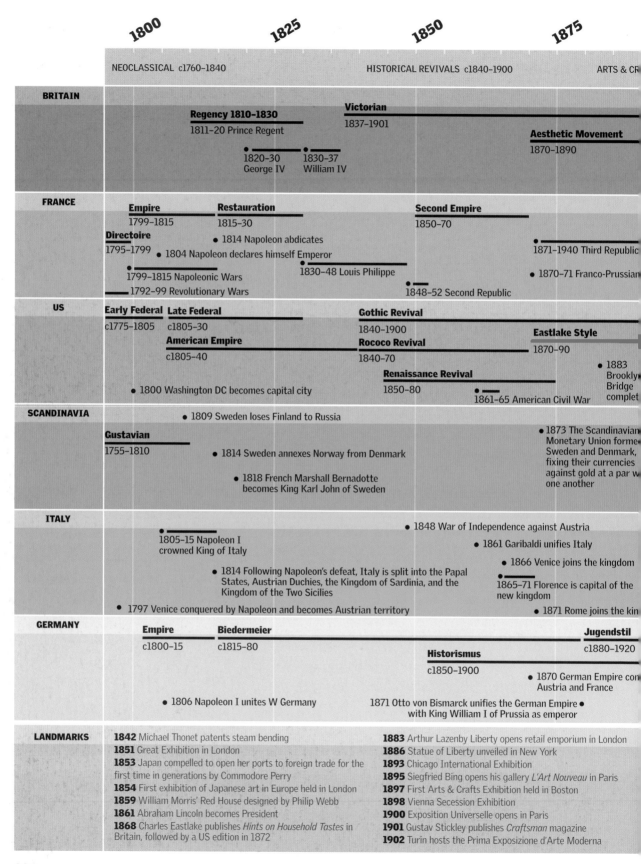

	1800	1825	1850	1875
	NEOCLASSICAL c1760–1840		HISTORICAL REVIVALS c1840–1900	ARTS & CR

BRITAIN

Regency 1810–1830
1811–20 Prince Regent

Victorian
1837–1901

1820–30 George IV   1830–37 William IV

Aesthetic Movement
1870–1890

FRANCE

Empire 1799–1815
Restauration 1815–30
Second Empire 1850–70

Directoire 1795–1799
• 1814 Napoleon abdicates
• 1804 Napoleon declares himself Emperor
1799–1815 Napoleonic Wars
1792–99 Revolutionary Wars
1830–48 Louis Philippe
1848–52 Second Republic
1871–1940 Third Republic
• 1870–71 Franco-Prussian

US

Early Federal c1775–1805
Late Federal c1805–30
American Empire c1805–40
Gothic Revival 1840–1900
Rococo Revival 1840–70
Renaissance Revival 1850–80
Eastlake Style 1870–90

• 1800 Washington DC becomes capital city
• 1861–65 American Civil War
• 1883 Brooklyn Bridge complet

SCANDINAVIA

• 1809 Sweden loses Finland to Russia

Gustavian 1755–1810

• 1814 Sweden annexes Norway from Denmark
• 1818 French Marshall Bernadotte becomes King Karl John of Sweden
• 1873 The Scandinavian Monetary Union forme Sweden and Denmark, fixing their currencies against gold at a par w one another

ITALY

• 1805–15 Napoleon I crowned King of Italy
• 1848 War of Independence against Austria
• 1861 Garibaldi unifies Italy
• 1866 Venice joins the kingdom
• 1814 Following Napoleon's defeat, Italy is split into the Papal States, Austrian Duchies, the Kingdom of Sardinia, and the Kingdom of the Two Sicilies
1865–71 Florence is capital of the new kingdom
• 1797 Venice conquered by Napoleon and becomes Austrian territory
• 1871 Rome joins the kin

GERMANY

Empire c1800–15
Biedermeier c1815–80
Historismus c1850–1900
Jugendstil c1880–1920

• 1870 German Empire con Austria and France
• 1806 Napoleon I unites W Germany
1871 Otto von Bismarck unifies the German Empire • with King William I of Prussia as emperor

LANDMARKS

1842 Michael Thonet patents steam bending
1851 Great Exhibition in London
1853 Japan compelled to open her ports to foreign trade for the first time in generations by Commodore Perry
1854 First exhibition of Japanese art in Europe held in London
1859 William Morris' Red House designed by Philip Webb
1861 Abraham Lincoln becomes President
1868 Charles Eastlake publishes *Hints on Household Tastes* in Britain, followed by a US edition in 1872

1883 Arthur Lazenby Liberty opens retail emporium in London
1886 Statue of Liberty unveiled in New York
1893 Chicago International Exhibition
1895 Siegfried Bing opens his gallery *L'Art Nouveau* in Paris
1897 First Arts & Crafts Exhibition held in Boston
1898 Vienna Secession Exhibition
1900 Exposition Universelle opens in Paris
1901 Gustav Stickley publishes *Craftsman* magazine
1902 Turin hosts the Prima Esposizione d'Arte Moderna

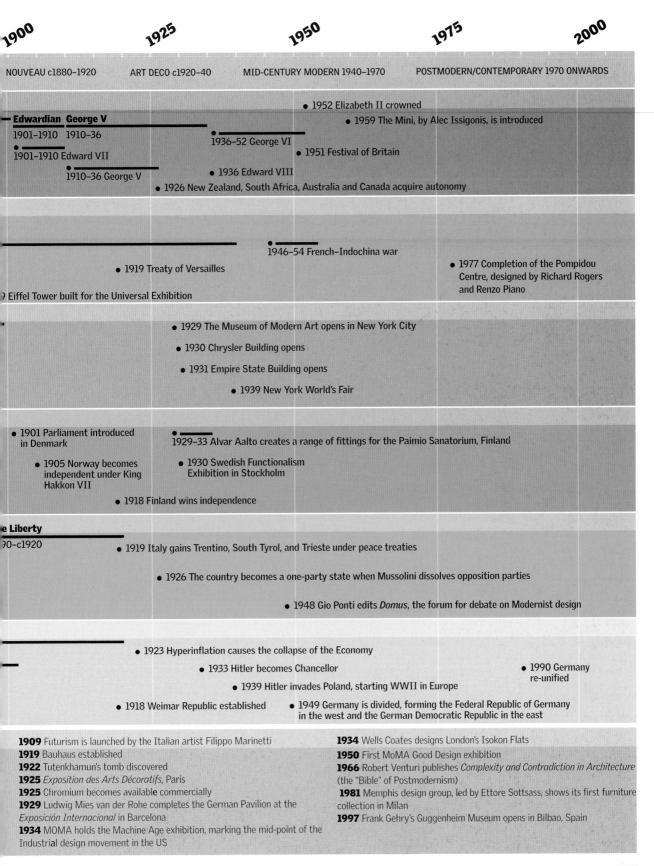

1900   **1925**   **1950**   **1975**   **2000**

NOUVEAU c1880–1920   ART DECO c1920–40   MID-CENTURY MODERN 1940–1970   POSTMODERN/CONTEMPORARY 1970 ONWARDS

● 1952 Elizabeth II crowned

Edwardian **George V**
● 1959 The Mini, by Alec Issigonis, is introduced

1901–1910   1910–36
1936–52 George VI

1901–1910 Edward VII
● 1951 Festival of Britain

1910–36 George V
● 1936 Edward VIII

● 1926 New Zealand, South Africa, Australia and Canada acquire autonomy

1946–54 French–Indochina war

● 1919 Treaty of Versailles

● 1977 Completion of the Pompidou
Centre, designed by Richard Rogers
and Renzo Piano

Eiffel Tower built for the Universal Exhibition

● 1929 The Museum of Modern Art opens in New York City

● 1930 Chrysler Building opens

● 1931 Empire State Building opens

● 1939 New York World's Fair

● 1901 Parliament introduced
in Denmark

1929–33 Alvar Aalto creates a range of fittings for the Paimio Sanatorium, Finland

● 1905 Norway becomes
independent under King
Hakkon VII

● 1930 Swedish Functionalism
Exhibition in Stockholm

● 1918 Finland wins independence

e Liberty
0–c1920

● 1919 Italy gains Trentino, South Tyrol, and Trieste under peace treaties

● 1926 The country becomes a one-party state when Mussolini dissolves opposition parties

● 1948 Gio Ponti edits *Domus*, the forum for debate on Modernist design

● 1923 Hyperinflation causes the collapse of the Economy

● 1933 Hitler becomes Chancellor
● 1990 Germany
re-unified

● 1939 Hitler invades Poland, starting WWII in Europe

● 1918 Weimar Republic established

● 1949 Germany is divided, forming the Federal Republic of Germany
in the west and the German Democratic Republic in the east

1909 Futurism is launched by the Italian artist Filippo Marinetti
1919 Bauhaus established
1922 Tutenkhamun's tomb discovered
1925 *Exposition des Arts Décoratifs*, Paris
1925 Chromium becomes available commercially
1929 Ludwig Mies van der Rohe completes the German Pavilion at the
Exposición Internacional in Barcelona
1934 MOMA holds the Machine Age exhibition, marking the mid-point of the
Industrial design movement in the US

1934 Wells Coates designs London's Isokon Flats
1950 First MoMA Good Design exhibition
1966 Robert Venturi publishes *Complexity and Contradiction in Architecture*
(the "Bible" of Postmodernism)
 1981 Memphis design group, led by Ettore Sottsass, shows its first furniture
collection in Milan
1997 Frank Gehry's Guggenheim Museum opens in Bilbao, Spain

Glossary

Acanthus A Mediterranean plant, *Acanthus spinosus*, with fleshy, scalloped leaves. From antiquity it was widely used for carved ornament such as decorative molding, notably in the Corinthian and Composite capitals of classical Greco-Roman architecture. In the 18th and 19th centuries, it was a particularly popular motif for furniture and metalwork.

Acid etching The technique of engraving a design into glass using hydrochloric acid. Broadly, the longer the vessel is exposed to the acid, the deeper the relief of the decoration.

Air twist Form of decoration employed from the 18th century on in the stems of drinking glasses, most notably English, in which spiral patterns are formed by elongating and twisting air bubbles introduced into the glass.

Apron The frieze rail of a table, the base of the framework of a piece of case furniture, or a shaped, and sometimes carved, piece of wood beneath the seat rail of a chair. It is also known as a skirt.

Armorial wares Ceramics decorated with a coat of arms. The term is most often associated with Chinese Export ware from the late 17th until the 19th centuries, which is often decorated with the arms and crests of Europeans or Americans.

Baluster A short post or pillar, such as a table leg, or one in a series supporting a rail and forming a balustrade. Usually of bulbous form, it was inspired by the shape of Classical vases and used since the Renaissance.

Bambocci chest Mostly made in Genoa in the 16th and 17th centuries, it is a storage chest decorated with elaborately carved human figures.

Banding A decorative strip of veneer in a contrasting colored or figured wood. Generally used around the edge of drawer fronts, table tops, and panels. In crossbanding, the contrasting wood runs at right angles to the main veneer. In feather, or herringbone, banding, two narrow strips of contrasting veneer run diagonally in opposite directions, thereby forming a chevron pattern.

Barley twist A form of decorative turning on furniture, and named after the spiraling shape of a barley sugar stick, which it resembles. It was used from the 17th century.

Batch The ingredients used to make glass, also known as the mixture.

Bergère French term for an informal, deep-seated chair of generous proportions. It usually has a caned or upholstered back and sides and a squab cushion.

Biedermeier A decorative style popular in Germany, Austria, and Scandinavia between c1815 and c1860. The name was invented by two German poets who wrote under the pseudonym Gottlieb Biedermeier, formed from a combination of *bieder* (meaning conventional or honest) and Meier, a common German surname. The solid, comfortable appearance of Biedermeier pieces was thought to mirror the unpretentious elegance of the German bourgeoisie. The

simple, geometric designs, which eschewed ornate decoration, were inspired by French furniture from the Empire period.

Bisque An unglazed form of porcelain with a matte surface, mainly used between c1860 and c1925 to make dolls' heads and ornaments.

Blanc de chine French term for a type of translucent white Chinese porcelain made from the late 17th century in the Fujien province of China under the late Ming dynasty. Typical wares included crisply molded figures, cups, and bowls, and they were widely copied by many European porcelain factories during the 18th century.

Bleu celeste A turquoise glaze used at Sèvres as a ground color on porcelain. Introduced in 1752, it was developed by Jean Hellot, decorator and chemist at Sèvres 1745–66. It was also used on 19th-century copies of Sèvres.

Bleu lapis A deep cobalt blue ground of almost purplish tone, introduced in 1753 at the Vincennes porcelain factory, France.

Bone china A form of porcelain developed in 1794 by the Spode factory in England. Containing up to 50 percent bone ash, it was more durable than soft-paste porcelain, and cheaper to mass produce than hard-paste porcelain. It is still made to this day.

Boulle A marquetry technique named after its leading exponent, French cabinet-maker André-Charles Boulle, which

involves the elaborate inlay of either brass on tortoiseshell (*première partie*) or tortoiseshell on brass (*contre partie*). It was employed on high-quality furniture from the late 17th century onward, and was particularly popular in the 18th and early and mid-19th centuries.

Boutis A French quilting technique in which wool or cotton is inserted into the quilt to create a raised design. In Provence the background is usually filled with corded channels and the quilts are double sided.

Breakfront The front of a piece of case furniture, such as a bookcase or a wardrobe, in which a center section protrudes further forward than the sections on either side.

Brilliant cut A popular cut for gemstones which, in standard form, have either 57 facets, or 58 if the gem is cut with a flat base. The term is also sometimes employed to describe American glass made from c1876 to c1914 that has been deep cut with bold, elaborate patterns and then highly polished to sparkle in the light.

Bureau plat French term for a flat-topped writing desk, often with a tooled leather insert (skiver) on the writing surface, and with a shallow frieze with drawers below it.

Cabriole leg An ornamental furniture leg with two curves forming an attenuated S-shape, like an animal leg. Popular from the late 17th century onward, especially for chairs, it is often terminated in a claw, claw-and-ball, paw, or hoof foot, and its "knee" is sometimes decorated with a motif such as a shell or a cartouche.

Cameo glass Type of glassware made of two or more separate layers of contrasting-colored glass, in which the top layers are carved or acid etched to produce a relief image and reveal the other color, or colors, below.

Canapé French term for a settee: an upholstered seat with a back and arms, for two or more people, and used from the late 17th century on.

Cartouche A framed panel or tablet based on the shape of a scroll, either convex or concave, and with a plain or decorated center—the latter sometimes in the form of an inscription, monogram, or coat of arms. Cartouches were widely used in Renaissance, Baroque, and Rococo ornament, but less so in the Neoclassical styles.

Chiffonier From the French term *chiffonière*, and originally used to describe a tall chest of drawers made in Britain from the 1750s on. The term also came into common usage as a description for small side cabinets or sideboards with drawers and a cupboard or cupboards below.

Chinoiserie A decorative style, popular in the 17th and 18th centuries, in which exotic motifs (often fanciful) derived from Chinese originals were applied to European furniture, ceramics, silverware, and textiles.

Console table A table with two legs supporting its front and its back fixed to the wall.

Corbel A wooden bracket, either plain or decorative, attached to an upright and used to support a horizontal feature, such as an arm on a chair, from below.

Cornucopia Also known as "horn of plenty" and a symbol of fertility and abundance since Classical times. A goat's horn, usually depicted overflowing with ears of wheat and fruit, the cornucopia was a popular decorative motif during the Renaissance, and also in the 17th, 18th, and early 19th centuries. On French Empire and American Federal furniture it was often employed as an emblem of peace and fortune, while in ceramics ribboned cornucopias were fashionable from c1750 to c1870 as wall-hung flower-holders.

Diaper A pattern consisting of repeated diamond, lozenge, square, or other geometric shapes—trellis and lattice patterns being two examples. It is particularly prevalent in *chinoiserie* and *japonaiserie* decoration, and was much-favored in the mid-19th century for use in furniture, floor tiles, ceramics, textiles, and wallcoverings as part of an overall decorative scheme.

Doucai Translated as "contrasted colors," it is a term for a delicate type of Chinese porcelain first made in the Chenghua period (1465–87) and distinguished by the application of an underglaze blue outline filled in with overglaze translucent colored enamels.

Electroplating A method of chemically depositing by electrolysis a layer of metal, usually silver but sometimes gold, onto an object made of base metal, usually nickel or copper. The technique was patented by G. R. Elkington in 1840, and superseded Sheffield plate as a cheap substitute for solid silver.

En camaïeu French term used to describe painting in different tones of the same color.

Escutcheon A protective and usually ornamental keyhole plate, which is sometimes in the shape of a shield.

Façon de Venise Glassware with elaborate applied decoration (*filigrana*) made in the 16th and 17th centuries in countries such as Britain, Germany, and the Netherlands, and in the style of high-quality Venetian glass.

Faïence French term for tin-glazed earthenware popular in Europe from the 16th and 17th centuries. Lightly baked and of a buff or pale red color, it was covered with white glaze in imitation of far more durable hard-paste porcelain.

Famille jaune, noire, rose, and verte French terms used to classify Chinese porcelain decorated in enamel colors by its palette. In *famille verte*, green and iron red predominate, but it also contains yellow, blue, eggplant-purple and black. *Famille jaune* uses *famille verte* enamels on a yellow ground, while *famille noire* is the *famille verte* palette on a black ground. *Famille rose* was dominated by pink or purple tones. From the early 19th century a style known as Rose Medallion was used. It features groups of figures or flowers in medallions surrounded by floral borders.

Fasces A decorative motif comprising a bound bundle of rods, often enclosing an ax-head. Originally an emblem of the authority of ancient Roman magistrates, it recurs in Classical-inspired styles of ornament.

Fauteuil A French term for a large, upholstered open armchair, first used at the court of Louis XIV, and particularly popular in the 18th century.

Fazzoletto An Italian word for a handkerchief vase: in other words, in the shape of a falling handkerchief.

Federal style The dominant style in American architecture and decorative arts from the Declaration of Independence in 1776 until c1830. Essentially Neoclassical, it was initially inspired by British designs, and in the early 19th century was much influenced by the French Empire style. More significantly, however, it developed within a Classical framework a vocabulary of ornament that drew for inspiration on imagery and motifs indigenous to the newly independent country such as the American eagle and views of the Hudson River.

Festoon A Classical decorative motif in the form of a garland of fruit and flowers tied with ribbons and/or leaves. It was revived during the Renaissance, and was a widely recurring motif in subsequent Neoclassical and Classical Revival styles during the 17th, 18th, and 19th centuries.

Filigrana Also known as *latticino*, and developed in Venice in the 16th century, it is a technique in which decorative threads of white or colored glass rods are embedded as twisted, crossed, or spiral patterns in glassware.

Finial A decorative turned or carved ornament surmounting a prominent terminal on any object, for instance a lid, and used to emphasize it. Typical forms include urns, acorns, pinecones, and *fleurs-de-lis.*

Flashed glass A thick layer of clear glass covered with a thinner layer of colored glass, and the latter often acid etched, cut, or sandblasted to create a pattern and reveal the layer of clear glass underneath.

Flatback An earthenware figure, or group of figures, with a flat, undecorated back intended to be placed against a wall, hearth, or mantelshelf, and therefore intended to be viewed from the front only. They were made in the mid-19th century mostly in Staffordshire but also elsewhere in England and in Scotland.

Fretwork A form of decoration comprising a repeat pattern of geometric forms, which can be incised, carved in relief, or, most commonly, pierced, as well as painted or printed. Dating back to ancient Chinese and Egyptian cultures, fretwork proved particularly popular on 18th-century *chinoiserie*, Rococo, and Gothic styles of furniture, notably by Thomas Chippendale.

Gateleg table A form of drop-leaf table. Introduced in the 16th century, it employed stretchered legs that pivot out like a gate to support the leaves of the table top.

Gather The blob of molten glass "gathered" on the end of the blowing iron, before being blown into the desired shape.

Gilding A decorative finish in which gold is applied to wood, leather, silver, ceramics, or glass. The process involves laying gold leaf or powdered gold (or silver) onto a smooth base such as gesso. Parcel gilding is the term used when only part of the object has been gilded.

Giltwood Wood that has been gilded (*see Gilding*).

Girandole An Italian term for an ornate giltwood candleholder that was popular with 18th-century Rococo and Neoclassical designers.

Goût grec A French term (literally, "Greek taste") describing the renewed interest in ancient Greece and Rome that resulted in the Neoclassical style of the late 18th and early 19th centuries.

Grand feu The colors green (from copper oxide), blue (cobalt), purple (manganese), yellow (antimony), and orange-red (iron) used to decorate tin-glazed earthenware until the 18th century, after which *petit feu*, or enamel colors, were more common. The earlier colors are known in French as *grand feu* because of the high temperatures necessary to adhere them to the tin glaze.

Ground The surface or background color of ceramics, onto which painted decoration is often applied.

Imari Japanese porcelain made at Arita from the late 17th century, and exported from the port of Arita. It features a complex overlapping of geometric or leaf-shaped panels dominated by underglaze blue, iron-red enamel, and gilding, and with other colors such as yellow, green, eggplant, and bluish black.

Intaglio Decorative technique for incising or engraving stone, ceramics, metalware, and glass, in which a pattern or motif is cut away to create the image in relief (standing proud).

Japonaiserie (or Japonisme) Exotic European designs based loosely on Japanese works of art, after Japan opened up the West in the 1850s.

Kakiemon In ceramics, the name given to a distinctive palette of colors comprising turquoise, dark blue, black, iron red, and yellow, and typically applied as sparse and asymmetrical decoration on a pure white ground. First applied to Japanese porcelain in the mid-17th century, it was much copied by European porcelain factories in the early 18th century.

Kangxi Chinese porcelain made during the reign of the Qing dynasty emperor Kangxi (1662–1722) at Jingdezhen in eastern China. Wares for the domestic and European export markets included blue and white; *famille verte, jaune,* and *noire; blanc de chine;* armorial wares; and, toward the end of the period, Chinese Imari and *famille rose* wares.

Lambrequin A decorative apron or fringe, originally based on the scarf worn across a knight's helmet and its heraldic representation, found on drapery, furniture, silver, or ceramics, and particularly popular in the mid-16th and early 18th centuries.

Lattimo An Italian term for "milk glass." An opaque white glass that resembles porcelain. Developed in Venice in the 15th century, in the 17th and 18th centuries it was also made in France (called *blanc de lait*), Germany (*Milchglas*), and

Britain, and was often decorated with enameling and gilding.

Marquetry A decorative veneer used on furniture, and comprising shaped pieces of wood of different colors and figuring, or other materials such as ivory, mother-of-pearl, or metal, pieced together to form a pattern or picture. The technique was perfected by the Dutch, who produced fine examples of floral pattern marquetry during the 16th century, and it enjoyed a resurgence of popularity during the late 18th and early 19th centuries.

Milk glass See Lattimo.

Millefiori Italian for "a thousand flowers," and a technique, often used in paperweights, in which tile-like cross sections of brightly colored glass canes are arranged in patterns (known as "set-ups") and embedded in clear glass.

Netsuke Ornamental toggles worn at the sash or waist of traditional Japanese clothing, and used to secure, via cords, an *inro* (seal case) or a pouch for carrying small personal possessions. Made from the early 17th to the late 19th century, netsuke were produced in various materials, including woven or braided metal, bamboo, and bone. Many were carved or shaped as figures, animals, or plants.

Okimono A small to medium-sized Japanese sculpture, often of ivory, but also of bone or wood, and designed to stand inside a *tokonoma* (display alcove). Made during the 19th and early 20th centuries, their intricately carved figural —human or animal—forms were often based on the small netsuke.

Ormolu An English term derived from the French term *or moulu*, meaning "ground gold," denoting a process of gilding bronze for decorative mounts.

Overglaze A technique in which enamels are painted onto fired and glazed porcelain, which is then fired again.

Parquetry A form of marquetry comprising a symmetrical, geometrical pattern made up of contrasting grained or colored woods. Often employed from the mid-17th to the late 18th century.

Petit feu enamels Colors fused to ceramic bodies by firing at low temperatures in the kiln. *See also* Grand feu.

Pressed glass Glass that has been shaped by being pressed in a mold. The technique was developed in the United States in the 1820s.

Putto (pl Putti) An Italian term for a chubby infant, either an angelic spirit (a cherub) or one of the attendants of Cupid or Eros. Widely employed as a decorative motif since the Renaissance.

Raising A metalware technique used to create hollow wares out of a flat disc or sheet of metal by hammering it over an anvil-like stake to gradually form sides of the required height and shape.

Rocaille The rockwork decoration that gave its name to the Rococo style originating in France. *Rocaille* was often used in asymmetric combination with shells, motifs reminiscent of splashing water, scrollwork, *chinoiserie*, and foliage.

Rose montée A faceted, flat-backed rhinestone, often mounted in a pierced metal cup, so that it can be wired onto clothes or jewelry.

Saber leg A leg with a gentle concave curve similar in profile to the blade of a saber, predominantly employed as the back legs of a chair, and widely used on Regency, Empire, and Federal furniture during the first half of the 19th century.

Schnelle The German name for a tall tapering tankard usually made of stoneware or faïence, and often with a pewter cover. It was the typical shape of the Siegburg potters of the 16th century and was often decorated in relief with biblical or mythical subject matter. Imitations were made in the 19th century.

Slip A creamy mixture of clay and water used as a finish on pottery, or as a medium for casting ceramic hollow wares and figures. Slips can be colored or uncolored, can be inscribed or engraved, and can provide an all-over finish, or be selectively piped or trailed over the surface to create an image or pattern.

Sommerso From the Italian for submerged, a glass technique that involves casing one or more layers of transparent colored glass within a layer of thick, colorless glass.

Sterling silver A British term for silver of at least 92.5 percent purity. Silver marked sterling in capital letters is usually American.

Stoneware A form of pottery, called *grès* in France and *Steinzeug* in Germany, and made from a mixture of clay and stone (usually feldspar), which, when fired at high temperature, renders the hard, dense, and durable body non-porous. Salt and lead glazes have often been applied for decorative effect, although the latter less successfully because of the high firing temperatures required in the kiln.

Strapwork A form of ornament comprising a pattern of intertwined, band-like forms, similar in appearance to twisted ribbons or, sometimes, stylized scrolling foliage, and also sometimes studded with other motifs such as rosettes or lozenges. Developed during the Renaissance, and often employed up until the early 20th century, it was particularly suited to plasterwork; furniture inlay and carving; and metalware engraving.

Stretcher A horizontal wooden rail or bar joining the legs of tables, stools, and chairs, designed to strengthen the construction. Stretchers can be left plain, or be embellished by turning or decorative carving.

Style rayonnant A style of ceramic painting developed in the late 17th century at Rouen, in France. The patterns, which on plate and dishes radiate inward from richly decorated borders, resemble engraved embroidery designs and are comprised of lambrequins, scrolls, festoons of flowers and leaves, and lacy arabesques. It was subsequently employed at various French faïence factories, including those at Nevers, Moustiers, and Marseilles, and also at the porcelain factory in Saint Cloud. It remained a popular style of decoration until the 1740s.

Tripod table A small, occasional pedestal table supported by three splayed legs. The form was particularly popular in late 18th-century furniture.

Underglaze Decoration applied to a ceramic body before, rather than after, firing in the kiln. Because of the high temperatures involved, the palette is limited—cobalt blue and copper for red being the main examples.

Verre de fougère (French: "fern" or "bracken glass.") An early type of glass in which potash from burnt bracken or ferns was used as the flux. The French equivalent of German *Waldglas*, it shares the same green/brown/yellow color, and was used for simple forms, often with shallow cut decoration.

Vitruvian scroll An undulating or wave-like repeat scroll pattern, originally used in Classical Greek architecture, most notably in friezes and as border ornament in Neoclassical and various Classical Revival styles of decoration since the Renaissance.

Walzenkrug The German name for a cylindrical tankard.

Wucai A five-colored Chinese palette for decorating porcelain. Developed during the Ming dynasty, it includes underglaze cobalt blue with iron red, yellow, turquoise, and green overglaze enamels.

Zanfirico rods Refers to the technique *filigrana a retortoli*, in which white and colored threads or ribbons are twisted together in a filigree within clear glass. It is commonly found in Murano glass. The term is a corruption of the name of early 19th-century Venetian art dealer Antonio Sanquirico.

Zopfstii The late 18th-century German term for Neoclassicism, which takes its name from Classical braided friezes and festoons—*Zopf* meaning "braid" in German.

Dealers and auction houses

Dorling Kindersley and the Price Guide Company would like to thank the following dealers and auction houses for permission to use images. It should be noted that inclusion in this book in no way consititutes or implies a contract or binding offer on the part of any contributing dealer or auction house to supply or sell the pieces illustrated, or similar items, at the price stated.

Abbreviations: TR = top right; C = center; TL = top left; TC = top center; BL = bottom left; BR = bottom right; BC = bottom center

Norman Adams Ltd.
8–10 Hans Road
London
England
SW3 1RX
www.normanadams.com
14 BR, 35 BC

Albert Amor
37 Bury Street
London
England
SW1Y 6AU
www.albertamor.co.uk
87 TR BL BR, 110 TR, 131 TC TR

Antique Glass @ Frank Dux Antiques
33 Belvedere
Lansdowne Road
Bath
England
BA1 5HR
www.antique-glass.co.uk
135 BCL

Art Deco Etc.
73 Upper Gloucester Road
Brighton
Sussex
England
BN1 3LQ
johnclark@artdecoetc.co.uk
106 TR

Aurora Bijoux
www.aurorabijoux.com
182 BL, 183 BC

Axtell Antiques
1 River Street
Deposit
New York
NY 13754
USA
www.axtellantiques.com
179 BL

Beaussant Lefèvre
32 rue Drouot
75009 Paris
France
www.beaussant-lefevre.auction.fr
38 BR, 41 TL, 65 L, 92 BL

Bébés et Jouets
c/o Lochend Post Office
165 Restalrig Road
Edinburgh
Scotland
EH7 6HW
bebesetjouets@tiscali.co.uk
158 L, 162 BC BR, 164 TC BL BR

Pierre Bergé & Associés
12, rue Drouot
75009 Paris
France
www.pba-auctions.com
107 TC

Auktionshaus Bergmann
Möhrendorfestraße 4
91056 Erlangen
Germany
www.auction-bergmann.de
35 TL, 38 BL, 77 TC, 78 BC, 95 TR, 96 BR, 97 TL TC BC, 99 TC TR

Bertoia Auctions
2141 Demarco Drive
Vineland NJ 08360
USA
www.bertoiaauctions.com
156 CR, 161 C CR BL BC BR, 162 CR, 163 C, 164 TR BC, 165 TL TR,

Beverley
30 Church Street
London
England
NW8 8EP
11 TL, 106 BR

Blanchard
86/88 Pimlico Road
London
England
SW1W 8PL
20 TR, 47 TR

David Bowden
Stand 07
Grays Antique Markets
58 Davies Street
London
England
W1K 5LP
91 BR, 172 BCR BR

T. C. S. Brooke
The Grange
Wroxham
Norfolk
England
NR12 8RX
14 TR, 96 BC

Bukowskis
Arsenalsgatan 4
Box 1754
111 87 Stockholm
Sweden
www.bukowskis.se
15 BR, 33 CR BL BR

John Bull (Antiques) Ltd
139A New Bond Street
London
England
W1S 2TN
www.antique-silver.co.uk
141 TL, 142 CR, 149 TC TR

Calderwood Gallery
1622 Spruce Street
Philadelphia
PA 19013
USA
www.calderwoodgallery.com
50 CL BL

The Calico Teddy
www.calicoteddy.com
156 L, 166 C BL BCR, 169 TL

Lennox Cato Antiques
1 The Square
Church Street
Edenbridge
Kent
England
TN8 5BD
www.lennoxcato.com
36

Cheffins
Clifton House
1 & 2 Clifton Road
Cambridge
England
CB1 7EA
www.cheffins.co.uk
65 R, 73 BL BCL, 75 BL BCR, 92 BC, 112 BC

T. W. Conroy
36 Oswego St
Baldwinsville
NY 13027
www.twconroy.com
79 BL

Graham Cooley
graham.cooley@metalysis.com
135 BCR

Susie Cooper Ceramics Art Deco at Gallery 1930
18 Church Street
Marylebone
London
England
NW8 8EP
www.susiecooperceramics.com
107 TR BR

Cristobal
26 Church Street
London, England
NW8 8EP
www.cristobal.co.uk
159 TR, 180 BL BR, 181 BL BR,
182 TR, 183 TL TC BL BR

Andrew Dando
34 Market Street
Bradford on Avon, England
BA15 1LL
www.andrewdando.co.uk
81 BL

Barry Davies Oriental Art Ltd.
PO Box 34867
London, England
W8 6WH
5 BL, 7 TL, 86 BL, 88, 157 R, 172
C BL BCL

Decodame.com
www.decodame.com
67 CR, 139 L, 151 TL

The Design Gallery
5 The Green
Westerham
Kent, England
TN16 1AS
www.designgallery.co.uk
16 TL, 107 BC

Palais Dorotheum
Dorotheergasse 17
1010 Vienna, Austria
www.dorotheum.com
7 TR, 23 R, 60 C BC, 62 BC, 63 BL
BC

Dreweatt Neate
Donnington Priory Salerooms
Donnington
Newbury
Berkshire, England
RG14 2JE
www.dnfa.com/donnington
6 TC, 7 TCL, 29 TC, 30 BC, 34 BC,
42 CR, 60 BR, 71 BR, 72 BR, 73
BR, 75 C, 81 BR, 89 CL C CR BR,
96 TR, 97 BR, 99 BR, 105 L, 108 L
CR R, 112 C CB CRB BCA BR, 114
BR, 119 TR, 122 BL, 125 BC, 126 C
BR, 127 TC BL, 129 TR BC, 140
BL, 145 BL, 148 BC, 149 BL, 152
BL, 153 TR BL, 171 TL, 173 TR,
177 BL

Cynthia Findlay
Toronto Antiques Center
276 King Street West
Toronto
Ontario
M5V 1J2
Canada
www.cynthiafindlay.com
151 TR

Auktionhaus Dr. Fischer
Trappensee-Schößchen
D-74074 Heilbronn
Germany
www.auctions-fischer.de
6 TR, 17 BR, 109 L CR R, 115 BR,
117 TR, 118, 119 TL BL, 120 BC
BR, 121, 122 BC, 125 TL, 126 BL,
127 BL BC, 128 BR, 134 CR BC BR

Galerie Hélène Fournier Guérin
18 rue des Saints-Pères
75007 Paris
France
68 TR, 76 BL, 92 TR BR, 93 TL TC

Fragile Design
14/15 The Custard Factory
Digbeth
Birmingham
England
B9 4AA
www.fragiledesign.com
21 TR

Freeman's
1808 Chestnut Street
Philadelphia
PA 19103
USA
www.freemansauction.com
15 TR, 16 BR, 17 TR, 24 B, 35 BR,
37 BL BR, 39 CR BL BR, 40 BL, 42
TR BL, 43 TL TR TRB CL BL, 57
CR BL BC BR, 61 TR, 62 TR, 63
TL, 64 L, 98 BL BCL BR, 142 BR,
145 TR, 150 BL, 174 BR, 175 C
BCL BR

Richard Gardner Antiques
Swan House
Market Square
Petworth
West Sussex
England
GU28 0AH
www.richardgardenerantiques.
co.uk
90 TL

Thos Wm Gaze & Son
Diss Auction Rooms
Roydon Road
Diss
Norfolk
England
IP22 4LN
www.twgaze.com
21 BL, 167 C

Sidney Gecker
226 West 21st Street
New York
NY 10011
USA
4 BR, 22 C, 63 TC, 152 BC, 153 BC

Galerie Girard
7 rue des Saints-Pères
75006 Paris
France
www.veronique-girard.com
139 CR, 140 TR

Gorringes
15 North Street
Lewes
East Sussex
England
BN7 2PD
www.gorringes.co.uk
83, 96 BL, 154 TR, C, BR, 155 TL,
159 TL, 178 TR

Halcyon Days
14 Brook Street
London
England
W1S 1BD
www.halcyondays.co.uk
171 BL, 179 BR

Harpers General Store
301 Maple Avenue
Mt. Gretna
PA 17064
USA
www.harpergeneralstore.com
166 BCL, 168 BL, 169 BL

Leanda Harwood Teddy Bears
www.leandaharwood.co.uk
6 TL, 168 BC, 169 TR

Jeanette Hayhurst Fine Glass
32A Kensington Church St.
London
England
W8 4HA
108 CL, 112 TR BL CR BRA, 113,
114 CL, 115 TC, 120 BL, 122 BR,
123 BL, 124 TR BL, 125 TC TR,
126 TR, 127 TL TR, 137 BC

Willis Henry Auctions Inc.
22 Main Street
Marshfield
MA 02050
USA
www.willishenry.com
178 BR

Holsten Galleries
Elm Street
Stockbridge
MA 01262
USA
www.holstengalleries.com
136 BL, 137 BR

John Howard @ Heritage
Heritage
6 Market Place
Woodstock
Oxon
England
OX20 1TA
www.antiquepottery.co.uk
80 BCR, 81 TL TC TR BC

Imperial Half Bushel
831 N Howard Street
Baltimore
MD 21201
USA
www.imperialhalfbushel.com
142 CRB

Ingram Antiques
669 Mt. Pleasant Road
Toronto
M4S 2N2
Canada
125 BR

James D. Julia Inc.
PO Box 830
Fairfield
ME 04937
USA
www.juliaauctions.com
128 BCR, 131 BR

Auktionhaus Kaupp
Schloss Sulzburg
Hauptstraße 62
79295 Sulzburg
Germany
www.kaupp.de
17 C, 66 BL,95 BL CR BC BR,149
TL,179 BC

Gallerie Koller
Hardturmstraße 102
Postfach 8031
Zürich
Switzerland
www.galeriekoller.ch
7 TC,12 BL,13 TR, 35 TC

Law Fine Art Ltd.
The Long Gallery
Littlecote House
Hungerford
Berkshire
England
RG17 0SS
www.lawfineart.co.uk
79 BCL, 89 TR

**Lawrence's Fine Art
Auctioneers**
The Linen Yard
South Street, Crewkerne
Somerset
England
TA18 8AB
www.lawrences.co.uk
91 BC, 138 R, 139 R, 148 BR, 149
BR

Claude Lee
The Ginnel Antiques Centre
off Parliament Street
Harrogate
North Yorkshire
England
HG1 2RB
www.redhouseyork.co.uk
93 BR, 105 C

**Andrew Lineham Fine
Glass**
www.antiquecolouredglass.com
98 BCR, 110 CL, 111 TL, 114 BL,
116, 119 BR, 120 CR, 129 BR

Lyon & Turnbull Ltd.
33 Broughton Place
Edinburgh
Scotland
EH1 3RR
www.lyonandturnbull.com
11 TR, 18 B, 24 TR, 39 CL, 40 TR,
42 CB BRA, 43 C CR, 47 BR, 51 C
CL, 74 BC BR, 90 BC BR, 99 BL,
129 C, 135 TR, 138 L, 142 BRA,
145 BC, 148 TR BL, 174 BL

Macklowe Gallery
667 Madison Avenue
New York
NY 10021
USA
www.macklowegallery.com
19 BR, 111 TC, 128 C, 141 TR

Mallett
141 New Bond Street
London, England, W1S 2BS
www.mallettantiques.com
125 BL

Mary Ann's Collectibles
c/o South Street Antiques Centre
615 South 6th Street
Philadelphia, PA 19147-2128
USA
19 BR, 111 TC, 128 C, 141 TR

Galerie Maurer
Kurfurstenstraße 17
D-80799 Munchen
Germany
www.galerie-objekte-maurer.de
150 BC BR, 151 BC BR, 138 CL

**R. & G. McPherson
Antiques**
40 Kensington Church Street
London, England, W8 4BX
www.orientalceramics.com
68, 69, 82, 84, 85, 86 BC, 91 TC

Auktionshaus Metz
Friedrich-Eber-Anlage 5
69117 Heidelberg
Germany
www.Metz-Auktion.de
77 TR BC, 97 TR

Mum Had That
www.mumhadthat.com
135 BL, 136 TL, 137 TR

Lillian Nassau Ltd.
220 East 57th Street
New York
NY 10022
USA
www.lilliannassau.com
115 TR

John Nicholsons
The Auction Rooms
"Longfield", Midhurst Road
Fernhurst
Haslemere
Surrey
England
GU27 3HA
www.johnnicholsons.com
103 BL

Northeast Auctions
93 Pleasant Street
Portsmouth
NH 03801 , USA
www.northeastauctions.com
14 BL, 47 TL BL, 53 TL, 57 TC, 153
BR

**Galerie Olivia et
Emmanuel**
Village Suisse
Galeries 24 et 58, 78
Avenue de Suffren
75015 Paris
France
www.artface.com/olivia
15 BR, 144

Ormonde Gallery
156 Portobello Road
London
England
W11 2EB
34 BL

Partridge Fine Arts plc
144–146 New Bond Street
London
England
W1S 2PF
www.partridgeplc.com
1, 2, 5 CL, 6 TL, 7 TL, 8 TR, 9 TR,
10 BL, 12 BR, 22 L, 23 L C, 26, 27,
28, 29 TL BR, 30 C BL, 31 TR BC,
32, 34 TC BR, 35 BL, 38 TL, 42
BC, 44, 45 C BL BCL BCR BR, 46
TR BL, 49, 52 BL, 53 TR, 54, 55,
58, 59, 68 BRA BRB, 70 BL, 71 CL
BL, 75 TR, 94, 97 BL

David Pickup
115 High St
Burford
Oxfordshire
England
OX18 4RG
42 CR, 50 BL BR, 86 BR

Salle des Ventes Pillet
1, rue de la Libération
B. P. 23,
27480 Lyons la Forèt
France
www.pillet.auction.fr
52 TR

Pook & Pook
463 East Lancaster Avenue
Downingtown
PA 19335
USA
www.pookandpook.com
29 BL BR, 61 C BL BC BR, 62 BL,
152 TR, 153 TL, 159 CR, 174 BC,
175 TR BCR, 177 TR

Quittenbaum
Hohenstaufenstraße 1
D-80801
München
Germany
www.quittenbaum.de
19 BC 104 BC, 134 BL, 137 BL

David Rago Auctions
333 North Main Street
Lambertville
NJ 08530
USA
www.ragoarts.com
5 CR, 9 BR, 18 CR, 25 TR, 50 CL
CR BL BR, 51 TR, 66 TR, 100, 101,
102 TC TR BR, 103 TL BC BR, 106
BL BC, 115 CL, 128 BL BCL, 130
TR BL BR, 131 TL BC

**David Rago/Nicholas
Dawes Lalique Auctions**
333 North Main Street
Lambertville
NJ 08530
USA
www.ragoarts.com
3 (DACS, ADAPG), 109 CL(DACS,
ADAPG), 123 CR (DACS, ADAPG),
132 (DACS, ADAPG), 133 TR

Rogers de Rin
76 Royal Hospital Road
Paradise Walk, Chelsea
London, England
SW3 4HN
www.rogersderin.co.uk
157 CL, 170 BC BR, 178 BC

Brian Rolleston Ltd.
104A Kensington Church Street
London, England
W8 4BU
www.brianrolleston.com
56

Rosebery
74–76 Knight's Hill
West Norwood
London, England, SE27 0JD
www.roseberys.co.uk
155 TR, 158 TR, 171 BC

Rossini SA
7 rue Drouot
75009 Paris
France
www.rossini.fr
74 BL, 176 BL BC BR

Hugo Ruef
Gabelsbergerstraße 28
80333 Munich
Germany
www.ruef-auktionen.de
68 CL, 78 BR

Sampson & Horne
20 Mount Street
London, England, W1K 3NN
www.sampsonhorne.com
7 TR, 65 CR, 68 TC, 71 CR, 73 TR
TC C BCR, 79 C BR, 80 BCL BR

Galerie Saphir
69 rue du Temple
75003 Paris
France
galerie-saphir@wanadoo.fr
179 TR

Sign of the Tymes
12 Morris Farm Road
Lafayette
NJ 07848
USA
www.millantiques.com
169 TC

The Silver Fund
1 Duke of York Street
London
England
SW1Y 6JP
www.thesilverfund.com
5 BR (ADAPG), 21 BR (ADAGP),
141 TC, 151 TC BL

Skinner Inc.
63 Park Plaza
Boston, MA 02116
USA
www.skinnerinc.com
91 BL, 157 L, 171 TR, 174 C, 175
BL, 176 TR, 177 TL TC BC BR

Sollo: Rago Modern Auctions
333 North Main Street
Lambertville
NJ 08530
USA
www.ragoarts.com
25 CR, 53 BR, 139 CL (ADAGP,
DACS), 150 TR, 154 BL (ADAGP,
DACS), 155 BR

Patricia Stauble Antiques
180 Main Street
PO Box 265
Wiscasset
ME 04578, USA
170 BL

Roxanne Stuart
gemfairy@aol.com
181 TR, 182 BC, 183 TR

Sumpter Priddy III, Inc.
601 S. Washington Street
Alexandria, VA 22314
USA
www.sumpterpriddy.com
48

Spencer Swaffer Antiques
30 High Street
Arundel
West Sussex
England
BN18 9AB
www.spencerswaffer.com
156 R, 170 TR

Take-A-Boo Emporium
1927 Avenue Road
Toronto
Ontario
M5M 4A2
Canada
www.takeaboo.com
111 TR, 123 BCR

Uppsala Auktionskammare
Eddagatan 10
753 32 Uppsala
Sweden
www.uppsalaauktion.se
33 BCL BCR, 35 TR, 39 TL TR

Galerie Vandermeersch
Voltaire Antiquités-Vandermeersch
SA
21 quai Voltaire
75007 Paris
France
76 TC TR BC BR, 87 TL, 92 TL, 93
TR BL

Victoriana Dolls
101 Portobello Rd
London
England
W11 2BQ
heather.bond@totalserve.co.uk
160, 161 TR, 162 BL, 163 TC TR
BL BR

Johannes Vogt Auktionen
Antonienstraße 3
80802 Munich
Germany
www.vogt-auktionen.de
77 TL

William Walter Antiques Ltd.
London Silver Vaults
Chancery Lane
London
England
WC2A 1QS
www.williamwalter.co.uk
10 TR, 142 TR BL, 143, 145 C BR,
146, 147

Woolley & Wallis
51–61 Castle Street
Salisbury
Wiltshire
England
SP1 3SU
www.woolleyandwallis.co.uk
13 BC, 18 TR, 20 BR, 41 TC, 62
BR, 64 CL CR R, 65 CL, 67 TL TR,
70 BR, 72 C, 77 BR, 78 C BL, 79
TR, 80 C BL, 90 TR BL, 91 TL TR,
93 BC, 99 CR BC, 102 BL BC, 103
TC TR, 104 CR BL, 105 R, 106 TC,
107 BL, 137 TC, 138 CR, 142 CRA,
155 TC BL

Bonny Yankauer
bonnyy@aol.com
180 BC

Robert Young Antiques
68 Battersea Bridge Road
London
England
SW11 3AG
www.robertyoungantiques.com
22 R, 63 TR BR

Von Zezschwitz
Friedrichstraße 1a
80801 Munich
Germany
www.von-zezschwitz.de
135 BR, 136 BC BR

Additional picture credits

The Art Archive
33 TR

The Bridgeman Art Library
© Fitzwilliam Museum, University
of Cambridge, UK/ The Bridgeman
Art Library
74 C

Thomas Dreiling Collection
130 BC

The following images are © DACS,
London and ADAGP Paris 2007:
5 BR, 21 BR, 3, 21 TR, 109 CL, 123
CR, 132 L C R, 139 CL, 154 L C TR.

All other images © The Price
Guide Company Ltd and
Dorling Kindersley

Index

Acknowledgments

From the author

The Price Guide Company would like to thank the following people for their substantial contributions to the production of this book:

Photographer Graham Rae for his patience, humor, and wonderful photography as well as John McKenzie, Andy Johnson, Byron Slater, Ellen MacDermott, and Adam Gault for additional photography.

Bob Bousfield for his workflow and technical assistance and Nick Croydon for his business advice.

All of the dealers, auction houses, and private collectors for kindly allowing us to photograph their collections, and for taking the time to provide a wealth of information about the pieces.

Auktionshaus Bergmann for its assistance in compiling the ceramics, glass, and silver marks sections of the Composite photos chapter.

The team at DK, Jackie Douglas for her support and advice, Victoria Short, and Janet Mohun for all their skill and dedication to the project, and Anna Fischel for her invaluable support.

We would also like to thank our team of consultants for their help in the execution of this book: John Axford, Woolley & Wallis, Salisbury, UK; Heather Bond, Victoriana Dolls, London; Dudley Browne, James D Julia Inc, Fairfield, ME; Beau Freeman, Linda Cain, Lee Young, Samuel T Freeman & Co, Philadelphia, PA; Jeanette Hayhurst, Jeanette Hayhurst Fine Glass, London; Mark Law, Michael Pick and Christopher Johnstone, Partridge Fine Arts Ltd, London; Andrew Lineham, Andrew Lineham Fine Glass, London; Robert McPherson, R&G McPherson Antiques, London; Stephen Miners and Yai Thammachote, Cristobal, London; Ron Pook, Pook & Pook, Downington, PA; David Rago, Rago Arts and Auction Center, Lambertville, NJ; Paul Roberts, John Mackie and Campbell Armour, Lyon & Turnbull, Edinburgh; Jeremy Smith, Sotheby's, London; John Walter, William Walter Antiques Ltd, London.

From the publisher

Dorling Kindersley would like to thank Caroline Hunt for proofreading, Hilary Bird for the index, and Mandy Earey for design assistance.